GLOBALISATION, LAW AND THE STATE

This book begins—as is customary in globalisation literature—with an acknowledgement of the definitional difficulties associated with globalisation. Rather than labour the point, the book identifies some economic, political and cultural dimensions to the phenomenon and uses these to analyse existing and emerging challenges to State-centric/territorial models of law and governance. It surveys three areas that are typically associated with globalisation—financial markets, the internet, and public contracts—as well as trade more generally, the environment, human rights, and national governance. On this basis it considers how global legal norms are formed, how they enmesh with the norms of other legal orders, and how they create pressure for legal harmonisation. This in turn leads to an analysis of the corresponding challenges that globalisation presents to traditional notions of sovereignty and the models of public law that have grown from them. While some of the themes addressed here will be familiar to students of the European process (there are prominent references to the European experience throughout the book), *Globalisation, Law and the State* provides a clear insight into how the sovereign space of States and their legal orders are diminishing and being replaced by an altogether more fluid system of intersecting orders and norms. This is followed by an analysis of the theory and practice of the globalisation of law, and suggesting that the workings of law in the global era can best be conceived of in terms of networks that link together a range of actors that exist above, below and within the State, as well as on either side of the public–private divide. The whole is an immensely valuable, innovative and concise study of globalisation and its effect on law and the state.

Globalisation, Law and the State

Jean-Bernard Auby
Translated from the original French by Rachael Singh

With a foreword by Gordon Anthony

•HART•
OXFORD • LONDON • NEW YORK • NEW DELHI • SYDNEY

HART PUBLISHING

Bloomsbury Publishing Plc

Kemp House, Chawley Park, Cumnor Hill, Oxford, OX2 9PH, UK

HART PUBLISHING, the Hart/Stag logo, BLOOMSBURY and the Diana logo are
trademarks of Bloomsbury Publishing Plc

First published in hardback, 2017
Paperback edition, 2019

A catalogue record for this book is available from the British Library.

Library of Congress Cataloging-in-Publication Data

Names: Auby, Jean-Bernard, author.

Title: Globalisation, law and the state / Jean-Bernard Auby.
Other titles: Globalisation, le droit et l'àetat English

Description: Portland, Oregon : Hart Publishing, 2017. | Includes bibliographical references and index.

Identifiers: LCCN 2016049545 (print) | LCCN 2016049863 (ebook) | ISBN 9781509903528
(hardback) | ISBN 9781509903535 (Epub)

Subjects: LCSH: Law and globalization. | Law—International unification. | Rule of law. |
International and municipal law.

Classification: LCC KZ1268 .A9313 2017 (print) | LCC KZ1268 (ebook) | DDC 341—dc23
LC record available at https://lccn.loc.gov/2016049545

ISBN: HB: 978-1-50990-352-8
PB: 978-1-50993-019-7
ePDF: 978-1-50990-354-2
ePub: 978-1-50990-353-5

Typeset by Compuscript Ltd, Shannon

Foreword

I first read Jean-Bernard Auby's outstanding book *La globalisation, le droit et l'État* 12 years ago. The chance to do so came by way of invitation to review the book—then in its first edition—for the *European Public Law* journal. I remember being keen to read the book not just because I was familiar with some of Professor Auby's other work—notably on public authority liability—but also because 'globalisation' was becoming an increasingly prominent term in public law scholarship. This terminological shift was something that had introduced public lawyers to a number of normative and empirical questions about globalisation, where literature from the social, economic and political sciences had already provided important and challenging insights. However, for public lawyers, the idea that there are self-sustaining processes above the level of the state, which engage the state as an 'input' and 'output' actor, was always going to give rise to discipline-specific questions about the nature, source and ordering of power. *La globalisation, le droit et l'État* was thus prominent among a number of legal texts that appeared at that time and which considered globalisation's implications for, among other things, legal institutions, constitutionalism and the creation of (public and private) legal norms.

The approach which informed the first edition of the book—and which has been carried forward for this, translated, second edition—was one that was intellectually pragmatic in the face of debates about the nature of globalisation. The various and well-known critiques of globalisation have long been informed by a range of conceptual and/or sectoral concerns, whether associated with green theory, democratic theory, human rights, cultural relativism, and/or economic development (among other things). Professor Auby's book acknowledges such concerns and that globalisation can rightly be regarded as problematic, although its more fundamental premise is that globalisation is a working reality that has important implications for legal principle and practice. In adopting this approach, the book identifies economic, political and cultural dimensions to the phenomenon—which is also said to have multiple stages and levels—and uses these to analyse a range of challenges for perceived legal orthodoxy. These include a blurring of the public/private distinction, an evolving role for international law and its institutions, the pursuit of accountability through 'global' administrative law principles, and the diminishing space of state sovereignty. These, and other issues, are analysed as aspects of an unavoidably changed legal landscape with far-reaching consequences for the operation of standards and values.

Of course, for UK public lawyers, the publication of the book in English comes shortly after the Brexit vote of 23 June 2016 and it is, in that sense, particularly timely. Although the UK and EU are only beginning to address the political, economic, legal and administrative difficulties that Brexit will entail, it is already clear that the process of UK withdrawal will, at some levels at least, be illusory rather than real. This is very much one outworking of the fact that different legal systems now have multiple points of intersection with one another, where the idea that a national system can disentangle itself from a supranational order is as fanciful as it is misleading. While it is yet to be seen whether Brexit will result in a 'hard' or a 'soft' UK 'departure', it is inevitable that EU law (which can be influenced by—and influence— norms of international/global law) will continue to have direct and indirect influences within the UK system. Brexit therefore provides a particularly striking example of the linkages that Professor Auby's book analyses, and those who wish to understand the challenges that Brexit will present will learn much from this illuminating text.

A final word about the book is one that is more personal in nature. After writing my review of the first edition, I was fortunate enough to meet Professor Auby at a number of conferences and, thereafter, to collaborate with him on a range of projects. The excellence that characterises this book is something that runs across all of Professor Auby's work, and I have been greatly privileged to have had the chance to work with him. It goes without saying that it has also been my privilege to write the foreword for this English language version of his book, which now complements the original French work, as well as versions that have been published in Spanish and in Chinese. I can think only that the translation of this book into English will further its already considerable influence on debates about the nature and dynamics of globalisation.

Gordon Anthony
School of Law
Queen's University
Belfast
September 2016

Contents

Table of Cases

Introduction

Our law here, their law there; one law on this side, another law on that side; international law and domestic law both overlapping and separate; English law and French law juxtaposed and strictly separate... Our accepted view of the legal world is two-dimensional.

Globalisation is gradually forcing us to abandon that conception.

The current trend of economic, cultural and technical globalisation has influenced, and indeed continues to influence, the law, generating new phenomena—intermingling, interconnection, transversality—that radically alter its shape. These phenomena are gradually drawing it towards a three-dimensional geometry that can easily be described as being less and less Euclidian.

The aim of this book is to discuss globalisation's legal dimension. It goes without saying that there are other aspects to the phenomenon, and that different approaches may be taken. Furthermore, decanting its legal aspects is a particularly difficult exercise, as globalisation gives the sense of being driven by economic forces, technical imperatives, even political motivations, rather than legal proposals. The fact that, in addition, it is composed of heterogeneous mechanisms, situated in quite different spheres, together with the fact that the reality of globalisation is only partly complete, also complicates matters. This book claims only to be an essay that aims to shed light on some aspects of the problem at hand.

A word on the method, which may cautiously be dubbed 'critical positivism'.[1] It strikes us that the 'globalisation of law' may only be approached as a subject from a position of relative or critical positivism. We can contribute to the legal understanding of legal phenomena at work here only through the usual positivist approach, which simply requires that no proposition be made without reference to a law, judicial decision, customary rule, contractual practice, etc—in short, confirmation in positive law. Conversely, it must not be forgotten that law does not tell us everything about social realities (of which it is but one level), or that social realities sometimes work contrary to that which the law formally states. The critical caution that an awareness of these facts demands must be exercised, especially when examining an evolving phenomenon, the balances of which are not readily identified

---

[1] *cf* Luc Wintgens, *Droit, principes et théories. Pour un positivisme critique* (Brussels, Bruylant, 2000).

and which—and this cannot be overemphasised—tends to destabilise tenets, principles and hierarchies that form the basis of our law. To analyse the globalisation of law when one's mind is full of the certainties one may have on ordinary technical issues is to run the risk of missing many things.

A balanced approach to the subject is all the more difficult in that, as regards globalisation and legal globalisation more specifically, there is the constant temptation to take an approach based on the value judgements that we each necessarily make on these phenomena. There is no need to emphasise the lively and numerous debates on globalisation. As regards the globalisation of law, there are naturally positions of principle, be they violently hostile or effusively supportive. For some, the globalisation of law drives our legal systems to deny some of their basic principles, particularly those relating to the welfare state. For others it is—at least in some respects—a good in itself, a goal to be achieved: this is the stance of those campaigning for the development of a global criminal law and international human rights protection,[2] and is frequently that of environmental law specialists who wish for a global law on a par with the worldwide environmental heritage to be protected.[3] Many, in truth, make a Manichean distinction between what would constitute 'good' globalisation—of values, human rights, the environment—and 'bad' globalisation—economic globalisation, or that which eats into state and corporate power and threatens the various protections associated with it.

The conviction behind this book is that globalisation and the globalisation of law are neither good nor bad in themselves. That they transform the frameworks in which our collective value systems are rooted, that they change the way in which the public good is formulated and implemented, is undeniable. However, the effects that they produce in doing so are sometimes positive, sometimes negative.[4] In any event, these are facts that must be studied as such before we concern ourselves with assessing them in order to judge the phenomena that cause them.

We must stress again that a collection of emerging realities will be discussed: we will be in the presence of processes rather than states; a

---

[2] eg, especially Mireille Delmas Marty. See, in particular, *Trois défis pour un droit mondial* (Paris, Le Seuil, 1997).

[3] See, eg, Michel Prieur, 'Mondialisation et droit de l'environnement' in Charles-Albert Morand (ed), *Le droit saisi par la mondialisation* (Bruxelles, Bruylant, 2001) 397.

[4] Economic globalisation, for instance, contributes to the development of emerging nations while deepening inequalities if it is not accompanied by a global redistribution strategy—see, eg, Zaki Laidi, *La grande perturbation* (Paris, Flammarion, 2004). It contributes to international prosperity, but also frees economic forces that are likely to threaten a number of essential protections: Pierre de Senarclens and Ali Kazancigil (eds), *Regulating Globalization: Critical Approach to Global Governance* (United Nations, United Nations University Press, 2007) 275ff.

developing system rather than an established one. We will describe the orientations at work rather than stabilised legal configurations.

Six years passed between the 2004 and 2010 French editions of this essay, which was published as part of the *Clefs Montchrestien* collection. The question arose as to whether the subject matter had evolved literally and metaphorically in the meantime.

The realities of economic, social and cultural globalisation have not been disproved. Even the 2008 financial crisis had no tangible effect on its trajectory: states undoubtedly appear to have regained the upper hand, but this does little to disguise the fact that the crisis was, by its very essence, transnational and that national control was confined within particularly narrow limits. The economic difficulties faced by developed nations have without doubt reduced migratory flows, but that reduction would appear to be limited and temporary.

Legal globalisation has also peacefully taken its course towards a growing interconnection of systems, national systems, international law and domestic law, etc. The vagaries of the discussions within the World Trade Organisation (WTO) show that economic globalisation is by no means a quiet river, but WTO law is not the only factor in the legal globalisation phenomenon.

The scope of the book's ambitions extends to describing the current status of a process that is far from complete. The transformations that globalisation brings about within the world's political, economic and legal organisation are on such a scale, and the phenomenon gives such a striking impression of only having displayed part of its potential, that analysts are necessarily compelled to sail the waters of conjecture and prediction. This is perhaps all the more true for law than it is for other spheres. The global legal space, the global legal system, have yet to offer up all their secrets, and our view of the world's legal structure is adapting little by little to what they gradually allow us to glimpse of their development.

According to one modern political philosopher, 'education, politics and law cannot keep up with the pace set by a globalised world'.[5] What is absolutely true, in any event, is that legal science chases after the changes that globalisation induces, using all its branches in a bid to understand what is happening. The task of overhauling existing concepts is undoubtedly considerable, and all the good will in the world will be needed to accomplish it.

First, we will examine how law is influenced by globalisation, before questioning the processes by which the globalisation of law operates (chapter 1). Next, we will discuss the main areas of legal globalisation (chapter 2) before describing its mechanics, the way in which norms and relations between

---

[5] Daniel Innerarity, *Le futur et ses ennemis. De la confiscation de l'avenir à l'espérance politique* (Paris, Climats, 2008) 114.

systems emerge therein (chapter 3). The question of power and legitimacy in the global legal space will then be considered (chapter 4). We will venture to formulate hypotheses on the operation of the global legal space (chapter 5) and the structure of a global law under construction (chapter 6). We will finish by offering a number of complementary points on the implications of globalisation for public law (chapter 7).

1

The Law as Influenced by Globalisation

B EFORE TACKLING THE question of how globalisation comes into contact with the law, or exerts influence over it (see 'II. The Globalisation of Law' below), we must first say a few brief words on what globalisation is (see 'I. What is Globalisation?' below). Indeed, there is a great deal of disagreement, not to mention frequent misunderstandings, as to the meaning of the term, which can come as no surprise, given the obviously complex developments at work. These in turn have a disruptive effective on the usual ways in which we understand the structure of the world.

I. WHAT IS GLOBALISATION?

Globalisation is a difficult phenomenon to characterise, because it is a complex orchestration of factors; identifying its general directions demands a certain amount of effort.[1] The few comments below strive to define the globalisation phenomenon, in a very general way, through its origins, nature and scope, together with its various levels.

In order to sum things up, reference must be made to the notion according to which globalisation places political, economic, social, etc systems in a state of growing interconnectedness; one may subscribe to the rather

---

[1] There is now a great deal of economic, sociological, political, etc analysis of globalisation. Anglophone library shelves are perhaps likely to crumble under their weight. Reference can be made, for instance, to the following works.

English: Ulrich Beck, *What is globalization?* (Cambridge, Polity Press, 2000); Saskia Sassen, *A Sociology of Globalization* (New York: W W Norton & Company, Inc, 2007); Jan Aart Scholte, *Globalization. A critical introduction* (London, Macmillan and New York, St Martin Press Inc, 2000).

French: Elie Cohen, *L'ordre économique mondial* (Paris, Fayard, 2001); Pierre de Senarclens, *La mondialisation. Théories, enjeux et débats*, 4th edn (Paris, Armand Colin, 2005); Jacques Levy et al, *L'invention du Monde. Une géographie de la mondialisation* (Paris, Presses de Sciences Po, 2008).

effective definition given by David Goldman, who describes it as 'the increasing interconnections amongst things that happen in the world'.[2,3]

A. Origins of the Phenomenon

i. The Economic Dimension

The globalisation trend is, first and foremost, obviously economic in nature.[4]

On this front, it is first characterised by an opening up of economic areas; an expansion of international trade. Since the end of the Second World War, international trade has grown by 6.5 per cent per annum in real terms, more rapidly than world production.[5] Average customs duties stood at 3 per cent at the end of the twentieth century, as opposed to 25 per cent in the 1960s.[6] Between 1979 and 1998, the total daily value of foreign exchange transactions went from US $100 billion to US $1,500 billion.[7]

However, economic globalisation is fuelled by realities other than those mentioned above which, by their nature, are not truly unique and can be found in other periods of history. What is much more specific to it is a drastic increase in the mobility of activities and firms—which have also more frequently become multinationals; mobility and a multinational character are not necessarily connected. The number of multinational companies continued to grow through the second half of the twentieth century. There were approximately 7,000 such companies by the end of the 1960s, and close to 45,000 in 1997.[8] The World Investment Report adopted by UNCTAD in 1999 registered close to 60,000 and stated that, with almost 500,000 subsidiaries, they accounted for approximately one-quarter of world production in 1998. Multinationals, which are primarily European, Japanese or American, sometimes wield considerable power: as recalled by Sabino

---

[2] David Goldman, 'Historial Aspects of Globalisation and Law', in Catherine Dauvergne (ed), *Jurisprudence for an Interconnected Globe* (Aldershot, Ashgate, 2003), 43.

[3] Another way of formulating the same concept is to say that, in a globalising world, there is a sort of 'universal immediacy': Daniel Innerarity, *El nuevo espacio público* (Madrid, Espasa, 2006) 224.

[4] Aside from the references provided in note 5 below, see, eg, Paul Hirst and Grahame Thompson, *Globalization in Question*, 2nd edn (Cambridge, Polity Press, 1999); Roland Blum, *Mondialisation: chances et risques*, Rapport de la Commission des Affaires étrangères de l'Assemblée Nationale, no 1963, 1999; Charles-Albert Michalet, *Le capitalisme mondial*, coll Quadridge (Paris, PUF, 1998); Pierre-Paul Proulx, 'La mondialisation de l'économie et le rôle de l'Etat' in François Crépeau (ed), *Mondialisation des échanges et fonctions de l'Etat* (Brussels, Bruylant, 1997) 125.

[5] Pierre de Senarclens, *La mondialisation*, 4th edn (Paris, Armand Colin, 2005) 75.

[6] Nicolas Baverez, 'A l'épreuve de la mondialisation' in Roger Fauroux and Bernard Spitz (eds), *Notre Etat. Le livre-vérité sur la fonction publique* (Paris, Robert Laffont, 2000).

[7] Scholte *Globalization*. (n 1) 86.

[8] ibid.

Cassese, General Motors' turnover prior to the company's setbacks in 2005 was greater than the GDP of states such as Saudi Arabia, Turkey or Poland.[9,10]

A corollary to the expansion of such transnational economic activity is the rise of the world economy's financial dimension. This has become preponderant, profitability being sought less through the internal growth of firms than it is through investments made on the global markets[11]—whence the growing significance of mergers and acquisitions realised on a global level.

To these trends is added the characteristic phenomenon of spatial dislocation or dislocation of economic activities, particularly financial and communication activities, typically shown by the modern globalisation of financial markets. These economic functions tend to be exercised with almost no link to a specific location, across networks—the Internet, in particular—which are absolutely global, and in the operation of which the location of operators is of relatively little importance. Pierre de Senarclens points out that Swissair's booking system is handled in India, while Siemens' IT e-maintenance service is operated from the Philippines.[12] In India today, e-services aimed at the external market employ 110,000 people and produce an annual turnover in the region of US $1.5 billion.[13] Ulrich Beck adds the following anecdote:[14] after 6pm, announcements at Berlin's Tegel airport are made from California, without airport users being any the wiser...

As for those (still dominant) activities that may only be exercised in specific locations (owing to the need for proximity to physical, administrative and relational resources, etc), globalisation nevertheless pushes for their movement. It manifests itself here in the form of competition between countries to host companies which are themselves looking for areas that are as welcoming as possible on a fiscal, legal and political level. In particular, this results in the relocation of those companies likely to move their installations in order to find the most advantageous locations in fiscal terms, trade regulations, etc.

[9] Sabino Cassese (2002) 'Lo spazio giuridico globale', *Rivista trimestrale di diritto pubblico* 2, 323.

[10] A report published in 1999 by an American think-tank, the Institute for Political Studies, showed that a significant proportion of the leading global economic bodies were made up of companies: see Gavin Anderson, *Constitutional Rights after Globalization* (Oxford, Hart Publishing, 2005) 22.

[11] See Charles-Albert Michalet, 'Les métamorphoses de la mondialisation. Une approche économique' in Éric Loquin and Catherine Kessedjian, *La mondialisation du droit* (Paris, Litec, 2000), 11.

[12] de Senarclens *La mondialisation* (n 5) 124.

[13] Jean-François Bayart, *Le gouvernement du monde. Une critique politique de la globalisation* (Paris, Grasset, 2004) 190. They now include a substantial proportion of legal services subcontracted by Western companies: *Le Monde*, 3 April 2009, 3.

[14] Beck *What is globalization?* (n 1) 15.

ii. Other Dimensions

As essential as they are, the economic developments mentioned above do not constitute globalisation in its entirety. There are other dimensions to globalisation, which are as follows:

a. Cultural and Ideological Dimensions

There is a cultural and ideological reality to globalisation.[15] That reality is founded on a technical substratum: the development of powerful communication tools (eg the Internet, satellite television) which have breathed life into Marshall McLuhan's 'planetary village' prophesy. World events are, broadly, experiences shared through common images and messages, even where the national media put their own spin on the items that they broadcast.

These broadly common communication tools are a vehicle for the shared values of cultural and ideological globalisation—and they are shared, even where there is a degree of variation in the ways in which they are understood, and all the more so in the ways in which they are embodied. Global values encompass economic competition and the consumer society on a global scale, but also the rule of law, the ethics of human rights, the protection of the world's ecological heritage, etc. The latter values are an equal part of a global ideology, on the same footing as those of opening up trade or competition, which values surround economic globalisation.

For example, it can be said that globalisation is just as much the worldwide television broadcasts of sessions of the International Criminal Tribunal for the former Yugoslavia (ICTY) as it is that of advertisements for Coca-Cola or Nike. These extremely diverse elements are like so many faces of cultural and ideological globalisation.

b. Social Dimension

There is also a social dimension to globalisation, in the sense of movements directly affecting the lifestyles and working habits of the planet's inhabitants.

This includes the dissemination of shared consumption habits fuelled by the growing mobility of individuals, whether through migration or tourism—and that is before we take account of the fact that, according to sociologists, we can identify 'emerging global classes', ie groups of persons who are not necessarily mobile, but contribute directly to global processes,

---

[15] Gérard Leclerc, *La mondialisation culturelle. La civilisation à l'épreuve* (Paris, PUF, 2000); Arjun Appadurai, *Modernity at Large: Cultural Dimension of Globalisation* (Minneapolis, University of Minnesota Press, 1997).

such as economic and particularly financial players, activist groups, NGO experts, etc.

Within the business world, economic globalisation concerns in particular the consequences that the mobility of economic activities has for employment flows, particularly from developed to developing nations.

The truth is that migratory developments are not new. However, what the experts do highlight is that globalisation generates new migratory flows and sometimes leads to proactive policies of emigration—one may cite the examples of South Korea and China, in recent times—or immigration, while illegal immigration and human trafficking thrive.[16]

B. The Nature and Scope of the Phenomenon

Everything that has just been stated relates in some way to the *symptoms* of globalisation without telling us a great deal about the nature of the phenomenon. A number of remarks must be added here with a view to identifying its nature and scope.

i. The Degree of Novelty in Modern Globalisation

There is much debate as to whether the globalisation we are currently witnessing is an unprecedented phenomenon. Some argue that the world witnessed a similar trend during the Renaissance; others associate it instead—or even cumulatively—with the birth of capitalism in the nineteenth century;[17] still others make the same assertion about ancient times.[18]

Lawyers are ill-placed to come to a conclusion in this debate. Nevertheless, an examination of these alternative views shows us that although history provides examples of earlier periods in which, for instance, trade opened up, setting the foundations of what we know today, the current realities are of a particular intensity and nature. While arguing that the world experienced wide-ranging globalisation in the nineteenth century, CA Bayly[19] concedes that current globalisation presents three unique characteristics: it is polycentric; the nation state has weakened while the markets have grown more powerful; and, the digital revolution has been such that the world's transitivity is now without parallel in its scale and dimension.

---

[16] Sassen, *A Sociology of Globalization* (n 1) 129 ff; Catherine Dauvergne, 'Illegal Migration and Sovereignty, in Dauvergne *Jurisprudence* (n 2) 187.

[17] eg CA Bayly, *The Birth of the Modern World 1780–1914. Global Connections and Comparisons* (Oxford, Blackwell, 2004).

[18] eg David J Bederman, *Globalisation and International Law* (New York, Palgrave Macmillan, 2008).

[19] Bayly *Modern World* (n 17).

With the strong expansion of international trade (detailed above), the expansion of communications does indeed constitute an unprecedented development that is absolutely strategic in terms of scope. As Thomas Friedman noted: 'The world is flat'.[20] Communication between individuals has been revolutionised in three stages: firstly, with the invention of the personal computer; next, the advent of the Internet; and, lastly, the creation of communication standards (such as FTTP and HTML) in the 1990s, which make computer software interoperable and allow users to work on content with anyone, anywhere.

ii. The Nature of the Globalisation Phenomenon

In order to form a clearer idea of the nature of the globalisation phenomenon, one must remember that it has its own specific players. However, the truth is that it is easier to characterise its mechanics though the processes that allow it to exist.

There are a great many specific players involved in globalisation. Firstly, there are those from international institutions (be they regional or global) that promote or regulate the economic, social and ideological openings in which the globalisation phenomenon consists. A significant proportion of international organisations are concerned here, but especially those which are in charge of economic exchanges worldwide or international human rights protection. Next come the world economic and/or cultural operators, including multinational corporations. Lastly, there are the many non-governmental organisations, including those which are the guardians of human rights or the environment, and which are not always powerless in the face of the might of those players mentioned above: Greenpeace, for instance, now has some 26 independent national and regional offices and a total of 55 offices in 55 countries, while its annual revenue stands at US $324 million.[21,22]

We will return to the issue of the significant place occupied by some private players, both in the world's economic and social life and in the conduct of public affairs in the modern world.

That said, the deeper nature of globalisation today also lays—perhaps above all—in the (social, economic, etc) processes that it brings to bear, and which are quite unique in light of that to which we had become accustomed in our civilisations.

---

[20] Thomas Friedman, *The World is Flat: A Brief History of the Twenty-First Century* (New York, Farrar, Strauss and Giroux, 2005).

[21] de Senarclens, *La mondialisation* (n 5) 47.

[22] Greenpeace 2014 Annual Report, at www.greenpeace.org/international/Global/international/publications/greenpeace/2015/ANNUAL_REPORT_2014.pdf.

The most striking aspect in this respect is spatial dislocation: the 'deterritorialisation' of economic and social activities and mechanisms.[23] What is at stake here is a rearrangement of territories, on the basis of a dislocation of certain activities. As Jarrod Wiener points out,[24] Internet technology affords a person located within the territory of State A the possibility of committing an offence in State B, without really being within the territory of State B. For example, a person located in State A can hack into the IT system of a bank located in State B and siphon funds into an account located in State C. A number of social realities which have traditionally been firmly rooted in a state's territory are also witnessing the same kind of dislocation: as explained by Olivier Roy, while religions have traditionally been connected to cultures, they now tend to be detaching themselves from their original territories and contexts.[25]

The second process that is so characteristic of globalisation is a process of denationalisation of companies and of the world as a whole. This phenomenon admittedly has sources other than globalisation: it also arises from more general developments affecting authority and power in our societies, which are currently witnessing a general—albeit relative—denationalisation trend. It has also been fuelled, quite naturally, by neoliberal policies to which a number of leading nations have subscribed, particularly during the 1980s and 1990s. However, globalisation brings with it a further, significant dimension: the opening up of economic areas, the dislocation of activities, etc which, in themselves, reduce a state's ability to control and regulate social processes. We will examine this issue in greater detail (see chapter 4) and qualify the preceding observation; in many respects, it is more a question of changes in the place occupied and role played by states than it is of their marginalisation. Globalisation nevertheless contributes to a degree of decline in the centrality of the state in our societies. Some argue that globalisation causes, above all, a sort of 'denationalisation' of states, which have increasingly come to serve specific ends or take part in processes that go beyond them. Therein lies the leading development that globalisation has imposed on them.

The third characteristic process is that which consists in the expansion of transnational realities and mechanisms. What is most striking here is the fact that, in the realities of the modern world, there is a relatively high level of social, economic and cultural amalgamation between different societies. Our supermarket aisles are full of foreign products that once had to be sought in their countries of origin; equally, the mere click of a button on

---

[23] Bertrand Badie, *La fin des territoires* (Paris, Fayard, 1995); *Un monde sans souveraineté* (Paris, Fayard, 1999).

[24] Jarrod Wiener, *Globalization and the Harmonization of Law* (London and New York, Pinter, 1999): preface.

[25] Olivier Roy, *L'islam mondialisé* (Paris, Le Seuil, 2002).

a television remote control allows us to flick from an English channel to a French, Italian or Egyptian one.

One counterargument is that this social, economic and cultural inter-penetration is especially marked in the European sphere and is much less frequently encountered in other parts of the world. This is true to an extent, and is the type of nuance that we will examine at this juncture.

iii. Globalisation's Limits and Contradictions

Globalisation generates many strong opinions. Its supporters see it as the tool for building global prosperity thanks to the market's revenge on those states that have dominated the world since the seventeenth century,[26] or through which global democracy and the world's civil society will triumph over the egotism of the nation state. Its detractors view it as the key to the final victory of the market, of capitalism, of multinationals, to the detriment of the Third World, the environment and/or national social protection measures.

However, globalisation is a phenomenon that is particularly resistant to this kind of sweeping, eschatological or cataclysmic judgement, as it is so full of contradictions and confined within what would appear to be enduring limits. It ceaselessly yields contradictory trends, as various political, economic or social battles unfold.

As one author[27] recalls, one of the sticking points in the debate within the World Trade Organisation (WTO), surrounding the Multilateral Agreement on Investment (MAI), was the US-led demand made by multinationals that a principle be included under which any substantial change in the conditions that led a company to invest in a given state shall be compensated by that state. American environmental protection groups provoked the response to that demand by mobilising their European counterparts. It was, in other words, the global environmental players who forced the global economic players to back down.

The various components of globalisation—economic on the one hand; cultural and social on the other—are constantly at odds. In particular, the contradictions between economic globalisation and the universalisation of human rights, as shown by Mireille Delmas-Marty,[28] constantly fuel the trend.

---

[26] See, eg, Daniel Yerglin and Joseph Stanislaw, *The Commanding Heights* (New York, Touchstone, 1999).

[27] Olivier Audeoud, 'L'Etat dans tous ses états', *Mélanges Borella* (Presses Universitaires de Nancy, 1999), 22.

[28] Mireille Delmas-Marty 'La mondialisation du droit: chances et risques' (Paris, Dalloz, 1999) 2.

Contradictions, then, but also limits. Even in the economic sphere, which nevertheless seems to be the engine driving the economic opportunities presented by globalisation, those same limits emerge. It is frequently noted that multinational companies, whilst being multinational in their activities, are often not so in the composition of their management teams. One author observes that the increasingly close ties between the Japanese and American economies have done little to bridge the chasm separating the different conceptions of entrepreneurial activity in each of the two countries.[29]

Globalisation's mechanisms are equally more or less marked depending on the region of the world and depending on the period.

The phenomena of spatial dislocation of activities, denationalisation of companies and growing transnationality are especially marked in those parts of the world which either are particularly vulnerable owing to the weakness of their state and national structures (as is the case for some parts of the Third World), or voluntarily expose themselves through deliberate regional agreements. Elsewhere, they will be less visible.

The intensity of these phenomena surely varies over time as well. Periods of international *détente* see them flourish: it is no accident that the emergence of what we now call globalisation came about when the Cold War came to an end. Conversely, the economic crisis which occurred in 2008 has certainly had the effect of slowing, perhaps even—relatively speaking— reversing the trend: this is because it resulted in states being less inclined to lend themselves to the various opportunities presented by economic globalisation—protectionist temptations can be difficult to contain—and because it drove them to establish national protection and recovery policies, which place them firmly back in the saddle—all within the fairly restrictive limits on what economic integration and international and European commitments allow to be done on a national level. It also, if not stemmed, then redirected migratory flows, as shown by the 2009 edition of the OECD's annual report, 'Trends in international migration.'

C. The Different Stages of Globalisation

In order to characterise the globalisation phenomenon, further indications of what may be termed a 'morphological' nature must be added to the above. The essential point is as follows: our understanding of globalisation must not be confined to its global, universal aspects; it must also be understood to act on many other levels, including regional integration and, in particular, the European construct.

---

[29] John Gray, *False Dawn. The Delusions of Global Capitalism* (London, Granta, 1998).

i. A Multilevel Phenomenon

Restricting globalisation to its worldwide manifestations (be they economic or otherwise), as is sometimes done, only scratches the surface. In reality, it is present on all levels of international society; it is, by its very essence, 'multilevel.'

As has been seen, that which is characteristic of globalisation involves an opening up, dislocation, transnationality, etc. As such, globalisation cannot be reduced to its most obvious worldwide expressions (the WTO, G20, etc). The position would be different only if it were to comply with the most traditional organisation of international society, in which the realities that go beyond national divisions rest on international institutions created for the purpose.

Globalisation questions and crosses the frontiers of national systems, and only partly follows the path of international institutions in the traditional sense. Its players and mechanisms are often of a different nature.

The result is that the mechanisms and phenomena that constitute globalisation are no more global than they are regional; no more regional than national; no more national than sub-national. The Internet is no more global than it is regional, national or sub-national; it is all of those things at once, as it can be used as much in relations between international institutions as it can in internal relations within local companies.

As explained in particular by Saskia Sassen,[30] the state is an essential component in the globalisation process. Moreover, the global can also be found on a local level. Sassen again shows that one of the essential infrastructures of the modern world's political and economic organisation is made up of a network of 'global' cities, the great world centres of financial and service-sector activities. The truth is that this presence of the global in local matters manifests itself in the considerable expansion of international co-operation between regional and local authorities, the expansion of which has been especially strong in a European context: where a French regional or local authority on or near the border enters into a co-operation project with a German, Italian or Spanish neighbour, the result is neither European, nor national nor local, but rather all of those things at once, and may indeed be characterised as global.

ii. The Vertical and Horizontal Nature of the Globalisation Trend

If we accept the above, it becomes clear that the phenomena linked to globalisation have both vertical and horizontal dimensions: globalisation is not a phenomenon placed 'above' national systems or local societies.

---

[30] *A Sociology of Globalization*, cited above.

Globalisation thus spans systems and societies horizontally, by creating the openings discussed above. It intensifies transnationality, whether it concerns transnational economic activities, intergovernmental networks or transnational activism, etc.

Naturally, it also has a vertical dimension as it spans systems and societies, producing its effects on all levels: local and global, regional and national. As we shall see below, it redistributes the cards between these various echelons, sometimes causing surprising role-reversals between the various levels.

The main elements that contribute to making globalisation a phenomenon whose consequences are both horizontal and vertical are summarised in the table below.

Conducting public affairs in a globalised context

	Vertical phenomena	Horizontal phenomena
International public entities	International institutions increasingly fulfilling traditionally national functions	Growing number of national networks of public institutions: — traditional administrative bodies — new types of regulators
Non-state international or transnational players	Growing role of non-state international players taking part in public affairs, including regulators	Growing role of non-state transnational players, sometimes fulfilling regulatory functions
National systems	National institutions increasingly fulfilling international functions	Transnational co-operation between national or international institutions

iii. Regional Integration and Globalisation

If we accept its validity, the analysis above raises (acutely so) the question of how to locate regional integration, and particularly the European construction, within the globalisation trend, and of knowing what meaning it takes on in relation to that trend.

In light of globalisation, the truth is that regional integration processes would all appear to have mixed meanings. They convey the various openings that globalisation involves and implies: for instance, quite clearly, development projects in the field of regionalisation on the American continent—Alena, Mercosur—'were designed and implemented in order to facilitate integration into the globalisation process and to respond to the new competitive conditions that it entails.'[31] In economic terms, it can be argued that regional integration has the advantage of placing national economies into the globalisation phenomenon with lower transaction costs than those incurred in the wider globalisation context.[32] What happens within those economies in terms of the opening-up of markets and cultures, spatial dislocation, etc is perhaps the most sophisticated aspect of globalisation. They are key elements in the fabric of globalisation.[33]

At the same time, such regional integration is also the construction of 'islands' of protection for certain markets, and for certain legal, economic, cultural particularities, etc.[34] In this sense, it gives the impression that they buck the trend. It must, in fact, be viewed as a level of globalisation; one of the contexts in which it unfolds.

One author[35] argues that international regionalisation may, in fact, be examined as a response to globalisation, on four levels. It corresponds to the need for regional areas to act on behalf of global organisations, whose implementation resources are limited. It responds to the globalisation of political agendas through the development of locally integrated political programmes. It allows all Member States to participate more effectively—albeit indirectly—in international forums. It is a means of ensuring the survival of the nation state, with a maintained, if altered, sovereignty.

iv. The European Construct and Globalisation

What we have noted above also applies to the European construct.

The latter is above all a tool used in freeing up the movement of goods, services and capital. While it achieves this opening-up in its own way, thus fulfilling—to use Jacqueline de la Rochère's excellent wording[36]—'a more specific role in identifying a need that must be expressed in terms of what is possible for the States concerned'. With its own decisions for the creation of the single market, and above all the abolition of exchange controls and the liberalisation of the financial markets in the 1990s, the European Union (EU) has made a significant contribution to the acceleration of the

---

[31] Blum, *Mondialisation* (n 4) 47.

[32] Gérard Kebadjian, *Les théories de l'économie politique internationale* (Le Seuil, 1999) 287.

[33] Louise Fawcett, 'Regionalism and global governance. An appraisal' in Pierre de Senarclens and Ali Kazancigil (eds), *Regulating Globalization: Critical Approach to Global Governance* (United Nations, United Nations University Press, 2007) 150.

[34] On this dialectic, see, eg, Roland Axtmann, *Globalization and Europe. Theoretical and Empirical Investigation*, (London and Washington, Pinter, 1998).

[35] Paul Taylor, *International Organization in the Age of Globalization* (London, New York, Continuum, 2003) 256 ff.

[36] Jacqueline de la Rochère, 'Mondialisation et régionalisation' in Loquin and Kessedjian, *La mondialisation du droit* (n 11) 150.

globalisation process.[37] In its own way, the European Community has been a stage in that process.[38]

Conversely, the EU can serve either as a defensive tool against globalisation, or as a tool in adapting globalisation to European realities: the Common Customs Tariff, the agricultural levy, the Common Agricultural Policy, etc have all served to protect the European Economic Area.[39] The EU is, insofar as its development allows, the seat of a common power that negotiates with global economic authorities. Furthermore, its purposes are mixed: in particular, faced with the WTO's single objective of global free trade, the EU sets down more complex values, of an integrationist nature, which it also strives to have recognised by the WTO.[40]

The fact nevertheless remains that the European construct is deeply vested with phenomena that are characteristic of globalisation: it is an integrated economic area; a broadly integrated cultural area; strict limits have been imposed on state control over the economy; transnational economic, social, cultural, etc realities are the common lot of the Union, etc.

The issue here is not one of knowing whether the EU is a global entity in itself; globalisation is a phenomenon that manifests itself on all levels of government institutions. However, in terms of globalisation taken as a whole, the European construct works both as a relay and as a turning point. Its historical trajectory in some ways makes it an advanced 'laboratory' for globalisation,[41] although that dimension naturally does not summarise that trajectory.

It can also be put another way. Were the EU a nascent state, we would have to treat it as such in our analysis and consider what the impact of globalisation would be on its development, on the same basis as other state institutions. However, the EU is not a nascent state, but something between a confederation and a federation; a group of states that has agreed to act together in the—primarily, but not exclusively economic—globalisation process, drawing the profits and minimising the negative effects thereof.

---

[37] de Senarclens, *La mondialisation* (n 5) 95.

[38] Axtmann, *Globalization and Europe* (n 34) 19; Olivier Audeoud, 'La construction communautaire, étape "régionale" au carrefour de la mondialisation et d'un fédéralisme inachevé' in Council of Europe/Conseil de l'Europe, *Les mutations de l'Etat-nation en Europe à l'aube du XXIᵉ siècle*, 1998.

[39] Philippe Manin, 'Mondialisation et structures étatiques: l'expérience européenne' in François Crépeau (ed) *Mondialisation des échanges et pouvoir de l'Etat* (Brussels, Bruylant, 1997) 150.

[40] See Thiébaut Flory, *L'Organisation mondiale du commerce. Droit institutionnel et substantiel* (Brussels, Bruylant, 1999) 213.

[41] On the two sides of the relationship between European construct and globalisation, see also: Michael Keating, 'Europe's Changing Political Landscape: Territorial Restructuring and New Forms of Government' in Paul Beaumont, Carol Lyons and Neil Walker (eds), *Convergence and Divergence in European Public Law* (Oxford, Hart Publishing, 2002) 3.

The opening effects that it brings about, just like the regulations that it seeks to put in place, are all realities linked to globalisation, and which may be treated as such in the examination below. The openings that it creates, the regulations that it seeks to put in place—these are all realities linked to globalisation, and will be discussed as such below.

II. THE GLOBALISATION OF LAW

Just as globalisation is a complex concept, so too the effect it has on law, which can be termed 'globalisation of law' or 'legal globalisation'. In seeking to understand legal globalisation, in addition to the doubts as to the substance of economic, ideological and cultural globalisation, there are further difficulties that derive from the depths of the law itself, which never accurately reflect the social phenomena that influence it.

We will first identify the main lines of emphasis concerning the pressure that globalisation brings to bear on the law and the process of globalising the law, and offering up a number of comments on the specific interest presented by the scientific theory of legal globalisation compared to others. We will first identify the main lines of emphasis concerning the pressure that globalisation brings to bear on the law, the process of globalising the law, together with the contradictions and limits of legal globalisation. Next, we will offer up a number of comments on the specific interest presented by the *scientific* theory of globalisation as compared with other hypotheses.

A. The Pressure that Globalisation Brings to Bear on the Law

In order to understand the kinds of tensions that globalisation elicits within the law, the basics of globalisation itself are a good starting point. Globalisation is the opening-up of economic, ideological, cultural, social, etc relations; and the growth of deterritorialisation, denationalisation and transnationality in the economic order (but not exclusively so) in a universe where new players (multinational companies, NGOs, individuals, etc) have risen to much greater heights than they had previously.

It is quite easy to see the kind of generalised pressure that these realities naturally exert on the law. At least three central axes emerge:

i. The tension in the direction of the development of norms and legal mechanisms, indifferent to the spatial location of the objects to which they apply

The objective openings offered by globalisation, such as the preoccupations of characteristic global players, push in that direction. For such players, in particular, the plurality of legal systems, the territorialisation of the law, are sources of cost, friction and even inconsistencies.

Globalisation thus exerts pressure in the sense of a harmonisation of rules; a reduction in the control over those rules that was wielded by the plurality of national systems. Leading operators push for a homogenisation of the rules governing international trade. As we shall see, the regulation of the Internet sits in part outside the scope of national laws. International criminal law includes common concepts to prevent those that it is designed to prosecute from sheltering behind domestic legal concepts. A natural trend towards harmonisation lies at the heart of legal globalisation.

There is necessarily a tension, in the sense of the denationalisation of the law, associated with the developments discussed above. A law that is less sensitive to national legal variations is naturally a law that is less dependent on specific state intentions. This does not mean that global law operates outside states—we shall return to this point in greater detail later. It means that states have less control or involvement in global law; that they are called upon, whether they like it or not, to accept more or less uniform rules without which the economic and other opportunities available in the modern world would be hampered; it means that they are also called upon to agree to international institutions producing laws that are partly beyond their control, etc.

ii. The development of norms—of compulsory rules or legal standards—concerning not states, as is traditionally the case under international law, but individuals, private groups (companies, NGOs, etc), even sub-national public authorities

While there is often an impact on states—including, as we shall see, occasionally on the functioning of the governmental machine—the purpose of globalising law is not to guarantee balance and peace between them, or a reduction in the development inequalities that separate them. Instead, it tends to address the practical problems faced by individuals and companies.

Highly characteristic of this development is the international and regional law protecting human rights, which has largely deviated from the prospects for more traditional international law to become a branch of law that mainly concerns individuals and private groups—both as beneficiaries of those rights and as players in their protection—and in which states are increasingly spectators, especially where there are legal penalties that elude them.

Conversely, this is also coupled with the emergence of non-governmental regulators, making rules and standards without being intergovernmental bodies or public international organisations. The rise of state players in the sphere of globalisation can indeed also be seen in the rise of those non-governmental regulators, which can characteristically be found in a number of fields such as standardisation or the Internet, where the main international legal rules are generated by such producers.

iii. The growing acknowledgement and development of transnational legal realities

The economic, social, cultural, etc interpenetration of national systems naturally results in such tension. Multinational companies are in essence transnational legal realities even though, taken individually, the legal mechanisms on which their organisation rests—found under corporate law, taxation law, etc—are almost all borrowed from national law. Cross-border pollution is regulated thanks to an interweaving of mechanisms borrowed from the national laws concerned, sometimes combined with elements of international law.

There is no end to the number of legal transnationality situations, the proliferation of which demands the involvement of the law. The number of people holding more than one nationality continues to grow.[42] The same can be said for the frequency of criminal offences with an international element.[43] Transnational marriages—and divorces—also continue to thrive.[44] Double taxation situations are increasingly common.[45]

A corollary to this legal interpenetration is the development of extraterritorial legal norms and solutions. Sabino Cassese opens his work on the crisis of the state[46] by noting that in 2002, the EU Competition Authority turned its attentions to a draft agreement between General Electric and Honeywell: although it involved two American companies, the draft had to be submitted to the Authority owing to the interests held by those companies on EU territory. The Authority's decision ultimately settled a dispute that was largely internal to the United States.

Extraterritoriality in a context of legal globalisation

Legal extraterritoriality situations are those in which the norms or rules of a given system produce effects outside the territorial scope of that system. They tend to develop in a context of legal globalisation, which raises a series of problems.

---

[42] Linda Bosniak, (2002) 'Multiple Nationality and the Postnational Transformation of Citizenship' 42 *Virginia Journal of International Law* 979.

[43] André Huet and Marie Koenig-Joulin, *Droit pénal international*, 3rd edn, (Paris, PUF, 2005) introduction.

[44] Volkmar Gessmer and Ali Cem Budak (eds), *Emerging Legal Certainty. Empirical Studies on the Globalization of Law* (Aldershot, Ashgate, 1998).

[45] Bernard Castagnède, *Précis de fiscalité internationale* (Paris, PUF, 2002) foreword.

[46] *La crisi dello Stato*, (Bari, Editori Laterza, 2002).

Symptoms of the development of legal extraterritoriality situations:

1. Increasingly frequent cases in which national economic regulations produce effects on partly external situations:
   — Cases involving antitrust legislation, environmental legislation or legislation protecting privacy (Gregory Shaffer, 'The Power of EU Collective Action: The Impact of EU Data Privacy Regulation on US Business Practice' (1999) 5 *European Law Journal* 419), etc.
   — In one sense, growing economic integration means that all national economic regulations may potentially have an extraterritorial impact: Stefano Battini, 'The Globalization of Public Law', *European Review of Public Law*, Spring 2006, 27.
2. Universal jurisdiction mechanisms that break with the traditionally strictly territorial nature of criminal law, be it those adopted by some national systems or those embodied by international criminal courts (see, eg, Ana Peyro Llopis, *La compétence universelle en matière de crimes contre l'humanité* (Brussels, Bruylant, 2003); Stéphane Chauvier, *Justice et droits à l'échelle globale* (Vrin—EHESS, 2006) 61 ff).
3. Cases in which national public bodies act outside the scope of their home territory at the service of international institutions (military or humanitarian interventions, etc) and which raise the question of whether, for example, their constitutional rules on human rights are applicable (Krysztof Wojtyczek, *Le champ territorial d'application d'une constitution nationale*, Séminaire de la Chaire MADP de Sciences Po (16 May 2008): www.sciencespo.fr/chaire-madp/sites/sciencespo.fr.chaire-madp/files/krzysztof_wojtyczek.pdf; Ann Peters, 'The Globalization of State Constitutions' in Janne Nijman and Andre Nollkaemper (eds), *New Perspectives on the Divide between National and International Law* (Oxford, Oxford University Press, 2007) 251.
4. Cases involving international legislation conferring extraterritorial effect to national administrative acts: while there is no obstacle in principle to the extraterritorial application of administrative law (see Mathias Audit, 'La compétence extraterritoriale du droit administratif' in AFDA, *La compétence* (Paris, Litec, 2009)), it is quite rare for an administrative act to be of an imperative nature for anywhere other than the issuing state; EU law nevertheless confers this effect to various national administrative acts—licences to produce and market merchandise, in light of the *Cassis de Dijon* judgment, for example—see Marie Gautier, 'Acte administratif transnational et droit communautaire' in Jean-Bernard Auby and Jacqueline Dutheil de la Rochère (eds), *Droit administratif européen* (Brussels, Bruylant, 2007) 1069.

The management of these frequent instances of legal extraterritoriality raises a number of problems:

1. Substantive problems, relating to:

   — Establishing the applicable law: in particular, when faced with extraterritoriality situations involving public law, it is a matter of establishing whether the conflict rules under private international law are likely to solve those problems. Some will answer in the positive, with the exception of those instances in which a national phenomenon produces effects in two states that have divergent interests.

   — The potential taking into account under national law of the extraterritorial effects of national regulations: one example can be found in the French *Code de l'urbanisme* (Town Planning Code), specifically Article L.121-4-1, which provides that 'the town planning documents applicable to border territories shall take into account the occupation of land in the territories of adjacent States'.

   — Issues of accountability, which are related to the fact that the national control mechanisms that apply to national regulations do not come into play with regard to another state's regulations although there are exceptions (the external accountability gap: Stefano Battini, *Extraterritoriality and Administrative Law*, Séminaire de la Chaire MADP de Sciences Po (16 May 2008): www.sciencespo.fr/chaire-madp/sites/sciencespo.fr.chaire-madp/files/stefano_battini.pdf).

2. Problems relating to judicial protection for those affected extraterritorially:

   — In the 2004 *Hoffman la Roche* case, the Supreme Court of the United States, ruling on the issue of whether a non-American claimant could bring an action before it against a non-American defendant, for events that took place and caused damage outside US national territory, answered in the negative (see Julie Allard and Antoine Garapon, *Les juges dans la mondialisation* (Paris, Le Seuil, 2005) 50).

   — Conversely, under the Schengen system, provision has even been made for a decision refusing residence, a deportation order, etc issued against a foreign national, which decision is made in State A on the basis of the foreign national's inclusion in a database compiled by State B of persons not to be admitted, to be challenged before the courts in State A and for those courts to rule on the lawfulness of a person's inclusion in that database, after requesting, where applicable, justification from State B (Marie Gautier (2005), 'Le dépassement du caractère national de la juridiction administrative: le contentieux Schengen' *Droit administratif*, May 7).

It is quite easy to understand that the phenomena described above bring about profound changes to the relationships between legal systems. Closely related to this is the fact that the more legal systems face external consequences, the more they themselves will produce external consequences, the less they are suited to controlling the legal processes that pass through them and, at the same time, the less the scope of their mechanisms is limited to that which is specific to them: they become both insufficient in scale and externally relevant![47]

B. The Processes of Legal Globalisation

According to Sabino Cassese,[48] what characterises globalisation is more the universalisation of rights than market globalisation. This statement is perhaps excessive, but one thing is certain: as discussed above, globalisation produces sweeping transformation within law and legal institutions. We shall summarise this here, but it is explored in greater detail in later chapters.

We have already noted that it is through the very processes that engender it that globalisation can best be characterised. That is also true of legal globalisation.

The overriding aim of this book is precisely to attempt to shed light on some aspects of the processes of legal globalisation. The issue will therefore crop up repeatedly.

i. The Main Orientations

The tensions that globalisation generates within the law bring about legal globalisation through processes that can generally be characterised as follows.

We shall see that the law of globalisation—globalised law—is made up of norms or rules often with unusual characteristics. They are sometimes unusual in terms of their creation, particularly in that the range of law-makers tends to expand—in particular, to accommodate non-governmental regulators. They are sometimes unusual in terms of their content, particularly where it must accommodate an implementation carried out through different legal traditions—one example is the very 'open' concepts conveyed by human rights law. They are often unusual in terms of the ways in which they are connected to each other and to norms under non-global law; we

---

[47] On this last point, see in particular: Stefano Battini (2006) 'The Globalization of Public Law', 18 *European Review of Public Law* 1, 27.

[48] 'Le droit administratif global. Une introduction', (2007) *Droit administratif* May, 17.

will look more closely at the phenomena linked to legal 'dehierarchisation' that are associated with globalisation. They are often unusual in terms of their implementation, particularly the way in which they often combine with national legal and other mechanisms, be they international or from another domestic legal system.

Perhaps even more than the rules of which it is composed, legal globalisation is characterised by the relationships between systems found therein. Three trends, which will be examined below, strike us as characteristic here. First, the trend of 'permeabilisation' affecting legal systems: globalisation renders legal systems more vulnerable to the penetration of external norms or rules. Next, the trend of competition between legal systems: globalisation makes their differences and similarities, advantages and disadvantages, both more visible and more significant in the eyes of the growing numbers of players who may find themselves immersed in a variety of legal contexts. Lastly, the trend towards the harmonisation of legal systems: confronted with and interpenetrated by each other, legal systems tend to harmonise their disparate solutions concerning the activities and phenomena affected by globalisation.

ii. Vertical and Horizontal Dimensions of Legal Globalisation

Just as the phenomena linked to globalisation can be both vertical and horizontal in nature,[49] so this applies in the legal sphere.

The current significance of the horizontal flows of legal transnationality has already been discussed. The numbers of players and situations straddling national legal systems continue to grow, bringing with them new legal challenges, be it by their nature or by their scale.

Legal globalisation also crosses legal systems vertically. It imbues them with international norms, but it also increasingly places the onus on legal systems for the practical implementation of those norms. It modifies the allocation of responsibilities between national systems and international legal bodies, etc.

iii. Between Old and New

The legal globalisation processes undoubtedly have a powerful transformative effect on the world's legal organisation. This does not mean to say that it has in any way transformed that organisation.

On the one hand, in order to solve new problems presented by globalisation, it goes without saying that the law sometimes draws on some of its most traditional mechanisms. As we shall see, for instance, the harmonisation

---

[49] Cf above, 'ii The Vertical and Horizontal Nature of the Globalisation Trend'.

of norms under economic globalisation is broadly based on national laws, which also occasionally transpose international models that have no legal force in themselves, without any external, pioneering, hierarchical pressure being exerted. As we shall also see, the sense that globalisation was in the process of completing a scenario in which an international trade law was developing independently of states, based on established trade practices and regulated through arbitration—in other words, the *lex mercatoria* scenario—always collides with the fact that state mechanisms are necessary in guaranteeing that arbitrators' rulings will be enforced.

On the other hand, it is clear that, in order to meet the challenges brought by globalisation, the law has built, not only on traditional mechanisms under international law (conventions, international institutions in a traditional form, etc), but also on new mechanisms that the latter has developed in the modern age: international courts open to private individuals, direct effect techniques, etc. International law's panoply of modern technology has been employed and, in truth, the management of the issues raised by globalisation may be viewed as having played a key role in its current development.

*iv. The Law of Regional Integration, European Law
   and Legal Globalisation*

We have accepted that regional integration is one level within globalisation; one of the contexts in which it unfolds; that within such regional integration, mechanisms can be identified that are quite typical in terms of the opening-up of markets and cultures, of spatial dislocation, all whilst being a level in the global edifice of public systems where the effects of globalisation are 'reworked', mitigated.

The law governing regional integration bears the marks. In an attempt to ensure the fluidity of economic relations between partners, it also helps to protect them against the outside world, and consequently constitutes one level in the legal organisation of international trade. Concerned first and foremost with the economic dimension, it necessarily comes to incorporate other values—if only because it has to regulate the cross-border labour flows, and therefore come close to the protection afforded by labour law.

This is true of the European construct and its law. The latter must be viewed (though this naturally does not summarise it in its entirety) as a vector for legal globalisation, but it is also a level in the world's legal architecture where legal globalisation occurs in part and is transformed.[50]

---

[50] Jean-Bernard Auby, 'The EU and Global Administrative Law' in Patrick Birkinshaw and Mike Varney (eds), *The European Legal Order after Lisbon* (London, Kluwer Law International, 2010) 57.

a. A Vector for Legal Globalisation

In the legal configuration of the European construct, the influence of processes that are characteristic of legal globalisation can clearly be seen. As noted by Christine Bertrand, the European construct is an 'example of legal globalisation.'[51]

Indeed, within that construct, we can see the characteristic processes of legal globalisation embodied even in enhanced forms.

Some of the most typical attributes of global law norms are reflected in European law. European law can be used directly by private individuals, be they companies, persons, groups, etc. It cuts through national systems both horizontally (it may be used by any person against any state) and vertically (it may form the basis of legal action brought by a non-governmental national player against European institutions; for instance in competition matters). It has a complex relationship with national laws, a relationship that does not obey the usual hierarchical rules.[52]

The same relationships between systems can also be found, much more markedly, in EU law. The permeability of national systems to EU law is not at issue: it is inherent to the European construct. Competition between legal systems is an obvious characteristic of the Community system in all fields where EU law creates openings without going so far as to harmonise rules.[53]

The EU is a transnational legal construct in itself.[54]

b. A Forum in which Globalisation is Co-produced

As a vector for globalisation, the European construct is also a forum in which globalisation is co-produced, transformed, 'tweaked'. It acts both as a 'firebreak' and a vehicle for globalisation.[55]

In various respects, the European construct is a vehicle for legal globalisation. It frequently serves as a kind of 'transmission belt' for global law—and

---

[51] Christine Bertrand, 'Mondialisation, Etat de droit et construction européenne' in Daniel Mockle (ed) *Mondialisation et Etat de droit* (Brussels, Bruylant, 2002) 141.

[52] On this issue, which will be examined later in this book, see, eg, Olivier Audéoud, 'La construction européenne, étape "régionale' au carrefour de la mondialisation et d'un fédéralisme inachevé", in Council of Europe/Conseil de l'Europe, *Les mutations de l'Etat-nation en Europe à l'aube du XXIe siècle*, 1998.

[53] Manuel Ballbé and Carlos Padros, *Estado competitivo y armonización europea* (Madrid, Ariel Sociedad Económica, 1997).

[54] François Ost and Michel van der Kerchove, *De la pyramide au réseau. Pour une théorie dialectique du droit*, (Brussels, Publications des facultés universitaires Saint-Louis, 2002) 65.

[55] It is 'worked by the contradictory unity between the fact that it is a stepping stone for globalisation but also a stakeholder that can influence its content': Pierre Bauby, 'La construction originale d'un intérêt general européen' in Olivier Delas and Christian Deblock (eds), *Le bien commun comme réponse politique à la mondialisation'* (Brussels, Bruylant, 2003), 45.

that does not apply solely to international trade law, the law of the WTO. In other areas, the EU serves as a tool in rendering compulsory for all Member States various norms of global law by which they were not all bound: this is what happened, for instance, in 1982, with the 1973 Washington Convention on the International Trade in Endangered Species of Wild Flora and Fauna.[56]

It acts as a 'firebreak' in that it works in adapting legal globalisation trends to the specific imperatives recognised by European nations—or at least it does so clearly in economic matters and in relations with the WTO: in matters regarding genetically modified organisms, for instance, in characteristic fashion. As regards the globalisation of human rights, however, the quest for autonomy and particularism is traditionally less significant, the desire for harmonisation being especially strong; but we know that, since *Kadi*,[57] the EU has reserved the right to brandish its own specific heritage in the field of the protection of human rights against global law when necessary.

C. The Contradictions and Limits of Legal Globalisation

Like globalisation more generally, legal globalisation is not a long, calm river. We have identified the contradictions and limits of the former above. However, law adds its own specific frictions and stumbling blocks.

i. The contradictions and limits of economic, social and cultural, etc globalisation also found in law

The contradictions of legal globalisation[58] are perfectly reflected, for instance, in WTO law, where the imperatives of economic globalisation collide with those (which are no less global) of the protection of health, with regard to the issue of genetically modified organisms, together with those surrounding the guarantees for the fundamental rules of labour law.[59] This is a duplication of the world, according to René-Jean Dupuy:[60] different values exert their various pressures on global law.

---

[56] Jean-Claude Gautron and Loïc Grard, 'Le droit international et la construction européenne' in Sociéte Française de Droit International, *Droit international et droit communautaire: perspectives actuelles* (Pedone, 2000) 11.

[57] Case C-402/05 *Yassin Abdullah Kadi and Al Barakaat International Foundation v Council of the European Union and Commission of the European Communities* [2008] ECR I-06351.

[58] Mohammed Salah, *Les contradictions du droit mondialisé* (Paris, PUF, 2002).

[59] Werner Meng, 'International Labor Standards and International Trade Law' in Eyal Benvenisti and Georg Nolte (eds), *The Welfare State. Globalization and International Law* (Berlin, Heidelberg, Springer, 2003) 371 ff; Jill Murray, 'Relabelling the International Labor Problem: Globalization and Ideology' in Dauvergne *Jurisprudence* (n 2) 129.

[60] 'Le dédoublement du monde' (1996) *Revue générale de droit international public* 2, 313.

The result thereof obviously depends only slightly on law itself. The globalised world is not a world without power. Dominant stakeholders make their domination felt: a domination that can be legal, political, ideological, etc.

It is hardly surprising that the main drivers of legal globalisation are Western. Western stakeholders are economically and politically dominant. They have also produced those political forms that are best adapted to globalisation models. It is in the European sphere that the Kantian model of 'peace through law' has most clearly been developed; it is therefore not surprising that some of the most characteristic legal globalisation mechanisms can be found there. This does not mean to say that they are lacking elsewhere, if only because—as is well known—some emerging nations have efficiently positioned themselves so as to profit from economic globalisation and, to that end, they have placed themselves in a legal position to make the most of the opportunities that it affords.

ii. The law's own specific contradictions and limits combined with those of globalisation

National legal systems each have their own particular balance, their own particular coherence, which put up varying degrees of resistance to legal globalisation by their nature and scale. We may think, for instance, of the varying difficulties encountered by European legal systems in accommodating the legal effects of Community directives.

Harmonisation and the legal interpenetration of legal systems may sometimes give the impression of setting the pace for national legal particularisms—whence the debate, to which we will return later, on the issue of whether the democratisation of global society ought to accompany, or even precede, the creation of a truly global law.[61]

D. The Scientific Scenario of Legal Globalisation and Its Rivals[62]

The theoretical situation can be summed up by stating that, alongside legal globalisation, there are two types of alternative theory that may account for the phenomena that it seeks to characterise.[63] Some may be called theories

---

[61] Benjamin Barber (1993) 'Global democracy or global law: which comes first?', 1 *Indiana Journal of Global Legal Studies,* 119, 119–24.

[62] Jean-Bernard Auby (2006) 'Globalisation et droit comparé' 8 *European Journal of Law Reform* 1, 43.

[63] For a different presentation and which, truth to tell, does not strike us as doing justice to that which the theory of legal globalisation has in its own right: Marie-Claire Ponthoreau, 'Trois interprétations de la globalisation juridique. Approche critique des mutations du droit public' (AJDA 2006) 20.

of the internationalisation of law, while others may be dubbed theories of the convergence of laws; neither type strikes us as being able to account for the current legal configuration of the world.

i. Increased international regulation of legal relations?

It is quite tempting to say, in order to characterise that legal configuration, that it is quite simply marked by an increase in the regulation of legal relations within global society by international norms. The particularity of today's legal world simply lies in the fact that law is drawn towards international law, domestic norms increasingly giving way to international ones.

Giuliana Ziccardi Capallo's work[64] is fairly characteristic of that line of thinking. The author argues that what characterises the current situation is nothing more than a sort of completion of the historic project under public international law, in the sense of the 'verticality', legality, integration and development of collective guarantees.

The phenomena of this internationalisation, the increasing overtaking of national rules by international norms are self-evident and indisputable. However, if we settle for simply stating that what we are witnessing is merely an internationalisation of law, the world's national laws being drawn towards an international dimension, and the subjugation of the world's laws to shared international values, it seems to us that we run the risk of missing at least two realities, to which we shall return in greater detail later.

The first is that, if we look closely, we find that it is increasingly through domestic law that international norms—which are steadily growing, admittedly—have an impact. The determining feature here is the fact that, particularly through direct effect mechanisms, international norms come to find within national legal—and particularly judicial—mechanisms a springboard for effectiveness that they struggle to find on an international level. It is an odd sort of 'internationalisation of law' whose secret depends so much on domestic law!

The second is that, if we look closely yet again, we can see that this international law, whose influence is increasingly felt in domestic law, has a growing tendency to distance itself from international concerns in order to busy itself with domestic issues—particularly practical issues, often of an administrative nature, concerning the environment, immigration, economic regulation, etc. It is an odd sort of 'internationalisation of law', in the context of which international norms are increasingly concerned with issues of domestic law.

---

[64] Giuliana Ziccardi Capallo *The Pillars of Global Law* (Aldershot, Ashgate, 2008)—we will return to this view: see chapter 7, 'C. The Quest for Theoretical Renewal'.

A *fortiori*, theories that see the triumph of public international law—or, on the contrary, of private international law—appear to be thoroughly unsuitable in today's realities.

Are we witnessing the triumph of public international law, of the management of things, beings and law by the international community through its political bodies? This is quite difficult to accept both for the general reasons mentioned above and because, indisputably, in what is unfolding before our very eyes, there is much that rests on private relationships, private mechanisms, a social and economic fabric in which states are largely absent. The Internet, international trade and standardisation broadly regulate themselves outside the scope of the mechanisms of public international law.

Are we witnessing the triumph of private international law which, particularly because it broadly holds in its hands the extremely important reality that is international trade, could be the principal regulator of the new legal world? This is equally difficult to accept, again for the general reasons evoked above, and also because, in what is happening today, so many phenomena are linked to the public sphere, public governance, public law. There is not a lot of private law in the globalisation of environmental law, or that of human rights, for example.

ii. Convergence of laws?

Under the umbrella term of 'theories of convergence of laws', the core of what is taking place in the modern legal world can be characterised as a movement of convergence of laws towards common standards, even the progressive creation of a global *ius commune*.

In truth, there are two versions of these conceptions. The first, which may be deemed optimistic, and which is an incarnation of cosmopolitanism, sees in this trend of internationalisation of law the signs of humanity's irresistible—though chaotic—progression towards a common law, the core or spirit of which will be the internationally recognised corpus of human rights. Mireille Delmas Marty's work embraces this view.[65]

In the pessimistic version of these theories of convergence of laws, what is currently playing out is more the gradual subjugation of all laws to principles and standards inspired by neoliberalism, essentially North American in origin. This is particularly the theory of 'hegemonic globalisation', the most famous spokesman of which is Boaventura da Sousa Santos.[66]

In both cases, these theories may be considered simplistic.

---

[65] In particular: Mireille Delmas Marty, *Trois défis pour un droit mondial* (Paris, Le Seuil, 1997).

[66] Particularly, Boaventura da Sousa Santos, *Law and Globalization from Below* (Cambridge, Cambridge University Press, 2005).

The former is simplistic in terms of its idealistic register. A certain amount of goodwill is required in order to think that international society would be guided on any significant level by a draft law. Furthermore, the theory of convergence of laws towards a common law tends to ignore the irreducible pluralism which is the very essence of any legal system; the international legal community has no reason to be more homogenous than domestic systems already are if we examine them closely.

The latter is a sort of conspiracy theory, which we can only accept if we ignore the fact that it is based on a combination of factors. It distorts reality by presenting the link between the opening-up of international relations and the progress of liberalism as a logical sequence. In such a conceptual framework, how can we explain China's position, which currently appears to be one of the systems best adapted to economic globalisation and cannot readily be accepted as a liberal system? Naturally, there is a sort of historical coincidence between the advances made, during the 1980s and 1990s, with international economic opportunities on the one hand, and the neoliberal policies of certain states on the other. However, even in accepting that each of these fuelled the other, the two phenomena were separate in nature, which proves the fact that some national systems remained separate from the latter whilst participating in the former.

Theories of legal globalisation are more realistic—and more relativistic. They regard the globalisation process as a complex, uneven evolution, separate from any comprehensive project. They themselves are not homogenous. Their proponents sometimes disagree on issues of particular importance. For example, on that concerning the place to be granted to the state: for some, we have already reached a stage of 'law without the state';[67] for others, the state remains an essential regulator in legal globalisation, although this may be subject to different modalities.[68]

We shall have ample opportunity to come back to all of the above.

---

[67] Gunther Teubner, *Global Law without a State* (Aldershot and Brookfield, Dartmouth, 1997).

[68] See, eg, Jarrod Wiener's demonstration (in *Globalization and the Harmonization of Law*; n 24), in which he argues that legal globalisation does not occur through an international unification of law, but rather through a harmonisation of solutions presented by national legal systems.

2

Areas of Legal Globalisation

I N TODAY'S FAIRLY broadly integrated international society, we could well think that there is no branch of law that remains unaffected by globalisation. Were we to imagine, for instance, that family law is not influenced by globalisation, we would find an immediate contradiction of such a view in the legal issues raised by the increasing number of binational divorces or international adoptions. Were we to suggest that bioethical issues are not impacted by globalisation, such a proposition would ignore the legal issues raised by the growing international trend of products derived from the human body, or even from embryos. Many more examples could be cited.

It is impossible to describe all of the issues impacted by legal globalisation in this book; we can only discuss those that are especially affected. We will do so by giving three characteristic examples, and going into some detail before broadening the scope of the discussion.

I. THREE CHARACTERISTIC EXAMPLES

The first two examples concern realities that can readily be seen as affected by legal globalisation: financial markets law and Internet law. As to the third—and this is where its interest lies—the same cannot be said intuitively: this is public contracts law.

A. Financial Markets Law[1]

i. Globalisation of Financial Markets

As we have already noted, and as events during the 2008 financial crisis made us fully aware, it is obvious that the globalisation of financial markets has been and, indeed, continues to be a major dimension in economic globalisation.

---

[1] Andreas Busch, *Banking Regulation and Globalization* (Oxford, Oxford University Press, 2009).

The progressive liberalisation of capital movements which gradually came about during the 1960s, and more swiftly during the 1980s, will have counted for a lot in the development of economic globalisation.

That liberalisation was fuelled by the gradual abolition of currency exchange controls between developed countries. For current payments, this abolition was achieved in 1958 between Organisation for Economic Co-operation and Development (OECD) countries. From the 1960s onwards, the OECD strove to extend the same liberalisation to capital movements.[2]

The liberalisation of capital movements in the European sphere was fully achieved in January 1994; from that date on, pursuant to Article 73 of the Treaty of Rome (now Article 56), all restrictions on capital movements and payments between Member States, or between Member States and third countries, were prohibited.[3]

Under WTO law, the free movement of capital is guaranteed by the General Agreement on Trade in Services (GATS) and the accompanying Annex to the GATS on Financial Services and, as regards investments linked to the trade in goods, by the General Agreement on Trade in Goods.[4]

On the basis of this twofold liberalisation, and owing to the boom in the use of electronic methods, a true globalisation of financial markets emerged, characterised by the globalisation of three factors: products (global bonds, swaps, etc), information and transaction processing systems; and intermediaries (banks, brokers, etc).[5]

This liberalisation–globalisation of financial markets led to the impressive expansion of those markets: some US \$1.2 billion are exchanged on the currencies market every day, while global financial assets represent approximately US \$160,000 billion, being three times the world's GDP. However, the crises soon followed, affecting financial institutions—the bankruptcy of Bankhaus Herstatt in 1974, for instance, or that of Banco Ambrosiano in 1983—which quickly affected states themselves: in 1982, Mexico announced that it was no longer able to pay its debts.[6]

The need for global regulation, to balance out global liberalisation, had emerged.

---

[2] Geneviève Burdeau, 'Le FMI et la surveillance de l'espace monétaire et financier mondial' in Eric Loquin and Catherine Kessedjian (eds), *La mondialisation du droit* (Litec, 2000) 268.

[3] Subject to which, aside from retail markets—and particularly the consumer loans market—European financial markets are highly integrated: see the Communication from the European Commission of 6 May 2004 on the subject.

[4] Peter Behrens (1999) 'The Institutional Architecture of Global Financial Markets', 6 *Maastricht Journal of European and Comparative Law* 3, 271.

[5] Jean-Baptiste Zufferey, 'La globalisation et ses effets en droit des marches financiers', in Charles-Albert Morand (ed), *Le droit saisi par la mondialisation* (Bruxelles, Bruylant, 2001) 228.

[6] Jarrod Wiener, *Globalization and the Harmonization of Law* (London and New York, Pinter, 1999) 41 ff.

ii. Global Regulation

The implementation of such regulation took a circuitous route, an examination of which is instructive.[7]

Leaving aside the unilateral strategies which consisted, on the part of some states—and the United States in particular[8]—in setting national restrictions, the scope of which was extended to all external transactions affecting certain national interests, it can be said that regulation came about on three levels.

The first consisted in disciplines that states accepted for themselves, in the context of the International Monetary Fund (IMF), concerning the management of their public finances and the organisation of the banking systems. The collapse of the Bretton Woods system, following the abolition of the convertibility of the dollar in 1971, rendered those efforts relatively ineffective.

The second level consisted in the markets' own attempts to self-regulate through the development of various prudential practices: for example, the rules and practices of the International Chamber of Commerce regarding documentary credit, or the fact that firms' access to international financial markets is subject to the acceptance of International Accounting Standards.[9]

The third level, which is the most effective in practical terms, consisted of defining—in line with unusual, partly governmental, partly non-governmental modalities—international banking standards, subsequently imported into domestic law.

A unique international body was a key stakeholder here: the Basel Committee on Banking Supervision, which, since 1964, has brought together the representatives of 26 central banks, all of which are now represented within the Bank for International Settlements.

From 1985 onwards, the Committee issued a series of directives on banking supervision,[10] the consequences of which were drawn by national legislations. In the European Union (EU), this was done first through directives, including that of 1972 concerning the supervision of financial institutions.

---

[7] In addition to the preceding references, see: Marie-Anne Frison-Roche, 'Le cadre juridique de la mondialisation des marchés financiers', *Banque et Droit* (1995) 47; Eilis Ferran and Charles Goodhart, *Regulating Financial Services and Markets in the 21st Century* (Oxford, Hart Publishing, 2001).

[8] Harald Baum, 'Globalizing Capital Markets and Possible Regulatory Responses' in Jürgen Basedow and Toshiyuki Kono (eds), *Legal Aspects of Globalization* (The Hague, Kluwer Law International, 2000) 77.

[9] See Behrens 'Institutional Architecture' (n 4). The standards set by the Basel Committee were overhauled in 2004 (Basel II).

[10] See Burdeau (n 2), and the work by Wiener *Globalization and the Harmonization* (n 6) 68 ff.

Other non-governmental authorities are also involved in the production of global regulations. This is the case for the International Organization of Securities Commissions (IOSCO), which brings together independent securities supervisors and private bodies responsible for regulating those same markets.[11] It also applies to the Berne Union, comprised of public and private export credit insurers.[12]

iii. Towards a Global Financial Markets Law

Global financial markets law is an especially interesting case. Not only does it concern a heavily globalised reality, but it also reflects a number of the characteristics of global law.

Firstly, we note that the regulation it produces consists of a mix of international and domestic norms. The directives adopted by IOSCO, for instance, owe their actual influence to the fact that domestic law incorporates or imitates them, or else uses them as an interpretative instrument, as shown by Dimitry Kingsford Smith.[13]

Secondly, we can see that a significant role is played therein by non-binding standards (market practices, Basel Committee directives, etc).

Conversely, there are some instances in which the international norms adopted by some states are specifically extended to other states, because market integration is such that, if they are not applied everywhere, they lose all effectiveness. This is the case in the fight against money laundering: compliance with the rules adopted by the Financial Action Task Force (FATF) is occasionally imposed on non-Member States, under the threat that they will no longer have access to the markets of the Member States.[14]

Thirdly, we can see the significant place occupied by various, non-interstate regulators in the production of rules, including the Basel Committee, which is neither a private entity nor an inter-governmental body, but rather a network of national regulators.

Fourthly, we can see that there is a not inconsiderable proportion of self-regulation, as those involved in the financial system themselves play a significant role in defining their professional disciplines.

Moreover, as is well known, this large degree of self-regulation has been heavily criticised by some, particularly European, states in the context of

---

[11] Dimitry Kingsford Smith, 'Networks, Norms and the Nation State: thoughts on Pluralism and Globalized Securities Regulation' in Catherine Dauvergne (ed), *Jurisprudence for an Interconnected Globe* (Aldershot, Ashgate, 2003) 93.

[12] Janet Koven Levit (2005) 'A Bottom-Up Approach to International Law-Making: the Tale of Three Trade Finance Instruments' *Yale Journal of International Law* 30, 125.

[13] See n 11.

[14] Heba Shams, *Legal Globalisation, Money Laundering Law and Other Cases*, Sir Joseph Gold Memorial Series, British Institute of International and Comparative Law (2004) 237 ff.

the financial crisis which began in 2008. They blamed it for the lack of regulation that allowed investment banks, not to mention commercial or high-street banks in off-balance-sheet strategies, to expand their portfolios of structured products, the failure of which was the central driving force behind the crisis.

Nevertheless, the global regulation of financial markets has yet to undergo any radical transformation.[15]

B. Internet Law

i. The Global Reality of the Internet

Like financial markets, the Internet is a powerfully global reality. We can readily comprehend the extent to which this particular reality can raise problems for the traditional segmentation of legal systems.

The dematerialised nature of the network raises major questions—for example, those concerning electronic signatures—but its transnational, 'deterritorialised' character raises even greater issues.[16]

It naturally engenders constant issues as to the law applicable in matters of contract, tort, criminal law, etc.[17] It also raises great difficulties for the implementation of intellectual property rules.

It exposes potential legal intervention to significant difficulties in terms of enforcement. We can remember, for instance, the matter of the neo-Nazi sites hosted by Yahoo. In its decision of 20 October 2000,[18] the *tribunal de grande instance* (regional court) at Paris ordered Yahoo to filter those sites in such a way that they could not be accessed from French territory. Shortly thereafter, the United States District Court for the North District of California refused to enforce that decision, holding instead that it was

---

[15] Although the idea of strengthening existing regulation was put forward in April 2009 at the G20 Summit in London.

[16] See, eg, Conseil d'Etat, *Internet et réseaux numériques* (La Documentation française, 1998); Thomas Hoeren, 'Electronic Commerce and Law—Some Fragmentary Thoughts on the Future of Internet Regulation from a German Perspective' in Jürgen Basedow and Toshiynki Kono (eds), *Legal Aspects of Globalization* (The Hague, Kluwer Law International, 2000) 35; Masato Dogauchi, 'Law Applicable to Torts and Copyright Infringement through the Internet', ibid 49.

[17] On the degree of originality of such issues: Bénédicte Fauvarque Cosson, 'Le droit international privé classique à l'épreuve des réseaux' in Georges Chatillon (ed), *Le droit international de l'internet* (Bruxelles, Bruylant, 2009) 55; Jack Goldsmith (1998) 'The Internet and the Abiding Significance of Territorial Sovereignty' *Indiana Journal of Global Legal Studies* 5, 475; David G Post (2002) 'Against "Against Cyberanarchy"' *Berkeley Technology Law Journal* 17, 1365.

[18] TGI Paris, référé, 22 mai 2000, *UEJF et Licra c/ Yahoo! Inc et Yahoo France*; see also Agathe Lepage (2002) 'Internet, territoires et Etat: le franchissement dématérialisé des frontières' *RGCT* numéro spécial, 47.

contrary to the First Amendment to the US Constitution, which protects freedom of expression.[19]

This immediately raised the question of whether the necessary legal disciplines could be on a par with the global scale of the Internet, as much in the relationships between network and users as between access providers and services, or between companies using the networks and the holders of intellectual property rights.

ii. The Emerging Internet Law

In order to guarantee those disciplines, a specific law was put in place—sometimes known as *lex electronica* or *lex networkia*—which presents some highly unusual characteristics.[20]

In terms of its substance, it draws heavily on established practices online—what is often called 'netiquette', more specifically—especially in contractual matters.

Broadly speaking, there are four main strands to this.

Some of the legal issues raised by the Internet are regulated by quite classic international agreements, such as the 1981 European Convention for the Protection of Individuals with regard to Automatic Processing of Personal Data, or the 1996 WIPO Copyright Treaty, which structures the protection afforded to electronic texts.[21]

Other issues are tackled, according to the phrase coined by Pierre Trudel, through 'template texts'. Some are template laws, such as the Model Law on electronic e-commerce drafted by UNCITRAL. Others are model contracts, the origins of which vary, such as that which the Council of Europe undertook to draft for transactions involving cross-border flows of personal data.

The third strand is very important: disciplines concerning access to networks and network interconnections are unusual in that they are composed of regulations whose production is mostly private or mixed—involving private and public entities. The task of defining standards allowing network interconnections is shared between non-specific bodies—including the International Organisation for Standardisation (ISO)—and specific

---

[19] *Yahoo! Inc v La Ligue Contre Le Racisme et L'Antisémitisme*, 145 F Supp 2d 1168, 1171 (N, D, Cal, 2001).

[20] In addition to the preceding references, see in Charles-Albert Morand (ed) *Le droit saisi par la mondialisation* (Bruxelles, Bruylant, 2001) the contributions submitted by Pierre Trudel ('La *lex electronica*', 221) and Evelyne Clerc ('La gestion semi-privée de l'Internet', 333).

[21] And requires that operators comply with all national laws at the same time: David G Post (1996) 'Governing Cyberspace' *Wayne Law Review* 43, 155.

bodies such as the Internet Society, which comprises businesses, public entities and foundations. In both cases, these are institutions governed by private law.

The regulation of this vital key to the network (ie domain names) is also ensured by a company governed by private law, but linked to the US government, created in the 1990s: the Internet Corporation for Assigned Names and Numbers (ICANN). The company ensures regulation, not through having regulatory powers but through a contractual structure, through a range of dynamic contractual references, according to Evelyne Clerc.[22]

ICANN (Internet Corporation for Assigned Names and Numbers)

ICANN is a part-private, part-public (and national) regulator.

— ICANN is a regulator
  — holding powers to regulate the allocation of domain names
  — holding real power to sanction that allocation: in the past, for example, it suspended the registration of sites ending with .iq (for Iraq) and .af (for Afghanistan).
— ICANN is a private company
  — ICANN is run by a board composed of representatives from local organisations responsible for domain names, and 'public interest' representatives.
— ICANN hosts governmental representations
  — ICANN has various committees, including a 'Governmental Advisory Committee' composed of a significant number of representatives from national governments.
— ICANN has links with the US Department of Commerce
  — to which it is bound by contract, the most recent version of which, headed 'Affirmation of Commitments', was signed in September 2009.

Criticisms levelled at ICANN

— ICANN is frequently criticised
  — the fact that such sensitive issues are handled by a private entity is occasionally called into question
  — however, there is also criticism of ICANN's links with the US government.

---

[22] ibid, 357.

— Its first CEO, Rod Beckstrom, ran the National Cybersecurity Center for the US Administration. He was succeeded by Fadi Chehadé in 2012.
— What are the alternatives?
   — some have suggested that the UN take charge
   — others argue for full privatisation.

See, *inter alia*:

— Lia Koletsou et al, 'The Role of Icann in Internet Governance: Friend or Foe', (2006) *European Review of Public Law,* Winter.
— Michael Froomkin, 'Wrong Turn in Cyberspace: Using ICANN to Route around the APA and the Constitution' (2000) 50 *Duke Law Journal* 17.
— ICANN website: www.icann.org

The fourth aspect is composed of specific mechanisms for dispute regulation and sanctions, instituted spontaneously on the Internet itself. In the absence of legal regulation, Internet stakeholders—servers, service providers, etc—had to implement their own disciplinary measures. Denial of access, in particular, was increasingly used to sanction abuses committed by various users.

iii. A Perfect Example of Globalising Law

Internet law constitutes a particularly interesting case in itself, and gives us an insight into the main characteristics of globalised law.

We must note in particular the highly composite nature of its structure, which combines traditional international agreements with purely contractual practices; traditional public regulation with purely corporate discipline.

A second notable aspect of Internet law is that it carries with it a considerable amount of self-regulation. This was intended from the very genesis of the Internet, even by the US government authorities. The message was heard loud and clear by private stakeholders—businesses and universities alike—who ensured the Internet's expansion. Internet law consequently appears to be highly decentralised—'Jeffersonian', to paraphrase David Post.[23]

At the same time, when taken as a whole, Internet law operates as much as 'co-regulation' as it does self-regulation. It is, in reality, produced jointly by public and private stakeholders. The role played by ICANN

---

[23] Post 'Governing Cyberspace' (n 21).

is based on an agreement binding it to the US government. The specific dispute-resolution and sanction mechanisms produced by the Internet are such that they will only serve to resolve minor disputes; when issues relating to consumer law, intellectual property law, etc begin to arise, internal regulation must pass the baton to state law.

This diversity is one property that merits closer examination.

C. Public Contract Law[24]

Public contract law is very different to Internet law, but equally interesting for various reasons chiefly because it concerns a subject which, *a priori*, does not appear to be especially affected by globalisation.

i. *Globalisation's Influence on Public Contract Law*

The area of public contract law has been impacted by globalisation via the following routes.

Firstly, public contractual relations are themselves increasingly internationalised.[25] Of course, they are not as open to the outside world as private commercial relations are. Be that as it may, public entities are also ever more frequently driven to seek partners on an international level: bodies that will grant loans on more favourable terms than those offered by national financial institutions; businesses that have expertise but do not own national businesses, etc.

As a corollary, public contracts are increasingly the subject of international concern, drawing closer attention and treatment from international institutions. Some of those institutions have developed active policies on opening public contracts for the purposes of expanding free international trade. This is the case for the WTO, with the Agreement on Government Procurement concluded during the Uruguay Round.[26] As for regional economic integration, this generally carries with it rules on the opening-up of public procurement: this is the case, obviously, for the European

---

[24] For a more in-depth analysis: Jean-Bernard Auby (2003) 'L'internationalisation du droit des contrats publics' *Droit administratif* August, 5.

[25] See Sophie Lemaire, *Les contrats internationaux de l'administration* (Paris, LGDJ, 2005); Malik Laazouzi, *Les contrats administratifs à caractère international* (Paris, Economica, 2008).

[26] Thiébaut Flory, *L'Organisation mondiale du commerce—Droit institutionnel et substantiel* (Bruxelles, Bruylant, 1999) 193 ff; Bernard Hoeckman and Petros Mavroidis, *Law and Policy in Public Purchasing—The WTO Agreement on Government Procurement* (Ann Arbor, University of Michigan Press, 1997); Evelyne Clerc, 'La mondialisation des marchés publics', in *Les marchés publics à l'aube du XXIe siècle* (Bruxelles, Bruylant, 2001) 141.

Union,[27] but also for NAFTA.[28] Naturally, there are also specific bilateral or multilateral agreements, for instance between Canada and the USA, or between the USA and Israel.[29]

Public contracts are also affected by the economic development and stabilisation policies led by international economic institutions, particularly as regards developing nations. For the World Bank, in particular, public contracts and public procurement private finance contracts for public facilities and services are all an essential level in economic development, which it works to promote and rationalise. Its assistance is often subject to the conclusion, by the states concerned, of certain kinds of contract, in accordance with appropriate procedures.[30]

To this may be added the fact that a number of public and private stakeholders in international economic relations have convinced themselves that international public contracts could not simply be left to the domestic law of the public entities concluding such contracts, and to such an extent that this has caused correlative legal adjustments.

The same applies to two fundamental issues. For investors, for the international contractual partners of public entities, as well as for those who finance them, there is the problem of guarding against policy reversals on the part of those entities. The classic problem of 'state contracts'—contracts concluded between states, particularly in the development sphere, and foreign companies, for the purposes of economic development—can be seen here in its entirety. Growth—the very sustainability of this tool for the development of less advanced countries—depends on the extent to which they can be guaranteed against the unpredictability of politically unstable states, without depriving signatory states of the power to change policy in the economic sectors to which the state contracts relate.[31]

---

[27] There is considerable literature on Community law on public contracts. For the French view on the subject, see, eg, Christine Bréchon's contributions to the *Juris-Classeur Europe*, and those by François Llorens and Pierre Soler-Couteaux to the *Répertoire Dalloz de droit communautaire*.

[28] Arie Reich, *International Public Procurement Law—The Evolution of International Regimes on Public Purchasing* (The Hague, Kluwer Law International, 1999), 261 ff.

[29] ibid 141 ff.

[30] Paul Lignières, *Partenariat public-privé*, 2nd edn (Paris, Litec, 2005); Tim Tucker, 'A Critical Analysis of the Procurement Procedures of the World Bank' in Sue Arrowsmith and Arwel Davies (eds), *Public Procurement: Global Revolution* (The Hague, Kluwer Law International, 1998) 139.

[31] Dominique Carreau, *Droit international*, 5th edn (Paris, Pedone, 1997), 170 ff; Prosper Weil, 'L'Etat, l'investisseur étranger et le droit international: la relation désormais apaisée d'un ménage à trois' in *Liber Amicorum Ibrahim F.I. Shihata* (The Hague, Kluwer Law International, 2000), reproduced in Prosper Weil, *Ecrits de droit international* (PUF, 2000); Charles Leben, *La théorie des contrats d'Etat et l'évolution du droit des investissements*, Recueil des Cours de l'Académie de Droit International, tome 302, (The Hague, The Hague Academy of International Law, 2003), 197; Sophie Manciaux, *Investissements étrangers et arbitrage entre Etats et ressortissants d'autres Etats* (Paris, Litec, 2004).

The second issue is that of combatting the natural tendency of states towards protectionism. As favourable as they are towards the expansion of international trade, states remain reluctant to open their public contracts to international competition: the stakes for their national economy—the political stakes therefore—are too great.

These concerns convinced international authorities that it was necessary to associate specific provisions concerning the opening-up of at least some public contracts with the general provisions on opening up international trade—hence EU law on public procurement and works concessions, and hence the WTO Agreement on Government Procurement, etc.

The internationalisation of public contracts is fuelled by a final, specific factor, which is the development of international contracts *between public entities*.[32]

We are currently witnessing extremely rapid growth in the number of international contracts concluded between public entities, be they state bodies or secondary public entities. Government networks,[33] which often encompass contracts, are the trend. Scientific, university or cultural public institutions conclude innumerable international co-operation agreements.[34] International co-operation between local governments[35] intensifies with each passing day, specifically in the European sphere, where it is actively encouraged by both the Council of Europe and the EU.[36]

ii. A Global Public Contract Law?

The logic and components of a global public contract law can be described as follows.

a. Public contracts and international norms

What is noticeable is the fact that public contracts are ever more frequently subject to international norms. And what is most striking is the fact that this subjection to international norms does not apply solely to international public contracts—although it does relate to such contracts first and foremost.

---

[32] On this subject, see the fascinating study conducted by Mathias Audit: *Les conventions transnationales entre personnes publiques*, LGDJ (2002), Bibliotèque de Droit Privé.

[33] eg: Anne-Marie Slaughter, 'Government networks: the heart of the liberal democratic order' in Gregory H Fox and Brad R Roth (eds), *Democratic governance and international law* (Cambridge, Cambridge University Press, 2000) 199.

[34] See Audit *Les conventions transnationales* (n 32) 140 ff.

[35] What French law awkwardly terms 'decentralised co-operation': awkwardly because the phrase gives no indication of the international nature of that co-operation.

[36] Christian Autexier, 'L'action extérieure des collectivités territoriales' in Francis-Paul Bénoit (ed), *Collectivités locales* (Paris, Dalloz, permanently updated).

It was in the aftermath of the Second World War, and more sharply from the 1970s onwards, that the trend towards internationalisation emerged in relation to state contracts. Denationalisation initially concerned dispute resolution: states increasingly agreed to arbitration, with the possible support of the Convention on the Settlement of Disputes between States and Nationals of Other States, signed in Washington in 1965. It then affected the context of the law through bilateral or multilateral investment agreements which then proliferated.[37]

Public contracts—or, at least to begin with, public procurement—quickly appeared to become subject to Community rules intended to ensure that such contracts were not the preserve of national businesses. The rules under the Treaty—free movement, free provision of services, non-discrimination, etc—all played a part here, prior to the emergence of the various aspects of the specific scheme applicable to public procurement contracts. The two series of factors are currently combined in the following way: for the time being, specific directives only govern markets and works concessions, but certain general rules under the Treaty apply to any public contracts that have an economic purpose.[38]

Public contracts are also affected, in a way that is not always easy to describe, by the rules of private international law that European law created in matters relating to the law applicable to contractual obligations: the Rome Convention of 19 June 1980, and the 'Rome I' Regulations of 17 June 2008.[39]

The third example is international contracts between public entities. In matters relating to co-operation between local authorities, and at least in the European sphere, there are a significant number of agreements which include specific local—and, more particularly, cross-border—co-operation projects. The most significant is the Framework Agreement signed in Madrid on 21 May 1980, under the auspices of the Council of Europe.[40] Many bilateral agreements establishing the rules governing cross-border local co-operation have been concluded within the scope of the Framework Agreement: *inter alia*, between France and Italy in 1993, France and Spain in 1995, and France and Germany in 1996.[41]

On a very different note, sometimes international human rights protection has consequences, more or less incidentally, for public contracts. This is

---

[37] On these historical developments, see Weil 'L'Etat, l'investisseur étranger et le droit international' (n 31).

[38] As per *Telaustria* case law: Case C-324/98 *Telaustria Verlags GmbH and Telefonadress GmbH v Telekom Austria AG* [2000] ECR I-10745.

[39] Sophie Lemaire, 'Le règlement Rome I du 17 juin 2008 et les contrats internationaux de l'administration', (2008) *AJDA*, p 2042–2045.

[40] Emmanuel Decaux, 'La convention-cadre européenne sur la coopération transfrontalière des collectivités locales et des autorités locales', (1984) *Revue générale de droit international public*, 557.

[41] See Audit *Les conventions transnationales* (n 32) 187 ff.

how, in the context of the International Labour Organisation, an agreement was concluded in 1949 on the social clauses in public contracts, supplemented by a Recommendation by the Organisation.[42] This is also how the European Convention on Human Rights and the European Court in Strasbourg have both sometimes had to rule on issues concerning public contracts. The connection obviously does not lie here in the presence of rules under the Convention specifically covering public contracts, or even contracts themselves: it is due to the universality of the Convention's material scope, through very general norms such as Article 6(1).[43]

b. International norms and domestic public contracts

There is a remarkable phenomenon in the fact that the internationalisation trend in public contract law also extends its influence to certain *domestic* public contracts.

This is because, while the international norms that come into contact with public contracts necessarily present international challenges (which would explain their emergence), sometimes they may only serve their own intended purposes by applying to purely domestic public contracts.

EU law on public procurement and works concessions, for example, makes no distinction. The relevant directives apply without exception to purely domestic public procurement and concessions: the resulting public procurement law is, for example, purely and simply integrated into the French Public Procurement Code, where it is 'mixed in' with existing domestic law.

Similarly, the contractual techniques and procedures that the World Bank strives to disseminate are not the preserve of international contracts. They remain unchanged in the face of the domestic or international nature of the arrangements of which they are a part. At most, we can say that in highlighting competition, they strive to ensure that national companies do not make such arrangements systematically.

c. The Internationalisation of Public Contract Litigation

It must be added that, while the relevant law is becoming increasingly international, litigation relating to public contracts is too. The natural monopoly held by national courts over such contracts is being eroded.

---

[42] Brian Bercusson (1999) 'Labour Regulation in a Transnational Economy' 6 *Maastricht Journal of European and Comparative Law* 3, 244.

[43] *Stran Greek Refineries v Greece*, Application no 13427/87, Series A no 301-B [1994] ECHR 48; *Doustaly v France* [1998] ECHR 32 (concerning a dispute between Nîmes and a site manager to whom the town was contractually bound).

This applies to international public contracts. Some international organisations that produce norms affecting public contracts have their own litigation mechanisms that may serve in settling disputes concerning such contracts. This is obviously the case for the EU, as Community courts can, via various avenues, hear disputes of that nature: in the context of competition law, and in that of actions for failure to fulfil obligations, for instance. But it is also the case for the WTO, whose dispute settlement mechanism is likely to come into play,[44] and has occasionally applied[45] to disputes involving public contracts. It is also the case for the provisions of the European Convention: as stated above, the European Court of Human Rights has in the past had to rule on cases involving public contracts.

Additionally, there is a trend whereby states are more willing to agree to their international contracts, or those concluded by other national public bodies, being subject to international arbitration.[46] This development has generally been observed for some time for state contracts,[47] in respect of which, as has been noted, investment agreements often provide for that type of settlement.

Moreover, on a multilateral level, the 1961 European Convention on International Commercial Arbitration expressly provides, under Article 2, the right of legal persons of public law to resort to arbitration for contracts relating to 'international trade transactions'. The 1965 Washington Convention established the International Centre for Settlement of Investment Disputes (ICSID), an arbitration body for international investment disputes between states and nationals of other states.[48]

While this may appear to be an exception, there are occasions when international public contracts elude the national courts of the signatory legal entity, not because they gravitate towards international litigation mechanisms but because they are 'left' to the other party's national courts.[49]

Traditionally, public contracts—at least those concluded by states—enjoyed the same jurisdictional immunity as the states themselves, and any disputes arising therefrom could not be heard by courts in another state.

---

[44] Annette Blank (1996) 'La contestation et l'Accord OMC sur les marchés publics' *Revue de la concurrence et de la consommation* 89, 23.

[45] In GATT case law, there was the matter of United States–European Community, involving a public procurement issue, on which the GATT dispute settlement bodies ruled in 1984 (GATT Panel Report, Panel on Value-Added Tax and Threshold, GPR/21, adopted 16 May 1984, BISD 31S/247); see Eric Canal-Forgues and Thébaut Flory, *Recueil des contentieux GATT-OMC* (Bruxelles, Bruylant, 2001) 179.

[46] See especially Gérard Teboul, 'Arbitrage international et personnes morales de droit public: brèves remarques sur quelques aspects de contentieux administratif'(1997) *AJDA* 25.

[47] Jean Combacau and Serge Sur, *Droit international public* (Paris, Montchrestien, 1999), 74; Weil *Ecrits de droit international* (n 31).

[48] Jean-Michel Jacquet and Philippe Delebecque, *Droit du commerce international* (Paris, Dalloz, 2001) 493.

[49] See Mathias Audit, 'La compétence extraterritoriale du droit administratif', in *AFDA, La compétence* (Litec, 2009) 69.

Over the course of the twentieth century, this classic concept gave way to a more restrictive view, in which immunity applies only to those acts that states make in their capacity as public powers, rather than those acts that they make as private legal persons.[50]

The result of this change of perspective is that immunity no longer covers certain public contracts whilst continuing to concern others. French case law grants immunity to public contracts that have the character of public law contracts, and particularly those containing clauses derogating from the generally applicable rules of law.[51] On the basis of the Foreign Sovereignties Immunities Act 1976, American law does not allow immunity for acts made in the context of commercial activities; this applies in particular to public contracts serving a commercial purpose.[52]

It must also be noted that this erosion of the monopoly held by national courts can also be seen, albeit on a lesser scale, in litigation relating to *domestic* public contracts.

The international procedures discussed above—be they those provided by EU law, the WTO or the European Convention—can also apply to domestic public contracts, just as they do to international public contracts.

In truth, they would tend to apply to purely domestic contracts. For example, when the European Commission instigates infringement proceedings in a case concerning public procurement, it generally relates to a procurement contract concluded purely and simply with a national company: the Commission clearly has the sense that the awarding of the contract to a national company may have resulted in a failure to comply with Community rules on opening up public procurement.

iii. Lessons to Be Drawn from the Globalisation of Public Contract Law

The globalisation of public contract law is instructive in a number of respects.

(a) Firstly, it is instructive in terms of its very existence, which shows that legal globalisation does not spare public realities. We shall return to this point in greater detail.

(b) Secondly, it is remarkable in that it also demonstrates the composite nature of global legal rules. The internationalisation of public contract law produces hybrid rules governing such contracts. Where national law had once created—with varying degrees of effectiveness or ingenuity— a set of relatively consistent rules based on certain balances,

---

[50] eg Pierre Mayer and Vincent Heuzé, *Droit international privé*, 7th edn (Paris, Montchrestien, 2001) 209 ff.

[51] ibid 212.

[52] Sarah Bon (1997) 'Deconstruction of National Sovereignty—Taking down the barriers between nations' *Princeton Law Journal* Fall.

internationalisation has introduced new legal 'germs', which are sometimes particularly disruptive.

(c)   Thirdly, it is remarkable in that it reveals the decline of the legal powers wielded by states over an issue which had previously fallen fully within their remit. In accepting that international institutions make rules applicable to their public contracts, and that courts other than their own rule on litigation relating to their public contracts, states consent to the fact that the production of the law governing those contracts is partly beyond the scope of their control.

This loss of control on the part of states over the production of the law governing their public contracts is also accompanied, as a corollary, by a challenge to their traditional privileges in those contracts.

In particular, where public contracts are subject to international arbitration, what is noticeable is that arbitrators are often reluctant to accept that they may be subject to special rules creating sovereign prerogatives for public authorities, such as unilateral amendment.[53] This was seen, for instance, in the arbitration proceedings relating to the use of the Channel Tunnel.[54]

Internationalisation tends to erode that which, in a public contract, is related to the inequality between the parties. This is confirmed in the development of international law on state contracts, where the validity of so-called 'stabilisation' or 'intangibility' clauses has gradually become accepted, under which the contracting state undertakes, for example, not to nationalise the co-contracting party's property, or not to increase their taxation or, more generally, not to render the performance of the contract more costly for the co-contracting party through new legislation.[55]

(d)   Fourthly, it must be noted that the international legal fabric which influences the law governing international public contracts is made up of truly enforceable legal rules. It is also made up of standards, rules of conduct, guidance and model laws proposed for the stakeholders concerned.

The World Bank's procedural guides are not contained in any compulsory legal act. Equally, the Model Law on Public Procurement drafted by the UN Commission for International Trade Law (UNCITRAL) is only a model.[56]

---

[53] See Gérard van Harten, *Investment Treaty Arbitration and Public Law* (Oxford, Oxford University Press, 2007).

[54] Gérard Marcou, 'La sentence arbitrale relative à la convention d'utilisation du tunnel sous la Manche par la SNCF et British Rail', *Annuaire français de droit international* (1997) 810.

[55] Pierre Mayer, *La neutralisation du pouvoir normatif de l'Etat en matière de contrats d'Etat* (Paris, Clunet, 1986), 5; Dominique Carreau (n 31) 179.

[56] Robert R Hunja in Arrowsmith and Davies, *Public Procurement* (n 30) 97. Note that the most recent version of the Model Law was published in 2014.

These standards, guides and models essentially have a cultural and political influence without any legal authority. This does not, however, mean that they are not imposed without a certain degree of force in practical terms. When the World Bank makes its assistance contingent on compliance with procedures that it has selected, these in fact quite naturally take on a great deal of authority.

(e) Lastly, it must be noted that global public procurement law rarely appears as a unified law. Instead, it more closely resembles a harmonisation law.

The concern common to the great majority of the internationalisation mechanisms evoked here is the opening up of public contracts. It is natural that such mechanisms should carry with them rules and standards, the principal concern of which is to guarantee transparency, publicity and competition in the conclusion of such contracts.

In truth, these rules and standards contribute to all the questions that national law well knows as key issues in this regard. Should it concern the way in which thresholds are applied in determining which public procurement procedure applied to the conclusion of a procurement contract, there is GATT and WTO case law on the subject.[57] Should it concern the issue of specifications, there is also a GATT–WTO doctrine on the subject,[58] but there is also a World Bank position.[59] As for the contract award criteria, and particularly the issue of whether non-economic criteria—eg social or environmental—may be used, there is EU law,[60] WTO law[61] and, for example, solutions put forward in the UNCITRAL Model Law.[62]

We must add that what can be called international public contract law is not strictly limited to the determination of such rules on competition and transparency. It sometimes concerns itself with the legal and judicial landscape likely to guarantee their effectiveness. EU public procurement law has set down its requirements with the 'remedies' directives,[63] but the WTO Agreement on Public Procurement also sets

---

[57] The matter of *United States–European Community*, mentioned above, concerned an issue relating to the taking into account of VAT in the application of said thresholds (GATT Panel Report, Panel on Value-Added Tax and Threshold, GPR/21, adopted 16 May 1984, BISD 31S/247).

[58] See Clerc, 'La mondialisation des marchés publics' (n 26).

[59] See Arrowsmith and Davies, *Public Procurement* (n 30) 15.

[60] In particular, Case C-513/99 *Concordia Bus Finland* [2002] ECR I-07213.

[61] Flory, 'L'Organisation mondiale du commerce' (n 26) 200.

[62] Arrowsmith and Davies, *Public Procurement* (n 30) 109.

[63] Dorthe Dahlgaard Dingel, *Public Procurement. A Harmonization of the National Judicial Review of the Application of European Community Law* (The Hague, Kluwer Law International, 1999).

down its own,[64] while the UNCITRAL Model Law contains its own stipulations in that regard.[65]

Similarly, the mechanisms recently adopted in the context of the OECD and the EU in the fight against corruption[66] convey, amongst their various essential objectives, that of overhauling the conclusion of public contracts.

To conclude, we should add that the harmonisation effects of the global law on public procurement contracts do not exclusively concern the rules governing those contracts. They also affect their legal conceptualisation.

For example, the concept of public procurement, which is of capital importance, is obviously strongly influenced by the various international instruments discussed above—and especially by EU law, the position of which is also analogous to that of the other instruments mentioned. Currently, the concept of public procurement has practically no independent national definition within the Member States of the EU. It is a prisoner of the EU definition. It could, where necessary, go beyond or be broader than it—although this is not the case under French law—but it cannot sustainably be more restrictive in scope without generating situations of uncertainty or legal insecurity for public procurement bodies—and especially in situations where, as in French law since the introduction of the Public Procurement Code in 2001, both EU and national rules are brought together in the same legal corpus. In such scenarios, at least, alignment on the EU definition is ultimately inevitable.

Even though, for the time being, it is only in a context of less legal supervision, internationalisation also makes its influence felt in the way in which concession contracts, arrangements involving private funding of public facilities or services, are examined. EU law has already tackled the issue of works concessions, for which it has consequently provided a definition.[67] On a global level, under the influence of the World Bank and the International Monetary Fund in particular, various contractual concepts have been disseminated concerning the private funding of public facilities and services, centred around the BOT scheme.[68] The European Commission has begun to develop a

---

[64] See Clerc, 'La mondialisation des marchés publics' (n 26).

[65] Arrowsmith and Davies, *Public Procurement* (n 30) 102.

[66] These will be discussed later: see below, this chapter, 'A Global Law of National Governance?'.

[67] Christine Bréchon-Moulènes et al, 'La concession de service public face au droit communautaire' (Paris, Sirey, 1992); Christophe Fourassier, 'Vers un véritable droit communautaire des concessions' (2000) RTD eur Oct–Dec 675.

[68] See Lignières (n 30) 18; Christian Bettinger, *La gestion déléguée des services publics dans le monde* (Paris, Berger-Levrault, 1997); Laurence Folliot-Lalliot, 'Vers une approche unifiée de la convention de délégation de service public (Etat d'avancement des travaux de la

doctrine on public–private partnerships which must inspire future legislation on concessions and similar contracts.[69]

It is interesting to add that, in both the sphere of procurement law and those matters relating to concession contracts, internationalisation does not fuel the common understanding of the typology of public contracts alone.[70] It also frequently contributes to other aspects of the legal conceptualisation of such contracts, for example that of the role played by the various stakeholders in the contractual arrangements concerned. The concepts of adjudicatory power, contracting authority, or public–private partnership, have all taken on legal perspectives from internationalisation, which in turn have benefited or been gradually imposed on national law.

II. THE KEY AREAS OF LEGAL GLOBALISATION

In order to continue our search for the basic forms of legal globalisation, we must now expand the perspective and identify the key areas where this trend is most strongly felt.

A broad examination shows that the principal impact points are trade, the environment, human rights and (national) governance.

A. Trade[71]

i. The Core of Legal Globalisation

Economic globalisation is at the heart of globalisation and, at the centre of economic globalisation, there lays the intensive development of international trade. Trade is the very core of globalisation.

Consequently, it is hardly surprising that it should be in the sphere of trade that the earliest symptoms of legal globalisation were observed, and that trade law should still strike many as the alpha and omega of legal globalisation.

Commission des Nations unies pour le droit international sur les projets d'infrastructure à financement privé)' (2003) *RFDA* 5, 893.

[69] European Commission (2009) Communication from the Commission to the European Parliament, the Council, the European Economic and Social Committee and the Committee of the Regions of 19 November 2009—Mobilising private and public investment for recovery and long term structural change: developing Public Private Partnerships COM(2009) 615 final.
[70] To the examples already given, we can add the gradual standardisation of co-operation contracts between public entities, which create the European instruments on local co-operation, and particularly the Madrid Agreement: see Audit, *Les conventions transnationales* (n 32) 169 ff.
[71] Marco d'Alberti, *Poteri pubblici, mercati e globalizzazione* (Bologna, Il Mulino, 2008).

What is true is that it is in this area that the trend towards the denationalisation of law has and continues to be embodied in the context of globalisation. There is indeed a trend towards the legal autonomisation of international trade, and that trend is inarguably an essential driving force behind legal globalisation.

The phenomenon must, however, be relativised and fleshed out.

ii. *The* lex mercatoria

The legal independence of international trade is both a platitude and the subject of a controversial theory: the *lex mercatoria*.

It is trite to state that customs occupy a significant place in the law governing international trade relations.[72] They are occasionally codified: with regard to sales, for instance, they take the form of International Commercial Terms (Incoterms), issued by the International Chamber of Commerce. They are occasionally recognised by international treaty law: for example, the 1980 United Nations Convention on Contracts for the International Sale of Goods (CISG) accepts the reference made to customs in order to determine the parties' intentions.

It is also in the international world of business, not the machinery of government, that the various standardisation and certification mechanisms are mainly developed. The extremely important International Standardization Organization (ISO) is a private law body.

The settlement of international trade disputes increasingly falls within the remit of the new form of 'independent' justice system that is international arbitration.

a. The *lex mercatoria* Theory

On the basis of these observations, which are undisputed, an extreme concept has developed with regard to the legal independence of international trade (which concept is far from being unanimously acknowledged): the theory of *lex mercatoria*. According to this theory, international trade is governed—or at least partly governed—by a third-party law, somewhere between international and domestic law, composed of customs within the international trade community and applied by the arbitration bodies that regulate it: law without the state.[73]

The theory of *lex mercatoria* may be considered to predate the globalisation trend, as it was first formalised by Berthold Goldman in 1964. However, trade globalisation has renewed interest in the *lex mercatoria*.

---

[72] See Jacquet and Delebecque, *Droit du commerce international* (n 48).
[73] Gunther Teubner (ed), *Global Law without a State* (Aldershot, Dartmouth, 1997), particularly the articles by Gunther Teubner (3) and Hans-Joachim Mertens (31).

The key idea behind it is that international trade increasingly regulates itself, though international arbitration based on the substantive rules of the *lex mercatoria*, which consist in[74] general principles such as good faith or the *pacta sunt servanda* rule, the customs of international trade, more or less codified trade practices, contractual practices that are routinely followed, etc, together with professional rules that are spontaneously followed or raised by private bodies renowned in the field.

b. Some Objections

The theory of *lex mercatoria* gives rise to an abundance of recurring theoretical, and theoretical–practical (as it is a matter of debating legal realities, not merely concepts) controversies.[75] For the purposes of the present analysis, it will suffice to draw out the following observations.

Nobody disputes the reality of the sociological statement on which the latest incarnation of the theory is based, ie the increase in the number of international trade disputes that are settled through arbitration and the application of the customs of international trade.

However, the theory of an 'a-national', 'stateless' law governing international trade sidesteps the fact that the factors on which the theory of *lex mercatoria* is founded can only take effect on the basis of state regulations which make them possible or make them sustainable in the long term.

International arbitration can only operate outside the scope of state law until such time as it needs the latter to guarantee the enforcement of its sentences. This is why the idea of an 'a-national', or floating, arbitration which is not governed by any national law—an idea that was quite stirring at one time—has almost been abandoned today.[76]

Furthermore, in substantive law, the 'independent' customs of international trade are, in actual fact, substantially recycled by state law, and thereby even find themselves in competition. As Laurent Aynès explains,[77]

---

[74] Jean-François Riffard, 'Mondialisation de l'économie et internationalisation du droit des affaires: une abdication de l'Etat de droit?' in David Monckle (ed), *Mondialisation et Etat de droit* (Bruxelles, Bruylant, 2002) 275.

[75] On the concept of *lex mercatoria* and the debate that it continues to spark, see, eg, in *Souveraineté étatique et marchés internationaux à la fin du 20ᵉ siècle, Mélanges en l'honneur de Philippe Kahn* (Paris, Litec, 2000) the articles by Eric Loquin ('Où en est la *lex mercatoria* ?' 23) and Alain Pellet ('La *lex mercatoria*, "tiers ordre juridique"? Remarques ingénues d'un internationaliste de droit public' 53). See also: Volkmar Gessner, 'Globalization and Legal Certainty' in *Emerging Legal Certainty: Empirical Studies on the Globalization of Law* (Ashgate, Dartmouth, 1998) 433; Michael Likosky (ed), *Transnational Legal Processes* (London, Butterworths, 2002); John Braithwaite and Peter Drahos, *Global Business Regulation* (Cambridge, Cambridge University Press, 2000).

[76] Gabrielle Kaufmann-Kohler, 'Mondialisation de la procédure arbitrale' in Morand, *Le droit saisi par la mondialisation* (n 20) 269.

[77] Laurent Aynès, 'L'influence de la mondialisation sur le droit des contrats' (1999) *Osaka Law Review* 46, 35.

faced with the threat of being overwhelmed by economic globalisation, states have chosen to adapt through a unification of law, a codification of customs under their auspices, by generating elements of a uniform law.

This process has taken two basic paths: international agreements; and the joint adjustment of model laws intended to be transposed into national legislations.[78] The work in these two areas has been done by three authorities in particular.[79] The Hague Conference on Private International Law has drafted a variety of agreements, including the Convention of 15 June 1955 on the law applicable to international sales of goods. Aside from the fact that it drafted the 1980 United Nations Convention on Contracts for the International Sale of Goods, UNCITRAL develops model laws, such as the 1985 Model Law on International Commercial Arbitration. UNIDROIT— an organisation founded in 1926 as an auxiliary body to the League of Nations—notably prepared the 1988 Ottawa Convention on International Factoring, and adopted the 1994 Principles of International Commercial Contracts.

We should not forget the fact, examined in particular by Horatia Muir Watt, that private international economic disputes increasingly reveal conflicts between economic regulations; as a corollary, states are increasingly involved in private international disputes, as *amicus curiae*, especially in those disputes brought before American courts.[80]

iii. The Global Law of International Trade

We must also note that the problem of the legal autonomisation of international trade law does not exhaust the influence of legal globalisation in this field.

Aside from its relative denationalisation, the global law of international trade presents other characteristics that echo the various observations made in the examination of three specific cases described above, and particularly of the following.

It is a composite law in terms of its sources, structure and production. It is composed in part of international norms, but only fully achieves its purpose by relying on domestic law (particularly when required for its enforcement

---

[78] Regarding the latter path, see in particular in Eric Loquin and Catherine Kessedjian (n 2), the contributions of Arlette Martin-Serf ('La modélisation des instruments juridiques' 179), Hans van Houtte ('La modélisation substantielle' 207), and Catherine Kessedjian ('La modélisation procédurale' 237).

[79] See Jean-François Riffard (n 74).

[80] Horatia Muir Watt (2003) 'Globalisation des marches et économie politique du droit international privé', *Archives de Philosophie du Droit* 243; *Aspects économiques du droit international privé*, Académie de Droit International de La Haye, Recueil des Cours (2004) 307.

apparatus) or even immersing itself therein (where it concerns the implementation of uniform law or model laws).

It is made by a wide variety of bodies and settings, be they national and international, public and private, corporate and non-professional. International trade law is typically the product of 'co-regulation'.

Moreover, in terms of its machinery, global trade law presents the essential attribute of being based principally on harmonisation rather than unification. It accomplishes this task by harmonising various solutions, striving to render them compatible, more than it does by unifying different laws—this is the case even when accomplished through the development of a uniform law. The model laws put forward in this context are always susceptible to reservations and adaptations, and leave aside issues that are often of great importance in establishing contractual balances. For example, the uniform law contained in the 1980 United Nations Convention on Contracts for the International Sale of Goods does not govern certain crucial issues such as the validity of the contract or the ownership of the goods sold; in addition, states may refuse to be bound by the part of the Convention on the formation of contracts, or the part on the effects of contracts.

B. The Environment

i. A Globalising Reality

Environmental issues are of course part and parcel of legal globalisation.

We have long known that marine or air pollution does not come to a halt at national borders.[81] We have long known that some sensitive areas must be protected against the covetousness of the machinery of internationalisation: the Antarctic, outer space, etc.[82]

In intensifying transactions, by shrinking land space, globalisation only increases the risks. The imbrication of economies, such as the greater movement of persons, renders our societies more vulnerable to health hazards: mad cow disease, for instance, suddenly became an international problem. In the words of Ulrich Beck,[83] we have entered the age of the world risk society.

---

[81] Rebecca Bratspies and Russell Miller (eds), *Transboundary Harm in International Law* (Cambridge, Cambridge University Press, 2006): reflections based on the 1941 *Trail Smelter* sentence, which established the principle that a state must not allow its territory to be used in order to cause pollution in the territory of a neighbouring state (the 'no harm' principle).

[82] Alexandre Kiss and Jean-Pierre Beurier, *Droit international de l'environnement*, 2nd edn (Paris, Pedone, 2000) 89.

[83] Ulrich Beck, *What is globalization?* (Cambridge, Polity Press, 2000) 39.

Furthermore, a sort of world consciousness—a 'cosmopolitan conscious-ness', as Ulrich Beck puts it—has developed in the face of such phenomena, which stimulates the development of increasingly powerful non-governmental organisations (NGOs): Greenpeace, the International Union for Conservation of Nature (IUCN), the World Wide Fund for Nature (WWF), etc.

All of this yields a global environmental law along the following lines.

ii. The Emergence of International Environmental Law

International environmental law took off in the 1970s, particularly with the 1972 United Nations Conference on the Human Environment, held in Stockholm, which, in addition to a general Declaration, adopted 109 Recommendations forming a global Action Plan, and a Resolution on the implementation of the Action Plan. Following the conference, treaties were concluded, on a universal or regional level, on various issues, particularly the protection of maritime habitats, wild fauna and flora. The second important stage unfolded in the 1990s and was marked in particular by the 1992 Rio Conference, also known as the Earth Summit, where a solemn declaration was adopted on, in particular, the reconciliation of economic development with environmental protection. In the wake of that conference, various agreements were adopted relating to climate change.[84]

The law born out of this (ultimately quite recent) occurrence presents the following particular characteristics.

a. Common Principles

It is increasingly based on a set of principles accepted, if not universally, at least broadly by the international community: a sort of *ius commune* of environmental protection.[85,86]

Amongst those principles, there is one whereby the environment may be considered as the 'common heritage of humanity'. Next, there is a series of operational principles around which the protection of that heritage tends to be structured: the prevention principle; the citizen participation and

---

[84] In addition to the work by Kiss and Beurier (n 82), see: in Denis Alland (ed), *Droit international public*, coll (Paris, PUF, 2000) 'Droit fondamental', the chapter titled 'Droit de l'environnement' by Laurence Boisson de Chazournes, 727 ff; Patricia Bernie, Alan Boyle and Catherine Redgwell, *International Law and the Environment* (Oxford, Oxford University Press, 2009).

[85] These principles feature not only in the treaties, but also more commonly in arbitral case law.

[86] Underlying the international efforts to protect the environment, there is the conviction that environmental assets are here and there 'global public goods'; we shall return to this concept later in the book (see chapter 4, 'B. Producing Public Goods under Legal Globalisation').

information principle; the 'polluter pays' principle; and the precautionary principle, although the latter remains highly controversial.[87]

b. Deterritorialisation

Under international environmental law, the 'deterritorialisation' of the law caused by globalisation, and the growing 'transnationality' that it elicits, can be seen especially clearly.

As stated by Laurence Boisson de Chazournes,[88] at the present time:

> environmental protection requires [...] that we transcend the spatial division of territoriality drawn by political borders. New strategies based on the concepts of 'ecosystem' and 'biosphere' have therefore been put in place, marking the ecological interdependence of the components of those systems on a regional, pan-regional and global level.

In concerning itself with areas the delimitation of which is linked to the ecological requirements that it is intended to face (eg the Mediterranean, which is protected against pollution under the 1976 Barcelona Convention; wetlands of international importance that are meant to be protected against various threats linked to urbanisation under the 1971 Ramsar Convention, etc), the international regulation of environmental protection often sets itself objectives which, *ratione loci*, ignore state divisions.[89]

c. Erosion of State Prerogatives

This is not the only level where international environmental law erodes the prerogatives that traditionally belong to state law. Let us simply note the following factors.

Firstly, we must note the extent to which international environmental law falls within the scope of the state prerogatives that it frames and guides. This is especially true in the European context. Firstly, the environment is a sphere in which the European Member States have agreed that secondary legislation beyond their control should be made. It is even one of the areas in which the most secondary legislation is issued.

European environmental law now goes so far as to focus on criminal legislation on environmental protection, as is the case for the Council of Europe Convention on the Protection of the Environment through

---

[87] See Kiss and Beurier, *Droit international de l'environnement* (n 82) 110 ff.

[88] n 83.

[89] There is a trend towards the regionalisation of international environmental law: see, eg, Tullio Treves, 'L'approche régionale en matière de protection de l'environnement marin' in *La mer et son droit, Mélanges offerts à Laurent Lucchini et Jean-Pierre Queneudec* (Paris, Pedone, 2003) 608.

Criminal Law, signed in Strasbourg on 4 November 1998. The Court of Justice, having accepted that the Community was competent to establish a framework for the repressive powers of Member States where necessary for the effective implementation of its environmental policy,[90] a draft directive was presented in 2007, intended to compel Member States to incriminate certain forms of damage to the environment and make provision for certain minimum penalties.[91]

Secondly, it must be noted that the environment is one of the areas in which individuals have been granted rights, by external norms, which they can exercise against states. At world level, a true right to a safe environment was enshrined by the 1998 Aarhus Convention on Access to Information, Public Participation in Decision-Making and Access to Justice in Environmental Matters.[92] In the European sphere, the rights of citizens in environmental matters are enshrined twice over: by EU law, by means of Directive 90/313/EEC of 7 June 1990 on freedom of access to environmental information; and by the law of the Convention, the European Court of Human Rights having accepted that the right to respect for private and family life, recognised by Article 8 of the Convention, included the right to a safe environment.[93]

Thirdly, in a similar vein, we must note that environmental law is a field in which NGOs have acquired a great deal of direct influence. Some NGOs have developed such widely acknowledged expertise in certain fields that they are involved—as experts, with no voting rights, naturally, but with a voice that is sometimes heeded—in the development of international regulations; this is the case for Greenpeace, for instance. They thereby take their place, within those limits and each on their own scale, amongst the non-state regulators that have emerged under globalisation.[94]

iii. Environmental Law and Globalisation

Environmental law occupies an extremely interesting place within the legal globalisation trend, reflecting the latter's ups and downs.

It also embodies some of globalisation's basic logic: in particular, that of a transnational law, largely indifferent to state lines and, as a corollary, that of a law, the development of which for the most part eludes states. This

---

[90] Case C-176/03 *Commission v Council* [2005] ECR I-07879.

[91] Comm. EC, 9 February 2007, n°IP/07/166. European Commission, IP/07/166, 9 February 2007

[92] Kiss and Beurier, *Droit international de l'environnement* (n 82) 93.

[93] *Guerra and others v Italy*, Application no 14967/89, ECHR 1998-I.

[94] See Anne Peters, Lucy Koechlin, Till Förster and Grette Fenner Zinkernagel, *Non-State Actors as Standard Setters* (Cambridge, Cambridge University Press, 2009).

twofold observation more obviously applies to the sphere of the EU than it does to others; it is, however, also true of those other spheres.

But environmental law also reflects the heterogeneity of legal globalisation and the occasionally antagonistic nature of the forces that drive it. Owing to the fact that the opening up of international trade and the development of international environmental protection do not necessarily pull in the same direction,[95] WTO law is currently seeking ways to reconcile its economic objectives with safeguarding the environment.[96] It is no easy task, and some examples testify to the fact that disputes brought before WTO bodies can result in regression in the field of environmental protection: for instance, the case where the USA was compelled, further to a complaint brought by Mexico, to give up a legal provision imposing tuna-fishing techniques designed to protect dolphins.[97]

C. Human Rights

i. A Global Issue

We need not labour over establishing that human rights have become a global issue.[98] The evidence is there for all to see, in the proliferation of international legislation, the expansion of increasingly perfected international protective measures, the international success of the 'ideology' of human rights that underpins the same legislation and measures.

We will settle for making an inventory—a Joycean stream of consciousness, as it were—of the main stages. The first historic steps are usually identified in the 1864 Geneva Convention on the law of war and humanitarian law, then in various provisions on minorities, which were included in the treaties concluded following the First World War.

The exponential expansion came after the Second World War and was reflected, *inter alia*, as regards general instruments[99] in the 1948 Universal Declaration; the 1950 European Convention; the 1966 UN Pacts on Civil and Political Rights and on Economic and Social Rights; the 1969 American Convention on Human Rights; the 1979 Declaration on Human Rights in

---

[95] However, they do sometimes: for instance, when the EU grants lower customs duties to developing nations that have ratified certain agreements, such as the Kyoto Protocol: Peter Mendelson (2008) 'Le commerce international au secours de l'environnement' *Les Echos*, 3–4 October.

[96] Flory, 'L'Organisation mondiale du commerce' (n 26) 200 ff.

[97] Pierre de Senarclens, *La mondialisation*, 2nd edn (Paris, Armand Colin, 2001) 152.

[98] See the works by Mirelle Delmas-Marty, and in particular *Trois défis pour un droit mondial* (Paris, Le Seuil, 1998); Alison Brysk (ed), *Globalization and Human Rights* (Berkeley, University of California Press, 2002).

[99] For more detail, see Frédéric Sudre, *Droit international et européen des droits de l'homme*, 9th edn (Paris, PUF, 2008).

Islam; the 1981 African Charter on Human and Peoples' Rights; the 2000 Charter of Fundamental Rights of the European Union; the 2001 Inter-American Democratic Charter; etc.

Alongside these general instruments, many specific conventions have also been adopted, for the most part at the instigation of the United Nations: the 1948 Genocide Convention; the 1965 Convention on the Elimination of All Forms of Racial Discrimination; the 1980 Convention on the Elimination of All Forms of Discrimination Against Women; the 1984 Convention Against Torture; the 1989 Convention on the Rights of the Child; etc.

There is a sort of international consensus, as shown by the fact that even the least democratic regimes strive to legitimise their actions from the viewpoint of guaranteeing human rights, for instance through the well-known manoeuvring that we see within the UN Commission on Human Rights or the Human Rights Council.[100]

There is no question that specific attitudes vary, but this does not mean that there is any less sharing of fundamental principles. There is, at the very least, a 'globalisation of the proclamation discourse', as it has been described.[101]

ii. Law and Human Rights

How does law tackle this increasingly obviously global issue? Three sets of comments may be made here.

a. Proliferation

Firstly, what is most striking is the outpouring of increasingly profuse and finely tuned legal measures dealing with the issue of human rights.

The proliferation of treaty-style norms is quite apparent; we need not go over it again. More interesting is the constant progress of legal 'technology' serving human rights. They are at the very heart of the concept of *jus cogens* that gradually permeates accepted public international law concepts; it is the core of the constitutional basis of public international law.[102]

The implementation of a number of human rights treaties is overseen by international organisations—the United Nations, the Council of Europe, the Organisation of American States—which sometimes have, for the purposes of that task, enhanced supervisory powers, such as the power to conduct

---

[100] Democratic opinion was shocked by the UN Human Rights Commission's decision, in 2003, to give the presidency to Libya. The Human Rights Council, which replaced the Commission in 2006, does not have a particularly remarkable record: Agathe Duparc, 'Les errances du Conseil des droits de l'homme', *Le Monde*, 14 April 2009, 2.

[101] Sudre (n 99) 91.

[102] eg Jan Klabbers, Anne Peters and Geir Ulfstein, *The Constitutionalization of International Law* (Oxford, Oxford University Press, 2009) 26.

investigations. Indeed, it is in the field of human rights that we may find some of the most advanced examples of international authorities having the character of genuine courts, access to which is open to individuals whose rights have been affected: the European Court of Human Rights, the Inter-American Court, etc.

In another development, global human rights law does not always settle for international mechanisms. It builds on domestic laws, uses them as relays. In all democratic systems, human rights treaties can be invoked before national courts, even if the potential of such citations varies depending on whether they serve to challenge national legislation or whether they can operate 'horizontally' against other private persons, etc. The direct effect of the European Convention on Human Rights (at least in some of the legal systems concerned) is such that it can be invoked on a day-to-day basis before domestic courts, sometimes with very powerful effects, such as those caused by Article 6.[103]

b. Standards

One of the main keys through which global human rights law influences legal systems lays is the gradual constitution of international standards, of a sort of common heritage for identifying principles to be safeguarded and violations to be fought against.

Not that there is a unified international law in this field. The contents vary from region to region, from convention to convention.[104] On some issues, such as religious rights, gender equality, there are some not inconsiderable divergences between one part of the world and another. Within even the most integrated systems, the harmonisation of rules relating to human rights varies depending on the issues in question; as Mireille Delmas-Marty puts it, in the ECHR system, 'harmonisation is rather weak in those cases that involve morality and religion, and stronger where the authority and impartiality of the justice system is in question'.[105]

The same can be said of the increasing number of points of approximation. For instance, although the rights proclaimed in the various great conventions vary, there is still a hard core of common principles: the right to life; the prohibition of torture and cruel, inhuman or degrading treatment; the prohibition of slavery; or the principle of non-retroactivity in criminal matters.[106]

---

[103] The implications of which, for example in French law, have been and continue to be disruptive; we shall return to this point later in the book.

[104] cf André-Jean Arnaud, *Critique de la raison juridique. Gouvernants sans frontières. Entre mondialisation et post-mondialisation* (Paris, LGDJ, 2003) 147.

[105] Delmas-Marty (n 98) 130.

[106] Gérard Cohen-Jonathan, 'Droits et devoirs internationaux des individus' in Denis Alland (ed), *Droit international public* (Paris, PUF, 2000) 573.

c. Challenge to States

It is essentially against the State that human rights are fought for and pro-tected: human rights are first and foremost a 'vertical' matter. Global human rights law therefore naturally encompasses a challenge to the legal preroga-tives of states, the main lines of which are as follows.

We must first note that the state finds itself increasingly and more com-pletely called into question. Its accountability with regard to its respect for human rights tends to ignore the traditional immunity that traditionally protected it. The UN ultimately accepted that the principle of non-interfer-ence in the internal affairs of states could no longer be invoked in the event of serious human rights violations, and that the mechanisms provided under Chapter VII of the Charter would be implemented in scenarios of purely internal violence: they were indeed, for example, in 1994 in the cases of Rwanda and Haiti.[107]

To this 'right of interference' in the internal affairs of states where serious human rights violations are committed, we must add the development of measures concerning the international criminal liability of individuals guilty of crimes against humanity, genocide, war crimes, etc. Indeed, with the international tribunals set up in 1993 and 1994 for the Former Yugoslavia and Rwanda, and the International Criminal Court established in 1998, these are mechanisms essentially intended to try governments, which cease to be protected by the immunity traditionally associated with the same.[108] Their influence extends even to governments in office: in 1999, the charges brought against Slobodan Milosevic constituted the first international legal proceedings against a head of state in office.

The state is increasingly and more extensively called into question. It is also circumvented by legal measures that overlook its institutions. Since Protocol 11 to the European Convention on Human Rights came into force in 1998, the Strasbourg Court has become a true, permanent court, able to hear individual cases brought before it by private individuals.[109]

For those reasons—and more besides—the state finds itself facing com-petition in the production of human rights and in their protection, from international enforcement mechanisms and international courts in particu-lar. However, it must also compete in a different way with the activities

---

[107] Fox and Roth, *Democratic governance* (n 33).

[108] Which, for example, the International Court of Justice recalled in its decision in *Demo-cratic Republic of Congo v Belgium* of 14 February 2002: 'it is firmly established that [...] certain holders of high-ranking office in a State, such as the Head of State, Head of Govern-ment and Minister for Foreign Affairs, enjoy immunities from jurisdiction in other States, both civil and criminal'; see also André Huet and Marie Koering-Joulin, *Droit penal international* (Paris, PUF, 2005) 249 ff; Philippe Sands (2001) 'Turtles and Torturers: the Transformation of International Law', *New York University Journal of International Law and Politics* 33, 527.

[109] Christine Bertrand, 'Mondialisation, Etat de droit et construction européenne' in Mon-ckle *Mondialisation* (n 74), 141.

of non-governmental organisations. Currently, the contribution of NGOs to the production and implementation of human rights is quite considerable.[110] During the 1970s, Amnesty International played a leading role in setting international standards concerning the prohibition of torture. NGOs are increasingly involved, as *amici curiae*, in matters brought before international courts, particularly the ECHR and the Inter-American Court. They play a significant role in monitoring compliance with human rights and in denouncing serious violations of such rights.

The globalisation of human rights law presents a great number of interesting characteristics, many of which are connected to what we have already seen in other fields mentioned above.

d. Harmonisation

As in the majority of other areas in which legal globalisation operates, a harmonisation trend, rather than one of unification, can be identified. Materially, it operates through major international standards (concerning the identification of human rights, and of violations to be combatted) rather than through single norms.

e. Domestic–International Dialogue

We have seen that global human rights law is built characteristically through a dialogue between domestic laws and international norms. International courts, for instance, are indeed a last resort where domestic courts do not give satisfaction: this is the case for the ECHR in Strasbourg, and is also how the International Criminal Court was conceived.[111] This means that the sanctioning of human rights violations, and the production of case law relating thereto, are often shared between international law and domestic law.

f. Control of States

This aspect naturally contributes to the lessening of state control over the mechanisms protecting human rights. Admittedly, this loss of control has its limits, the most basic of which concerns the fact that international mechanisms for protecting human rights only exist because they have been created, undertaken by states.[112] However, in the field of human rights, we

---

[110] Andrea Bianchi, 'Globalization of Human Rights—The Role of Non-State Actors' in Teubner, *Global Law* (n 73) 179; Peters et al *Non-State Actors* (n 94).

[111] Grégory Berkovicz, *La place de la Cour pénale internationale dans la société des Etats* (Paris, L'Harmattan, 2005).

[112] Beate Rudolf, (1999) 'Considérations institutionnelles à propos de l'établissement d'une justice pénale internationale' *Revue française de droit constitutionnel* 39, 451.

can specifically observe the phenomenon (and we shall return to this later) whereby some mechanisms created by states—on that basis, they are masters of those mechanisms—are not under their control and make law that is sometimes highly disruptive for their national traditions without states being able to object very much as the only way out would be to withdraw completely from the legal mechanism in question—which would often seem quite out of proportion.

g. Variety of Instruments

That said, it is important to add that the globalisation of human rights law occurs through a combination of conventional methods and new mechanisms. Materially, human rights law derives mostly from fairly traditional international agreements, although it draws on new sources and inspiration: case law from international courts, the groundwork done in developing enlightened international opinion, in particular.[113] As we have seen, it also draws on all sorts of new material and is immersed in various major strides made in international legal technology.

h. Conflict with Other Sides of Legal Globalisation

One final remarkable aspect must be mentioned here. It is the fact that the globalisation of human rights may often find itself in conflict with other sides of globalisation, particularly the globalisation of trade or, more broadly, economic globalisation[114]—indeed, to such an extent that, for some, economic globalisation in its very essence conspires against human rights.[115]

In particular, we know that the WTO has hosted and continues to host bitter debates on the subject, pitting those (often developed states concerned by the competition they face from states with less exacting requirements in terms of wages and working conditions) that would introduce minimum standards for respecting workers (particularly concerning child labour) against those that defend state freedom in that area, or the need to avoid contaminating the logic of the liberalisation of trade with other considerations.[116]

---

[113] Bianchi, 'Globalization of Human Rights' (n 110).

[114] Jean-François Flauss, *Le droit international des droits de l'homme face à la globalisation économique* in *Commerce mondial et protection des droits de l'homme*, Publications de l'Institut international des Droits de l'Homme (Bruxelles, Bruylant, 2001) 217; Ernst-Ulrich Petersmann, *Multilevel Trade Governance in the WTO requires Multilevel Constitutionalism* in Christian Joerges & Ernst-Ulrich Petersmann (eds), *Constitutionalism, Multilevel Trade Governance and Social Regulation* (Oxford, Hart Publishing, 2006) 5.

[115] See, eg, Umberto Allegretti, *Diritti e Stato nella mondializzazione* (Troina, Città Aperta, 2002).

[116] Mireille Delmas-Marty, 'Commerce mondial et protection des droits de l'homme' in *Commerce mondial et protection des droits de l'homme* (Bruxelles, Bruylant, 2001) 1; Werner

The issue of combining the liberalisation of trade and the protection of workers' rights can be found in EU law,[117] but in line with slightly different arrangements. EU legislation in the area of labour law first developed with the aim of harmonising the corresponding standards of protection in the interests of free trade and equal economic competition. However, it was subsequently enhanced with specific objectives, not linked to the sole concern of eliminating possible trade barriers, such as eliminating discrimination between men and women.[118]

D. (National) Governance

The globalisation trend has incontrovertible consequences for international governance—we shall have ample opportunity to come back to this point later. There are, however, consequences for *national* governance, and we shall discuss the issue here.

i. The Impact of Globalisation

One might imagine *a priori* that national governance—the way in which states organise and operate their political and administrative institutions— would remain exempt from globalisation. This is not the case, for reasons that fall into two categories.[119]

On the one hand, international institutions in charge of economic development convinced themselves, in this modern era, that one of the prerequisites for such development was the existence of a rule of law, likely to guarantee the security of economic relations. Specifically, the World Bank and the International Monetary Fund have thrashed out that jurisprudence between them.[120]

Meng, 'International Labor Standards and International Trade Law' in Eyal Benvenisti and Georg Nolte (eds), *The Welfare State, Globalization and International Law* (Berlin, Heidelberg, Springer, 2003) 371 ff; Jill Murray, 'Relabelling the International Labor Problem: Globalization and Ideology' in Dauvergne *Jurisprudence* (n 11) 129; see also nn 58 and 59, chapter 1.

[117] But also in the context of the North American Free Trade Agreement: Marie-Ange Moreau and Gilles Trudeau (1995) 'La Clause sociale dans l'accord de libre-échange nord-américain' *Revue international de droit économique* 3, 361.

[118] Brian Bercusson, 'Labour Regulation in a Transnational Economy' (1999) 6 *Maastricht Journal of European and Comparative Law* 3, 244.

[119] Jean-Bernard Auby, 'Globalisation et droit public' in *Mélanges offerts à Jean Waline, Gouverner, Administrer, Juger* (Paris, Dalloz, 2002) 135.

[120] Julio Faundez, Mary E Footer and Joseph J Norton (eds), *Governance, Development and Globalization* (Oxford, Blackstone Press Limited, 2000); Bonnie Campbell, 'Reconceptualisation de l'Etat au Sud. Participation démocratique ou managerialisme populiste' in François Crépeau (ed), *Mondialisation des échanges et fonctions de l'Etat* (Bruxelles, Bruylant, 1997) 168; Patrice Dufour, 'L'assistance économique et financière de la Banque mondiale dans le

On the other hand, the rise of the international preoccupation with human rights, evoked above, naturally led to the idea that those rights could only really flourish within a minimum framework of democratic institutions. It is in this spirit, for example, that United Nations bodies now make themselves the proponents of democracy as an instrument for international peace.[121]

Taking as its starting point the idea, expressed by the European Court of Human Rights, that the core of the organisation's common values rises in 'the principles characterising a "democratic society"',[122] the Council of Europe has adopted improved instruments for monitoring compliance with those principles on the part of states, particularly through monitoring procedures, handled by the Parliamentary Assembly or the Council of Ministers.[123]

Armed with these two concerns regarding economic development and human rights, the EU has made democracy and the rule of law conditions to be imposed on nations wishing to accede to the Union.[124]

We shall return to this later in the book.

ii. A Global Law of National Governance?

By those means and for those reasons, a global law of national governance has been hammered out. It affects a whole spectrum of issues, from public administration methods to the very organisation of the state itself.

Firstly, it is a vehicle for the requirement as to the rule of law—or at least, and as has been highlighted above, a technical, instrumental conception of the rule of law,[125] the components of which are: the observance of property rights; the guarantee of investments; the creation of stable regulatory frameworks for economic activities; and access to justice.

'Good governance', as conceived by international economic institutions, is also subject to imperatives relative to transparency in public administration and, for instance, in budgetary procedures, as recommended in the 'Code of Good Practices on Fiscal Transparency' published by the International Monetary Fund in 1998[126] and updated in 2007.

---

cadre des opérations de restauration de l'Etat' in Yves Daudet (ed), *Les Nations unies et la restauration de l'Etat* (Paris, Pedone, 1995), 79.

[121] Fox and Roth (n 33); Richard Burchill, *Democracy and International Law* (Ashgate, 2006).

[122] *Handyside v United Kingdom*, Application no 5493/72 [1976] ECHR 5.

[123] Giovanni Michele Palmieri (2006) 'L'internationalisation du droit public. La contribution du Conseil de l'Europe' *Revue européenne de droit public* 1, 51.

[124] Jacques Chevallier, 'La mondialisation et l'Etat de droit', *Mélanges Philippe Ardant, Droit et politique à la croisée des cultures* (Paris, LGDJ, 1999) 325.

[125] François Crépeau, 'La difficile insertion de l'Etat de droit dans le paradigme de la mondialisation' in Monckle *Mondialisation* (n 74) 399.

[126] Benoit Chevauchez (1999) 'Le Fonds monétaire international et la transparence budgétaire' *Revue française de finances publiques* 67, 231; Marie-Christine Esclassan, 'Le modèle

It includes the principle of good administration, which requires that matters be handled impartially by administrative authorities and within reasonable timeframes, etc. This principle is put forward especially in the European sphere, by both the Council of Europe[127] and the EU, the latter having also converted it into a right recognised by the Charter of Fundamental Rights.[128]

According to its proponents, 'good governance' also entails the fight against the corruption of public officials. It is under the banner of that conviction that various international and European measures have been established, particularly the 1997 Convention on Combating Bribery of Foreign Public Officials in International Business Transactions, developed by the OECD.[129]

iii. Global Law on Governance, State Organisation and State Institutions

Global law on governance not only carries with it various requirements relative to public administration, but also impacts directly on the organisation of the state and the democratic operation of state institutions.

Public international law today goes so far as to place amongst its objectives the development of democracy in the world, and the protection thereof in scenarios where it faces serious threats. As recalled above, the international community responded vigorously on two occasions to military coups: in Haiti in 1994 and Sierra Leone in 1998. Those who wonder about the basis of international law's competence in taking an interest in the democratic nature of national political regimes receive the reply that it lays in the right to political participation, recognised by the major treaties on human rights protection: the Universal Declaration; Pact on Civil and Political Rights; regional conventions, etc.[130]

The international consensus that tends to emerge focuses, it must be said, on a particular model of democracy: that of pluralist democracies, with

---

français de finances publiques à l'épreuve de l'internationalisation du droit et de la politique' in Michel Bouvier (ed), *Réforme des finances publiques, démocratie et bonne gouvernance* (Paris, LGDJ, 2004) 361.

[127] Palmieri, 'L'internationalisation du droit public' (n 123).

[128] Loïc Azoulai, 'Le principe de bonne administration', in Jean-Bernard Auby and Jacqueline Dutheil de la Rochère (eds), *Traité de droit administratif européen*, 2nd edn (Bruxelles, Bruylant, 2014) 667.

[129] Philippe Cavalerie, 'La convention OCDE du 17 décembre 1997 sur la lutte contre la corruption d'agents publics étrangers dans les transactions commerciales internationales' (AFDI, 1997), 609; Didier Jean-Pierre, *La lutte contre la corruption des fonctionnaires et agents publics*, (Paris, Dalloz, 2000)

[130] Fox and Roth, *Democratic governance* (n 33): see in particular the Introduction; Yves Daudet, 'La restauration de l'Etat, nouvelle mission des Nations unies?' in Daudet *Les Nations unies* (n 120) 17.

its own characteristics in the modern era, and which go beyond the mere election of a government by universal suffrage to include: the existence of written constitutions separating powers and guaranteeing individual rights; the 'judicialisation' of political and administrative relations (constitutional review, judicial review of the administration, etc); the existence of the liability of public decision-makers; the separation of political and economic powers, etc.[131]

Global law on governance sometimes pushes in the direction of the institution of a degree of decentralisation. International bodies, for example, often hold it up as a good way to democratise political regimes or, more crudely, to circumvent ineffectual and corrupt governments.[132]

iv. Reasons for the Meeting of National Governance and Legal Globalisation

That legal globalisation should affect national governance is a remarkable phenomenon in itself, the subject being so far removed from the globalisation of economic transactions which are often considered the be-all and end-all of globalisation. It is easy to understand why that is so. The organisation and operation of the state are under the sway of globalisation because they are obviously the keys to safeguarding human rights and because—although this is not as immediately apparent—they are definitely key to the development of economic relations. This is no less surprising. Globalisation touches the very heart of states and national sovereignty.

Nevertheless, owing to that particular purpose, global law on governance is not composed of many compulsory norms. It is generally more jurisprudential than normative. It underpins the philosophy of certain organisations, arming them with standards for conducting their activities—this is especially true for major international economic institutions. The force of pressure exerted by those institutions does, however, sometimes confer singular force to those standards; we need only think of the discussions, which have been ongoing for quite some time, between the EU and Turkey on the democratisation of the latter's institutions.

---

[131] Martin Shapiro (1993) 'The Globalization of Law' *Indiana Journal of Global Legal Studies* 1.

[132] Jean du Bois de Gaudusson, 'La décentralisation menacée par la (bonne) gouvernance' in *Mélanges offerts à Franck Moderne* (Paris, Dalloz, 2004) 995; Alain Ménéménis, 'L'assistance constitutionnelle comme condition de la restauration de l'Etat' in Daudet *Les Nations unies* (n 120) 41.

3

The Mechanics of Legal Globalisation

NOW THAT WE have identified the main areas in which legal globalisation operates, and established the principal effects that it produces in those areas, we will now attempt to characterise those effects in a more systematic way.[1]

This will lead us to consider two sets of issues. What is clear, first of all, is that globalisation contributes to the transformation of normative processes in the international sphere (see 'I. Normative Processes'). There is also clear evidence that it also contributes to transforming relations between systems within that same remit ('II. Systemic Relations').

I. NORMATIVE PROCESSES

For the reasons that we strove to identify in chapter 1, globalisation sparks various transformations within law; changes that affect the production of norms, their content, and their effects—in other words, normative processes.

We shall see that, on many levels, globalisation actually strengthens or relays developments that already exist in what can roughly be described as the modern nature of international law and European law. It is clear that modern international law, and even more so European law, have moved away from more traditional intergovernmentalism in order to embrace new normative processes, in which other players, other types of norms, and other models producing legal effects have gradually been included.

Globalisation acts as a catalyst for this new, modern form. The interdependence between systems and levels, the expansion of transnational situations and the emergence of various private stakeholders, etc, which can be attributed to globalisation, also bolster and add extra dimensions to it.

The corresponding lines of developments within normative processes can be described as affecting the creation of norms, their content and effects.

---

[1] Maria Rosaria Ferrarese, *Diritto sconfinato, inventiva giuridica e spazi nel mondo globale* (Bari, Editori Laterza, 2006).

A. Creating Norms

One of the basic characteristics of law engaged in the globalisation process is the multiplicity and diversity of its makers. However, the development that this process causes or fuels also concern the ways in which law is made.

i. Producers of Norms

a. States

As the usual pivots in the production of law, states exert a more restricted control over the creation of global law, as we have seen in the various cases evoked in previous chapters.

As André-Jean Arnaud writes,[2] state law is *relayed*, particularly by that produced by regional integration, and which presents the greatest similarities with it, such as that produced by private economic powers; it is *supplemented*, for instance by the law created by international financial institutions to ensure the regulation of economic transactions which they alone oversee; it is *supplanted* where principles relating to governance, the rule of law or human rights that are binding on the international stage.

This loss of control for states must not be exaggerated—and we will return to this point later—but it does exist. It is due not only to the emergence of competing regulators, but also to the fact that states are increasingly involved in institutions and procedures that make law, in their name as it were, but over which they sometimes have very little control.

Non-state players and regulators under globalisation

The growing weight of non-state *players*

— *Main types of non-state player becoming increasingly important:*
  — multinational corporations
  — international professional organisations
  — non-governmental organisations:
    — in the field of human rights: eg Amnesty International, Human Rights Watch, International Committee of the Red Cross, etc (Alma Kadragic, *Globalization and Human Rights* (Chelsea House Publishers, 2006), 61 ff)

---

[2] André-Jean Arnaud (1997) 'De la régulation par le droit à l'heure de la globalisation' *Droit et société* 35, 11.

- — in the environmental sphere: eg Greenpeace, etc
- — in combatting corruption: eg Transparency International
- — sometimes have a genuine part to play in the production of norms (see below 'Law-making methods'). Furthermore, they play an essential role in information gathering, monitoring, running aid programmes, etc (David J Bederman, 'Diversity and Permeability in Transnational Governance' (2007–2008) *Emory Law Journal* 201).

But also:

- — entities responsible for outsourced public tasks
- — local governments involved in international policies
- — the 'warlords' ('key players in the current "privatisation of war", particularly present on the African continent … who maintain close ties with international terror networks and transnational companies trading in raw materials, defying existing state structures or establishing themselves in so-called "failed states" as warlords in search of profit': Anne Peters, 'Le droit international public expliqué aux enfants' in Emmanuelle Jouanet, Hélène Ruiz Fabri and Jean-Marc Sorel (eds), *Regards d'une génération de juristes sur le droit international* (Paris, Pedone, 2008) 303).
- — etc.

The emergence of non-state *regulators*

- — *Main types of non-state regulators:*
  - — entities with ties to state institutions (eg Basel Committee, Internet Corporation for Assigned Names and Numbers (ICANN), International Organization for Standardization (ISO)
  - — international professional organisations; for example:
    - — business organisations against corruption: Extractive Industries Transparency Initiative (EITI), Partnership against Corruption Initiative (PACI), Wolfsberg Anti-Money Laundering Principles, Equator Principles, Global Impact
    - — professional organisations in the construction world, which produce standard rules and contracts for cross-border projects: International Federation of Consulting Engineers (FIDIC), European Construction Industry Federation (FIEC), Institute of Civil Engineers (ICE), etc (Saskia

> Sassen, *A Sociology of Globalization* (New York, WW Norton & Co, 2007) 214 ff)
> — in maritime affairs: International Maritime Committee
> — some non-governmental organisations having acquired recognised expertise—in environmental matters or human rights—which enables them:
>   — occasionally to be involved in the drafting of inter-state conventions, or of secondary legislation (with no voting rights)
>   — occasionally to draft private legislation, to propose codes of conduct, guides to treaty interpretation, etc (Ann Peters, Lucy Köchlin, Till Förster and Greta Fenner (eds), *Non-state Actors as Standard Setters* (Cambridge, Cambridge University Press, 2009); eg the 1997 Maastricht Guidelines on Violations of Economic, Social and Cultural Rights, which build on the 1987 Limburg Principles on the Implementation of the International Covenant on Economic, Social and Cultural Rights; the Montreal Principles on Women's Economic, Social and Cultural Rights 2002; the Princeton Principles on Universal Jurisdiction 2001
> — others, eg, international sports organisations (international federations, Olympic committees, etc) (Michael J Beloff (2005) 'Is there a lex sportiva?' *International Sport Law Review* 3, 49; Antonio Rigozzi, *L'arbitrage international en matière de sport* (Basel, Helbing et Lichtenhahn, 2005)).

b. New Regulating Entities

Within globalisation we are witnessing an expansion in the range of institutions making regulations. The most remarkable aspect is the place occupied by a growing number of private entities—or, in any event, bodies which are neither state, intergovernmental, nor governmental; nor are they international public entities (see table above).

The privatisation of regulation

We have already noted, in particular, the role that such entities play in the regulation of trade, or the Internet. In the same vein, along with the examples given above, there is the role played by authorities such as the World Economic Forum (with its annual meeting in Davos) or ratings agencies which, in other contexts, produce standards for the international regulation of those relations.[3] We may also mention the rapid expansion of private arbitration centres.[4]

As Gunther Teubner writes, the law's centre of gravity is moving towards private systems of rules, and global law is increasingly reliant on independent resources: multinationals, global legal consultants, funds, associations, etc.[5]

The traditional players on the international scene are bound to adapt increasingly to these developments. This is evidenced, for instance, by the partnership policy in which the United Nations is now engaged vis-à-vis non-governmental organisations (NGOs), some of which are making a growing contribution to the production of norms on an international level. In 1997, the UN Secretary General expressed his desire to establish partnerships with the private sector and, in July 2000, the UN launched its Global Compact programme, an initiative aimed at associating multinational firms, trade unions and NGOs with the Organisation's activities.[6]

Self-regulation

It must be noted that a frequent corollary to this trend towards the 'privatisation' of regulations is a situation of more or less pronounced self-regulation in the sectors concerned. However, it is never full self-regulation.[7] In these cases where non-state regulation occupies an important place, the prevalent model is in reality one of 'co-regulation', in which private and state regulation—or that provided by public international organisations—work together and complete each other. Summarising research on the legal measures that now provide a legal framework in transnational relations for debt recovery, the reinsurance market, banking relations custody disputes, immigration, etc, Volkmar Gessner and Ali Cem Budak[8] note that almost nothing has been identified in these areas that may genuinely be defined as 'autonomous non-state law-making'. They also note that, on the various

---

[3] Jan Aart Scholte, *Globalization. A critical introduction* (London and New York, Macmillan, 2000), 148 ff.

[4] Reza Benakar, 'Reflexive Legitimacy in International Arbitration', in Volkam Gessner and Ali Cem Budak (eds), *Emerging Legal Certainty: Empirical Studies on the Globalization of Law (Onati International Series in Law and Society)* (Aldershot, Ashgate, 1998), 347.

[5] 'Un droit spontané dans la société mondiale?' in Charles-Albert Morand (ed), *Le droit saisi par la mondialisation* (Brussels, Bruylant, 2001), 197.

[6] Jacques Chevallier (2003) *L'Etat postmoderne*, Paris, LGDJ, coll *Droit et société* 41.

[7] *cf* the case of the Internet—see above, chapter 2, 'B Internet Law'.

[8] Gessner and Budak, *Emerging Legal Certainty* (n 4) see introduction.

issues open to legal globalisation, there remains 'a mix of state and non-state regulations'.

A brief word here on the question of *lex mercatoria*. What gives the impression that international trade is, through that phenomenon, governed by an 'independent' law is essentially both the sociological reality of the development of international arbitration, and the fact that the norms considered part of the *lex mercatoria* are most often universally recognised, sharing a sort of common legal nature (good faith; *pacta sunt servanda*). These two factors would carry little weight were they not backed up by state law. Arbitration is only effective owing to the possibility of relying on a state penalty as a last resort: the *lex mercatoria* needs the coercive force of state legal orders, as is accepted even by the proponents of the theory.[9] As for the substantive principles of *lex mercatoria*, these are in fact fairly vague directives,[10] carrying only relative substantive weight compared with that brought by the various international agreements and model laws that have already been mentioned.[11] It is no exaggeration to say that the *lex mercatoria* draws its (relative) independence from the support it finds in national law.[12]

These provisos in no way detract from the fact that some international activities are now subject to co-regulation, a significant proportion of which is made up of self-regulation or regulation by non-state authorities.[13] As an example, a not inconsiderable part of the compliance with certain basic norms under labour law—concerning child labour, for instance—rests on codes of conduct adopted by certain multinational corporations, under the terms of which they refrain from employing certain practices.[14]

c. Intergovernmental Networks and Judicial Bodies

Lastly, it must be added that even in the 'classic' state and intergovernmental frameworks, the identity of the various law-makers tends to change.

The inter-state bodies that produce norms in the international sphere cannot be reduced by any stretch to the classic diplomatic conferences and intergovernmental authorities of international organisations. A growing role is played by national administration networks, or regulators independent of states—we will come back to this. Many international organisation bodies

---

[9] Eric Loquin, 'Où en est la *lex mercatoria*?' in *Souveraineté étatique et marchés internationaux à la fin du 20ᵉ siècle, Mélanges en l'honneur de Philippe Kahn* (Paris, Litec, 2000) 41.

[10] Pierre Mayer (2000) 'Actualité du contrat international' *Les Petites Affiches* 5 May.

[11] See below, chapter 2, 'The *lex mercatoria*'.

[12] *cf* Jarrod Wiener, *Globalization and the Harmonization of Law* (London and New York, Pinter, 1999) 161 ff.

[13] Xavier Dieux *et al*, *L'autorégulation* (Brussels, Bruylant, 1995).

[14] See eg Egal Benvenisti and George Nolte (eds), *The Welfare State. Globalization and International Law* (Berlin, Heidelberg, Springer, 2003), 411 ff.

now have the structure and functions of genuine global administrative authorities—we will also come back to this.

This is coupled with the proliferation of courts and quasi-judicial bodies, which is one of the most striking characteristics of the current developments on the international legal scene.[15] A growing proportion of international law-making comes from that very source.

The overall situation is most forcefully summed up by Zaki Laidi:[16]

> Traditionally, the international system was regulated by the international law binding states, and the more informal *lex mercatoria*, binding private players. The configuration is much more complex. On the one hand, this is because *lex mercatoria* has expanded considerably. On the other hand, it is because, between the traditional treaties between states and *lex mercatoria*, a considerable number of normative instruments have been developed, issued by transnational networks of players, hybrid arrangements between public and private actors, national regulators bound by international arrangements, regulation activity by private players on behalf of public authority. Furthermore, there is a growing social normativity which originates neither from states nor market participants, but rather from non-state transnational players.

ii. Law-making Methods

It is clear that the multiplication and diversification of law-makers brings with it various changes in the ways in which laws are made.

a. Dispersion

The most obvious here is the phenomenon of dispersion. The sources of law having multiplied and diversified, this has not resulted in less law, as might be thought if we were to believe globalisation equals deregulation, to which the decline of the state could potentially lead. On the contrary, as Mireille Delmas-Marty points out, there has been a proliferation of norms, for instance in the field of human rights.[17]

The dispersion as to the purpose of those norms, their spatial scope, their origins, etc results in a situation of considerable legal fragmentation, to borrow the title of the International Law Commission's 2006 report.[18]

---

[15] Eg José E Alvarez (2003) 'The New Dispute-Settlers: (Half) Truths and Consequences *Texas International Law Journal* 38, 405.

[16] *La norme sans la force. L'énigme de la puissance européenn* (Paris, Presses de Sciences Po, 2008) 83.

[17] Mireille Delmas-Marty, 'La mondialisation du droit: chances et risques' (Paris, Dalloz, 1999) 2.

[18] International Law Commission (ILC), 'Fragmentation of International Law: Difficulties Arising from the Diversification and Expansion of International Law, in Report of the International Law Commission, 58th Session (2006)' UN Doc A/61/10 (2006).

This does not mean that there is no structure at all. It is interesting to note, for instance, that whatever the sphere in which the legal globalisation trend can be seen, we can identify as a minimum that law is organised in such a way that certain norms make the rest possible: they play the role of secondary rules, within the meaning of Hart's concept of law. As an example, in the legal globalisation of trade on a European level, an essential role is played by the 1968 Brussels Convention on jurisdiction and the enforcement of judgments in civil and commercial matters: in ensuring a sort of free movement of judgments, it really serves as a kind of legal infrastructure.[19]

That said, those structures as can be identified are not necessarily founded on a hierarchy of norms operating in ways that are familiar to us. We will return to this point shortly.

b. Blurring the Lines: Proliferation and Diversification of Law-makers

Another thing that is also quite remarkable is the fact that the proliferation and diversification of law-makers, and the places where laws are made, frequently results in making the identification or characterisation of roles in normative processes much more difficult.

Who is the legislator? Who is the executive? Where are the normative powers? Where are the 'sanctionary' powers? How are the various roles shared between international law and domestic law? All the examples that we have examined show that such distinctions tend to be blurred in the context of legal globalisation. For instance, in all situations where there is a certain degree of self-regulation, the players responsible for that self-regulation act both as legislators and executive powers, normative and sanctioning bodies—we need only look at the Internet's legal structure!

In all the examples that we have mentioned, a combination of international and domestic law can be seen, in line with an allocation of roles in which only an *a posteriori* examination serves to reveal any logic; several decades ago, few would have imagined that national governance or good administration would become matters of international law. This is an important point, and we will come back to this later.

In addition to all of the above, there are uncertainties as to the allocation of roles between the various institutions that are specifically responsible for making global law in the various fields that it impacts. Take, for instance, the doubts currently surrounding the limits of the WTO's powers: to what extent must it include environmental concerns? Is it well placed to concern itself with the international regulation of competition?[20]

---

[19] Anthony McGrew, 'Global Legal Interaction and Present-Day Patterns of Globalization' in Gessner and Budak *Emerging Legal Certainty* (n 4), 325.

[20] Thiébaut Flory, *L'organisation mondiale du commerce. Droit institutionnel et substantiel* (Bruxelles, Bruylant, 1999) 200 ff.

B. Norms and Their Content

It is certainly not from the point of view of their content that norms influenced by globalisation processes are most evidently remarkable. Nevertheless, they do present a number of particularities in this area. We can highlight several of these, which are related to their purpose and to their wording.

i. Purposes

In all of the interconnections that it induces between systems, the interdependence between the various levels, globalisation forces international legal norms to focus on purposes that are often new and transversal.

The most striking aspect here is the way in which law, influenced by globalisation, tends to rely on a new vision of territories. We have seen, for example, how globalising law on the environment is based on new 'territorialisations', broadly unaffected by national boundaries: maritime zones, hydrographic basins, etc.

In order to push European legal co-operation forward, two avenues are pursued: the first consists of gradually neutralising the traditional territorial structure of criminal law by deciding that the link between an offence and the territory of a given state does not excuse that state from co-operating; the second consists of redefining criminal territorialisation by deciding to consider Community territory as a single judicial area.[21]

New customs territories, protected ecological areas that do not match the perimeters of traditional state or interstate activities, judicial areas that are also removed from the state's remit such as the European judicial area—globalisation induces a new legal territorialisation on a par with the 'deterritorialisation' phenomena that instigate it; public action is trying to adapt.

ii. Wording

In international law-making, does globalisation lead to certain particular traits that concern the wording of norms; the legal conceptualisation of reality on which they are based? Yes, in part. Without dwelling too much on the fact that they do sometimes contradict each other –global trade law coming into friction with global environmental law, for instance, or with human rights—two factors above all must be mentioned here.

---

[21] Robert Roth, 'Droit pénal transnational: un droit pénal sans Etat et sans territoire?' in Morand, *Le droit saisi par la mondialisation* (n 5) 131.

a. The Use of General Standards

As the norms under globalisation are intended to govern local legal realities that are often very different, as they often have what can be called a 'multi-system' nature, they often take on the character of fairly general standards, of open concepts that can be amalgamated into different legal cultures, and which thereby leave room for manoeuvre for those different legal cultures in terms of their implementation. As has often been observed, this is broadly how ECHR law operates.[22]

There is a downside to this situation, which we will revisit later, as it is an important factor in the structuring of legal relations in globalisation. The concepts that systems of rules under legal globalisation draw upon in order to encompass the multinational legal realities that they cover, are often erected as 'non-state concepts'—ie embodying their own meaning and significance, to which national systems must subsequently adapt. The phenomenon can be seen in ECHR law: in the context of the application of Article 6 ECHR, for instance, specific concepts of what is a trial, or what are civil or criminal cases, have been hammered out, with which national laws must now come to terms.[23] It is also present in EU law. The Court of Justice regularly states that such and such a concept—being linked to national concepts—must be understood as an 'autonomous concept of Community law', ie has a definition under Community law that must not coincide with that of any of its national counterparts. This sort of 'federating conceptual gap' concerns, for instance, the concept of 'public law body' in establishing the scope of Community rules on public procurement.[24]

b. The Use of Guidelines

For the same kinds of reasons, as regards their authority, their legal 'force', globalisation's norms are frequently characterised by the fact that they constitute standards of behaviour—guidelines—rather than mandatory rules of behaviour.

It is not especially useful for us to dwell on this aspect, except to note that it is in line with this general development of law which increases its soft law dimension, which Paul Amselek perfectly describes as 'the non-authoritarian direction of behaviour'.[25]

---

[22] See eg: Gérard Marcou (ed), *Les mutations du droit de l'administration en Europe*, (1995, Paris, L'Harmattan, coll 'Logiques juridiques'), 331 ff.

[23] Frédéric Sudre, 'Le recours aux 'notions autonomes' in Frédéric Sudre (ed), *L'interprétation de la Convention européenne des droits de l'homme* (Brussels, Bruylant, 1998), 93.

[24] *inter alia*: Case C-373/00 *Adolf Truly GmbH and Bestattung Wien GmbH* [2003] ECR I-01931.

[25] Paul Amselek (1982) 'L'évolution générale de la technique juridique dans les sociétés occidentales' *Revue de droit public*, 278.

C. The Effects of Norms

The phenomena associated with globalisation fuel some of the developments in modern international normative processes that can be found in the field of the effects of norms. Globalisation contributes to transformations in the sphere belonging to the recipients of international norms, the connections between those norms—and with domestic norms—and they implementation.

i. Recipients

By connecting systems as it does, globalisation constantly intensifies the ties between sub-state entities, going over states' heads, as it were. We can see that it fuels the modern trend for such entities to emerge as such on the international legal stage.

Globalisation provides a powerful boost to this modern trend in international norms, whereby they are increasingly aimed at individuals, and to non-state entities more generally[26]—even going so far as to view them as both beneficiaries and targets; this is how, along with the almost banal fact that the citizens of states bound by major human rights measures frequently have the right to claim them directly, there is also the fact that governments have become individually liable for certain major crimes under nascent international criminal law.

We should also add that it would be a mistake to believe that this legal 'outcrop' of private individuals is only to be found in the human rights sphere.[27] It can also be seen in international economic law, in which the possibility for private individuals to assert their rights (aside from the more classic diplomatic protection techniques) is increasingly encountered in the field of arbitration and transnational investment agreements.[28] The history of EU citizenship provides an especially striking example. On the basis of economic concerns expressed in the Treaty by the principles of free movement of workers and non-discrimination, various rights—be they social rights or different protective measures—have gradually emerged, benefitting individual EU citizens who can directly assert those rights in accordance with an intellectual and legal mechanism similar to that used by the US

---

[26] See eg Benedict Kingbury, Nico Krisch and Richard Stewart (2005) 'The Emergence of Global Administrative Law' 68 *Law and Contemporary Problems* 3–4, 23.

[27] What is characteristic here is, in truth, not only the fact that individuals are direct beneficiaries of right but also that they are 'perceived as such owing to their inherent nature as human beings' (Pierre-Marie Dupuy, 'Dynamique des droits de l'homme et société civile internationale' in Gérard Cohen-Jonathan, *Libertés, justice, tolérance, Mélanges en hommage au Doyen* (Brussels, Bruylant, 2004), 747).

[28] Gérard Cohen-Jonathan, 'Droits et devoirs internationaux des individus' in Denis Alland (ed), *Droit international public* (Paris, PUF, 2000) 573.

Supreme Court in establishing links between free trade between federated states and national social security schemes.[29]

Incidentally, the 'private individual' thus emerging under globalising law is not only an isolated individual holding the majority of classic human rights. It also refers to companies: this is true for economic law,[30] but also human rights law in some instances, particularly through property law. It also relates to private non-profit groups: charities, NGOs, etc; and, occasionally, sub-state entities—local authorities in particular, to which European law—EU law and the conventions signed within the framework of the Council of Europe—recognises various prerogatives, particularly regarding cross-border co-operation.[31]

ii. Connections

Modern law has seen, and indeed continues to see, relations between international norms, and between international norms and domestic law, evolve significantly according, in particular, to the concessions made by states to the development of an international legal structure. The globalisation trend has contributed to that evolution, owing particularly to the interdependence between the systems and levels that it creates and maintains. It thereby also contributes to two contradictory trends.

a. Globalisation and Direct Effect

The areas most affected by globalisation are those in which direct effect is most frequently encountered.

Dominique Carreau explains[32] that the choice areas for the direct application of international legal norms are: EU law; human rights protection within the framework of the Council of Europe; the status of foreign nationals where this is regulated by establishment conventions; the rules applicable to foreign property where this is regulated within the framework of a bilateral agreement; and international economic relations in which either the most-favoured-nation clause or the national treatment clause will apply.

We can see immediately that these different areas contain most of legal globalisation's footholds.

---

[29] Sybilla Fries and Jo Shaw (1998) 'Citizenship of the Union: First Steps in the European Court of Justice' 4 *European Public Law* 4, 533.

[30] Occasionally, in the context of public international economic disputes, this includes the law governing certain free-trade agreements which sometimes allows private parties to challenge national regulations before dispute-resolution panels. This is the case for the NAFTA framework: see Paul Schiff Berman (ed), *The Globalization of International Law* (Aldershot, Ashgate, 2005), introduction XIII.

[31] See above, chapter 2, Public contracts and international norms and below, chapter 4, III Globalisation and Territorial Pluralism: the Global–Local Dialogue ff.

[32] Dominique Carreau, *Droit international*, 5th edn. (Paris, Pedone, 1997), 494.

b. Globalisation and Normative Hierarchies

On the other hand, those areas in which globalisation acts most strikingly also belong to those in which an analysis easily reveals a degree of uncertainty in normative hierarchies.

This is the case in the field of human rights. Suffice it to mention here the highly complex tiers made up of United Nations law, European Convention law, EU law and national laws, as shown by European and national case law. The *Kadi* decision, on the one hand, with national case law such as *Solange*[33] on the other, show us that this tiering is not hierarchical in reality; rather, it rests on a sort of reciprocal hierarchical link, which is better characterised by saying that it contains a sort of mirroring mechanism.

Another good example is provided by the relations between WTO law and EU law. In *Portugal v Council*,[34] the European Court of Justice accepted that WTO agreements did not in principle feature amongst the norms in the light of which the Court reviews the lawfulness of acts performed by EU institutions.[35] As explained by Frédérique Berrod,[36] the WTO dispute settlement system uses the impossibility of pleading or arguing directly on the basis of national and European courts in order to operate: national or EU courts cannot intervene to enforce an obligation resulting from WTO agreements, and thus leave every latitude to negotiators and panellists to settle disputes. We are far from the model in which conflicts of norms must be resolved in favour of the hierarchically superior norm but, in this way, mutual concessions may be negotiated so as to achieve a balance allowing compliance with the ultimate purpose of the global norm.

Relations between norms under legal globalisation: models of the 'double mirror effect' Impossible or undesirable hierarchies

It would appear that some legal 'layers' in the multilevel governance model can ultimately no longer be situated—other than rather artificially—in any hierarchical models.

However, it may be argued that clearly accepted hierarchical relations develop to a certain extent, with national laws increasingly giving

---

[33] BVerfGE 37, 271 2 BvL 52/71 Solange I-Beschluss.

[34] Case C149/96, *Portugal v Council* [1999] ECR I-08395.

[35] Jean-Claude Gautron and Loïc Grard, 'Le droit international dans la construction européenne' in Société française pour le Droit international, *Droit international et droit communautaire. Perspectives actuelles* (Paris, Pedone, 2000) 108 ff.

[36] Frédérique Berrod, 'La Cour de justice refuse l'invocabilité des accords OMC: essai de régulation de la mondialisation' (2000) *Revue trimestriel de droit européen* July–September, 419. See also: Gaëtan Verhoosel, *National Treatment and WTO Settlement. Adjudicating the Boundaries of Regulatory Autonomy* (Oxford, Hart Publishing, 2002).

way to international law, the precedence of universal international law over regional international law being clearly accepted, etc. National case law that accepted the primacy of subsequent national law over a given international norm is becoming increasingly rare (eg: Giuliana Ziccardi Capaldo, *The Pillars of Global Law* (Aldershot, Ashgate, 2008) 187 ff). Some modern constitutions declare themselves subordinate to international law, or simply to international law on human rights (eg Anne Peters, 'The Globalization of state Constitutions', in Janne Nijman and André Nollkaemper (eds), *New Perspectives on the Divide Between National and International Law* (Oxford, Oxford University Press, 2007, 251)).

Nevertheless, in certain cases, it would appear that the hierarchy stutters, or slips; it struggles to impose itself.

1. The leading example is given by the *relations between EU law and the constitutions of the various Member States.* As we know, the key issue here is the extent to which, and the way in which, national courts, and particularly national constitutional courts, will be able to protect a proportion of national constitutional law, which would be exempt from the primacy of EU law. We know that some states have embarked on such a course. First, the Italian Constitutional Court which, in 1965 and 1984, accepted that it was able to review Community acts where the fundamental principles of the Italian legal order and the inalienable rights of human beings are at stake. Equally, with its three well-known decisions in 1974 (*Solange I*), 1986 (*Solange II*) and 1992, there is Germany's federal constitutional court, which ultimately accepted in general terms its duty to review the constitutionality of EU law (Constance Grewe & Hélène Ruiz-Fabri, *Droits constitutionnels européens* (Paris, PUF, 1995) 131 ff; Joël Rideau, *Droit institutionnel de l'Union et des Communautés européennes* (Paris, LGDJ, 2006) 1032 ff).

Faced with the risks of irresolvable conflicts that these positions contain, other constitutional courts settle for tackling the problem from a procedural angle: this was the case for French constitutional case law which, initially, only dealt with the problem via the rule according to which the ratification of treaties—EU or otherwise—which infringe the basic conditions for exercising national sovereignty requires a prior constitutional amendment. Then the Constitutional Council, from its 2004 *Loi pour la confiance dans l'économie numérique* decision onwards, adopted a position similar to that of the German Constitutional Court (Rideau, ibid 1131 ff).

2. The relations between EU law and national laws are not the only example of these impossible or undesirable hierarchies.

Kadi truly showed that in spite of its principle of deference to UN law, EU law could not refrain from checking compliance with Community principles relative to human rights in decisions made by EU authorities, even those taken in enforcing a decision of the UN Security Council (Jean-Paul Jacqué, 'Droit constitutionnel national, droit communautaire, CEDH, Charte des Nations unies. L'instabilité des rapports de système entre ordres juridiques' (2007) *Revue française de droit constitutionnel* 3).

As their relations currently stand—and may naturally change in the event of the Union acceding to the ECHR—ECHR law and EU law are clearly not part of a same hierarchy.

As we have seen above (iii Connections), relations between EU law and WTO law also struggle to be placed within a same hierarchical model.

The reality of the 'double mirror' effect

Everything therefore shows that, in some scenarios, the relationship between the various levels of norms cannot be viewed in purely hierarchical terms. A norm that is superior in principle only prevails insofar as it does not come up against a hard core in the norm that is, in principle, inferior; the hierarchy is neither absolute nor general.

In certain scenarios, the two bodies of norms bow to and respect each other (for instance, though efforts made to achieve compatible interpretations). In some way, they occasionally rely on each other: in substantive terms, this is how relations between EU law and Member States' national constitutions are best understood.

They are thus like mirrors held up to one another, the reflection of one in the other creating a double mirror, with none of the reflected realities definitively imposed.

This view is made all the more acceptable in that it tallies with the fact that global law, like global governance, is based around a multilevel model in which the various levels interact, interconnect, interoperate.

iii. Implementation

We can see that, in those areas most affected by globalisation, law sometimes produces unusual implementation mechanisms, but also often relies on the more traditional mechanisms provided under state or inter-state law.

In all of the main areas of legal globalisation, we can identify specific implementation measures. Focusing on sanctioning mechanisms, global trade law has the WTO panels; human rights have the Courts of Human Rights and the International Criminal Court; environmental law has the International Tribunal for the Law of the Sea, etc. Occasionally, these institutions take their place within classic international organisations—this is the case for the WTO's dispute settlement system, although this is quite specific in terms of its technology. It is very often the case for international arbitration, but it is also—and even more unusually—the case for Internet dispute resolution systems: 'cyberspace's adjudicatory structures', to borrow Pierre

Trudel's phrase,[37] are for the most part dispute settlement systems internal to the various networks, as we have seen above.

At the same time, the implementation of globalisation's norms borrows heavily from ordinary systems provided by state or inter-state law. In the main, it falls to domestic laws, often in their most ordinary configurations, to implement and sanction global law on the environment, public procurement, governance, financial markets,[38] etc. As Sabino Cassese points out,[39] in the global legal sphere, states retain the executive function—and strongly in any case. As for the judicial function, states also broadly have the last word; the enforcement of penalties always depends on this in any case, and always as a last resort.

II. SYSTEMIC RELATIONS

As we have seen, the globalisation trend fuels various developments in normative processes on the international stage. However, what marks out the mechanics of legal globalisation perhaps lays less in the formation of norms, their content and effects, than it does in the processes for their transmission, their movement, and their intrusion into national legal systems.

This is where we come on to the issue of relations between systems within legal globalisation. As we shall see, this covers three major trends in this respect: a 'permeabilisation' of legal systems; competition between those systems; and harmonisation of those systems.

A. 'Permeabilisation' of Legal Systems

In the various mechanisms competing with legal globalisation, several are of crucial importance and can be grouped together around the notion of a growing permeability of legal systems. In figurative terms, legal systems have traditionally had 'immune systems' in which, even where they have to welcome foreign bodies (because it simply is not possible to seal a system off from the rest of the legal planet), their fundamental balance is always restored, external agents being easily absorbed or reduced. In the globalisation sphere today, our legal systems have to accommodate the intrusion of external elements to such an extent and in such a way that they find

---

[37] Pierre Trudel, 'La *lex electronica*' in Morand, *Le droit saisi par la mondialisation* (n 5) 221.

[38] In the latter case, see eg Dimitry Kingsford Smith, 'Networks, Norms and the Nation State: Thoughts on Pluralism and Globalized Securities Regulation' in Catherine Dauvergne (ed), *Jurisprudence for an Interconnected Globe* (Aldershot, Ashgate, 2003), 93.

[39] Sabino Cassese, *Lo spazio giuridico globale* (Bari, Editori Laterza, 2003).

themselves profoundly altered from the inside, to the point where their very identity can be called into question.

i. The Monolithic View versus the Reality of Legal Systems

There is, in theory, a monolithic—or at least an elitist—view of the organisation of legal systems, which consists in considering that they are essentially sealed off from one another; that each accepts as law only those norms that it has itself made, and deems all others to be inoperable.[40]

a. Legal Systems are Permeable

The reality is quite different. An examination of the facts shows that legal systems are not always impermeable.

They always accept, to a lesser or greater extent, the intrusion of norms that they themselves have not made. All national systems do so insofar as they accept international legal norms entering their ambit, although they do this in various ways, depending in particular on whether they work on the basis of dualism or one or other of the various types of monism.

The permeability phenomena are not to be found exclusively in the relations between national legal systems and international law. They can also be seen in relations between national systems.

One example is the fact that states sometimes accept that a contract performed on their territory, and any disputes arising therefrom falling under the jurisdiction of their courts, can be governed by foreign law; this is the result, paradoxical in commonsensical terms, of traditional rules on conflicts of laws and jurisdictions.

All in all, there is nothing exceptional about foreign norms penetrating a given legal system; it is, in fact, quite normal.

b. Capacity for Resistance

However, this natural phenomenon is traditionally doubled up by another, which compensates for the trend. It is the fact that, faced with intrusion of external norms, legal systems have what can be called immune systems. Aside from the fact that they have in theory accepted that intrusion, at any one original point—by ratifying a treaty or accepting a custom—they have resistance and, substantively, assimilate the intruder norms at the cost, where applicable, of certain arrangements with them.

---

[40] See François Ost and Michel van de Kerchove, *Le système juridique entre ordre et désordre* (Paris, PUF, 1988) 189.

This resistance varies, but takes the form of at least two types of mechanism.

The first relates to the fact that a legal system faced with the importation of external norms will sometimes state that those norms shall not be able to contravene certain fundamental principles, deemed inviolate. This is what happens when, pursuant to rules applicable to international contracts, the law applicable to the contract may be set aside where its application is manifestly incompatible with the public policy considerations of incumbent on the court hearing the matter.[41]

The second related to a legal system's faculty for modulating the application of intruder norms, by amalgamating these with national concepts. This is what happens, for instance, when international law accepts that the application of norms that it has imposed be subject to standards, the content of which falls to national systems to determine; the 'urgency' which allows this or that measure vis-à-vis a foreign national, for example. In this kind of scenario, the national system can draw all or part of the sting from the intruding norm by moving the markers for its application.

These mechanisms are such that legal systems generally agree on arrangements with what is coming from outside without much difficulty, through a deeply assimilatory approach. It is the comfort of this approach, even the possibility thereof, that legal globalisation calls into question.

ii. The Multiplication of Vectors

One of the properties of legal globalisation is that the vectors for legal 'penetration' are multiplied within domestic systems, and increasingly effective vectors are even developed within those systems.

More so than in the context of classic inter-state relations, it is in the wake of legal globalisation, that advanced technologies of international law facilitating the intrusion of international norms in domestic systems have developed. There are, for instance, those that influence conditions for the *applicability* of international norms in the domestic legal order: applicability in line with simplified procedures—as in the case of Community regulations, the applicability of which relies simply on their publication; recognition of the immediate effect of certain provisions, etc. There are also those that influence conditions for the *justiciability* of international norms within the domestic legal order: direct effect, which we have discussed above.[42]

---

[41] As is provided, for instance, by Article 16 of the Rome Convention on the Law Applicable to Contractual Obligations 1980.

[42] Patrick Daillier, 'Monisme et dualisme: un débat dépassé?' in Rafâa Ben Achour and Slim Laghmani (eds), *Droit international et droit interne. Développments récents* (Paris, Pedone, 1998) 9.

Naturally, the best illustrations of such advanced technologies are to be found in EU law. Moreover, in this respect, it produces a ripple effect with regard to other spheres of international law.[43]

Even so, EU law brings an additional refinement in its relations with domestic law, which is the following. In deciding that only certain EU norms would have direct effect, the Member States accepted that the regulation of relations between their national laws and EU law fall within the remit of the latter (which must also ensure that the norms produced by the EU are shared between acts that have direct effect and those that do not).[44]

In addition, an examination of EU law also reveals that the strengthening of vectors for the penetration of external norms does not only affect relations between international norms and national systems. It also extends to relations between national systems, through which, for instance, mutual recognition mechanisms—such as those resulting from the case law in *Cassis de Dijon*.[45] Through such mechanisms, State A finds itself bound to import norms laid down by State B—to take them as its own—when it was not at all involved in making them.

iii. Weakening Resistance

The impact of the phenomena described above is amplified by the fact that, conversely, legal globalisation weakens resistance on the part of legal systems for various reasons, and principally the following:

a. A Uniform Application of the Law under Globalisation

The first relates to the fact that legal globalisation encompasses growing pressure in the sense of a uniform—or at least relative homogeneous—application of the law. This pressure clearly manifests itself in the development, as we have previously seen, of 'uniform law' in the sphere of international trade.

Even more pervasive manifestations can be mentioned. They can be seen, be it within EU law or WTO law, in the fact that both laws produce their own definitions, which are transnational by their essence, of certain concepts that define various public action requirements which have been acknowledged as buffers to the liberalisation of trade. In terms of public

---

[43] Gautron and Grard, *Le droit international* (n 35).

[44] Deirdre Curtin and Ige Dekker, 'The Constitutional Structure of the European Union: Some Reflections on Vertical Unity and Diversity' in Paul Beaumont, Carole Lyons and Neil Walker (eds), *Convergence and Divergence in European Public Law* (Oxford, Hart Publishing, 2000) 59.

[45] Case C-120/78 *Rewe-Zentral AG v Bundesmonopolverwaltung für Branntwein (Cassis de Dijon)*, [1979] ECR 00649.

policy, public health requirements, etc, EU law and WTO law tend to produce their own definitions and therefore establish a uniform law of sorts in respect of those areas.[46]

Public order exceptions, states and legal globalisation

Here we touch on one of the most remarkable mechanisms for vertical interpenetration between systems, which encompasses legal globalisation. It follows from the fact that many international systems imposing obligations on states afford them the possibility of avoiding all or part of those obligations where states invoke various public interest imperatives: public policy, public health, etc. However, as far as we are concerned here, the key to such a mechanism lays beyond that. It is found in the fact that, alongside the international system and the institutions that protect it, states consequently more or less share the responsibility of defining what their public interest, public policy, public health imperatives are (see above).

The mechanism itself operates as follows. While accommodating a margin of appreciation for states—which, in theory, still have the option of having their own conception of public policy, public health, etc (note that such recognition was made explicit by, for example, the European Court of Justice in the *Omega* case of 2001, on the issue of human dignity)—European or international authorities reserve the right to verify that the imperatives invoked by states are indeed of such a nature as to constitute an exception provided by the international system, and that the gaps that states want in relation to the usual rule are required by the imperatives put forward, proportionate and not discriminatory.

Thus, what is in theory a tool for the protection of state sovereignty becomes an avenue by which the definition of national public policy is Europeanised and internationalised (see, eg, on the Community definition of public policy: Case 30/77, *Regina v Bouchereau* [1977] ECR 01999; Case C-340/97 *Ömer Nazli, Caglar Nazli and Melike Nazli v Stadt Nürnberg* [2000] ECR I-00957: 'the concept of public policy presupposes, in addition to the disturbance of the social order which any infringement of the law involves, the existence of a genuine and sufficiently serious threat to one of the fundamental interests of society').

It ought to come as no surprise, as it well reflects the interconnection between the various levels for conducting public affairs that globalisation creates. There is no longer a purely national public order or public property; but in truth, there is no longer a purely international public order

---

[46] Thiébaut Flory, 'Les facteurs non-économiques dans la jurisprudence de la CJCE et des instances de l'OMC' (1999) Colloque Jean Monnet, 21–22 October.

either. There is an ensemble of models containing several definitions—multilevel models of general interest and public policy.

See: Abdelkhalek Berramdane, 'L'ordre public et les droits fondamentaux en droit communautaire et de l'Union européenne' in *Territoires et libertés, Mélanges offerts à Yves Madiot* (Brussels, Bruylant, 2000) 1570; Chahira Boutayeb, 'Une recherche sur la place et les fonctions de l'intérêt général en droit communautaire' (2003) *Revue trimestrielle de droit européen* October–December, 587; Marion Castillon and Régis Chemain, 'Les réserves d'ordre public en droit communautaire' in Marie-Joëlle Redor (ed), *L'ordre public: ordres publics ou ordre public. Ordre public et droits fondamentaux* (Brussels, Bruylant, 2001); Thiébaut Flory, *L'organisation mondiale du commerce. Droit institutionnel et substantiel,* (Brussels, Bruylant, 1999); Thomas Hamoniaux, *L'intérêt général et le juge communautaire* (LGDJ, 2001) 105 ff; Gisele Kapterian, 'A critique of the WTO jurisprudence on "necessity"' (2010) *International & Comparative Law Quarterly* 59, 89; Mustafa Karayigit, 'The Notion of Services of General Economic Interest Revisted' (2009) 15 *European Public Law* 4, 575; Georges Karydis, 'L'ordre public dans l'ordre juridique communautaire: un concept à contenu variable' (2002) *Revue trimestrielle de droit européen*, January–March, 1; Bob Kieffer, *L'OMC et l'évolution du droit international* (Brussels, Larcier, 2008); Jeronimo Maillo Gonzalez-Orus, 'Beyond the Scope of Article 90 of the EC Treaty: Activities Excluded from the EC Competition Rules' (1999) 5 *European Public Law* 3, 387; Nicolas de Sadeleer, 'Les clauses de sauvegarde prévues à l'article 95 du Traité CE' (2002) *Revue trimestrielle de droit européen*, January–March, 53.

b. Legitimacy of Global Standards

The second factor to weaken the resistance put up by national legal systems stems from the fact that legal standards under globalisation often have a high degree of legitimacy. This is especially true of those relating to the liberalisation of trade, as they are generally taken as guarantors of economic prosperity; the same can be said for those concerning human rights, given the broad consensus relative to such rights.

One significant consequence of this state of things is that these standards produce spill-over effects when they are incorporated into national legal systems—we shall return to this later.

c. Transnational Realities

The third factor weakening the defences of national legal systems relates to the fact that situations, organisations, players, etc emerge, sitting astride two or more legal systems and thus avoiding the control of those systems, be it one or other or all of them.

This is the case of multinational corporations, whose activities, for instance, are often only understood with great difficulty by national tax authorities. But it is also the case for cross-border administrative organisations, such as tend to develop in the European context: where local authorities located on either side of a border agree to establish a common economic area, or common local facilities, or to co-ordinate their urban planning policies. These organisations are a challenge for national legal systems, as shown in the contortions performed by French law in this regard.[47] This is because they drive the national legal systems involved to accept that what is increasingly a public reality falling within their remit is also subject in part to norms belonging to a neighbouring system.

The extraterritorial legal mechanisms and realities generally tend to develop under globalisation[48] and increasingly raise problems—even where the extraterritorial effects that permeate legal systems are desired by those systems. This is how, a number of years ago, the Russian government agreed that licences for the marketing of pharmaceutical products granted by the US Food and Drug Administration constituted an authorisation to distribute the products in Russia.[49]

iv. New Ways to Assimilate External Norms

The two phenomena discussed above—the development of factors in the penetration of external norms, and the decrease in resistance on the part of legal systems—have one highly significant consequence, which is that once external norms have permeated them it becomes increasingly difficult for legal systems to make the arrangements whereby they traditionally succeeded in assimilating such norms.

a. A Higher Level of Confrontation

This is especially so since the level of confrontation tends to increase, in the sense that it is fundamental levels within legal systems that are affected by external norms introduced by globalisation.

---

[47] See Christian Autexier, 'L'action extérieure des collectivités territoriales' in Francis-Paul Benoit (ed), *Collectivités locales* (Paris, Dalloz, regular updates); Renan Le Mestre (2008) 'Le nouveau cadre juridique de l'action extérieure des collectivités territoriales françaises' *Mélanges Fenet*, 727.

[48] See chapter 1, 'Extraterritoriality in a context of legal globalisation'.

[49] Anne-Marie Slaughter, 'Government networks: the heart of liberal democratic order', in Gregory H Fox and Brad R Roth (eds), *Democratic governance and international law* (Cambridge, Cambridge University Press, 2000) 199.

In the spheres most marked by globalisation, the norms put forward by globalisation tend increasingly to exert pressure on the basic values of those systems. Requirements under EU law in the area of competition question the very concept in French law of what traditionally constitutes a public service.[50] International standards relative to fair trial, as expressed in particular under Article 6 of the European Convention on Human Rights, unbalance various independent administrative authorities whose operating rules had previously been carefully weighed up and which had appeared to embody a fortunate exceedance of more classic forms of government activity. The requirements set down by EU law in *Factortame* drove English law to give up the principle whereby injunctions could not be granted against the Crown.[51] *Francovich* forced Italian law to abandon the distinction between the violation of rights and of interests, which traditionally structures the law on administrative liability.[52]

Quite logically, in certain scenarios the confrontation comes about on a constitutional level. The creation of the European single currency, a characteristic instrument in the liberalisation of trade, compelled some European states to amend their respective constitutions. Community case law forced Germany to abandon constitutional rules barring women from the military—or at least forbidding women from using arms.[53]

b. Forms of Subsidiarity

In such a situation, a major problem concerns subsidiarity, ie the existence and organisation of an area of legal freedom left to a legal system where globalisation's legal norms affect important aspects of that system.[54]

This is the meeting point for constitutional reservations in the relations between EU law and national laws, and case law through which, inspired by the German Constitutional Court, various constitutional courts have sought to 'sanctuarise' a proportion of national constitutional norms without clashing head-on with Community law.[55]

The insulation technique can also be found here, whereby certain principles imported into national laws by Community law only apply to situations governed by that law,[56] or even the margin of appreciation recognised to

---

[50] Louis Dubouis, 'Droit administratif et droit communautaire: deux cultures juridiques?' in *Mélanges Philippe Ardant* (LGDJ, 1999) 443.

[51] See Paul Craig, *Administrative Law*, 5th edn (London, Sweet & Maxwell, 2003) 874 ff.

[52] Angela Siciliano (1999) 'State Liability for Breaches of Community Law and its Application within the Italian Legal System' 5 *European Public Law* 3, 405.

[53] Case C-285/98 *Tanja Kreil v Bundesrepublik Deutschland*, [2000] ECR I-00069.

[54] Mireille Delmas-Marty and Marie-Laure Izorche (2000) 'Marge nationale d'appréciation et internationalisation du droit', *Revue internationale de droit comparé*, 753.

[55] See above, this chapter, 'Relations between norms under legal globalisation: models of the "double mirror effect"'.

[56] eg: Gérard Marcou (ed), *Les mutations du droit de l'administration en Europe* (Paris, L'Harmattan, 2000), 31.

states by the European Convention on Human Rights in the implementation of its principles,[57] etc.

B. Competition between Legal Systems

i. Competition as a Characteristic of Legal Globalisation

One of the structural characteristics of legal globalisation is that legal systems find themselves in fierce competition. The reasons behind this situation are easily identified.

a. National Systems as Options

A certain number of international players are in a position to establish competition between legal systems because they are able to choose to be in the orbit of this or that system depending on their preferences.

This phenomenon is well known in the economic order. Many companies and investors have the possibility of moving their activities in order to place them where, in their view, they will be able to operate at maximum profit. Economists put it this way: the more globalised the economy, the more what can move—companies or capital—establishes competition between what does not move—institutions, taxation, etc.[58]

However, it would be a mistake to think that this competition between systems only occurs in the economic sphere. 'Forum shopping'—the search for the most favourable legal system—can involve many other aspects of legal life. It is sometimes possible, in divorce matters, to place oneself under the auspices of a law that is more favourable than that under which one married.[59] In Europe under the Schengen Agreement, the abolition of border controls has allowed foreign nationals to seek out the most generous systems in terms of asylum law—effectively 'asylum shopping'; the Dublin Convention put a brake on the practice, setting criteria for identifying the state responsible for examining applications for asylum.[60]

---

[57] Alain Didier Olinga (1995) 'La théorie de la marge d'appréciation dans la jurisprudence de la Cour européenne des droits de l'Homme' *Revue trimestrielle des Droits de l'Homme* 567; Mireille Delmas-Marty and Marie-Laure Izorche (2000) 'Marge nationale d'appréciation et internationalisation du droit' *Revue internationale de droit comparé*, 753.

[58] Jean-Louis Guigou, in *Construire la dynamique des territoires* (Paris, L'Harmattan, 1997).

[59] Pierre Mayer and Vincent Heuzé, *Droit international privé*, 7th edn (Paris, Montchrétien, 2001), 267.

[60] Clothide Maminho (ed), *The Dublin Convention on Asylum: Its Essence, Implementation and Prospects* (Maastricht, European Institute of Public Administration, 2000).

b. Direct Competitive Effects

To this must be added the fact that globalising law itself fosters competition between legal systems.

It does this on a minor level through a variety of legal techniques, such as national treatment, the importance of which under WTO law is well-known,[61] and the use of which has also been recommended by the OECD in its 1976 Declaration on International Investment and Multinational Enterprises. In essence, this technique leads to a comparison between the national legal system, which it extends, and other solutions which may be less favourable.

In the context of EU law, competition between legal systems is taken much further. Firstly, it is simply encouraged by the main freedoms: for example, as stated by the Court of Justice, freedom of establishment inherently includes the search for the least severe system.[62] It is also done, only more forcefully, through the mechanism that is mutual recognition, and through the principle of the law of the country of origin.[63] As has been shown in one study,[64] from the time when EU law, with the *Cassis de Dijon* decision and the 1985 White Paper, decided to base what would become the internal market on the mutual recognition of national economic regulations, those regulations found themselves in direct competition: by its very nature, the mechanism incites players to place their activities under the least restrictive regulations, which necessarily compels the others gradually to adapt.[65]

ii. Factors for Selecting a Legal System

That said, we can only form an accurate idea of the realities of competition between legal systems if we acknowledge that it is not simply a race between the most lenient or the most deregulated systems.[66]

---

[61] See, eg, Dominique Carreau and Patrick Julliard, *Droit international économique*, 4th edn (Paris, LGDJ, 1998) 230 ff.

[62] Case C-212/97 *Centros Ltd v Erhvervs-og Selskabsstyrelsen* [1999] ECR I-01484. See also Case C-196/04 *Cadbury Schweppes plc and Cadbury Schweppes Overseas Ltd v Commissioners of Inland Revenue* [2006] ECR I-07995: in the Court's view, establishing a company in a Member State with low taxation is legitimate, so long as said establishment is not fictional— see Bernard Castagnède, *Précis de fiscalité internationale* (Paris, PUF, 2002) foreword.

[63] Mathias Audit (2006) 'Régulation du marché intérieur et libre circulation des lois' *Journal du droit international* 4, 1333.

[64] Manuel Ballbé and Carlos Padros, *Estado competitivo y armonización europea* (Barcelona, Ariel Sociedad Económica, 1997).

[65] Norbert Reich (1992) 'Competition between Legal Orders: A New Paradigm of EC Law' *Common Market Law Review* 29, 861.

[66] The issue is a complex one, and fuels theoretical debates amongst economists as well as lawyers: see, eg Horatia Muir Watt (2003) 'Globalisation des marchés et économie politique du droit international privé' *Archives de Philosophie du Droit*, 47, 243.

We know, for instance, that choices of location made by multinational companies are far from being based solely on considerations such as taxation levels and public subsidies in the various states where they may contemplate investing. Many other factors compete in hammering out these decisions, both non-legal (political stability, geography) and legal (labour regulations, environmental regulations, the quality of the legal system, the nature of relations with the authorities, etc)[67]—all in all, a number of different legal 'comfort' factors.

iii. Consequences

What are the consequences of this marked competition between legal systems, brought about by globalisation? Two sets of observations may be made at this juncture.

a. Strategies of the States

Faced with the realities of competition between them, legal systems can adopt two types of adaptation strategy. They can opt for savage competition, through fiscal or regulatory dumping practices, for instance. However, this particular strategy can be dangerous, as it can lead to indeterminate profiteering and ultimately weaken all competing states. This is the reason why, for example, both the EU and the OECD are concerned with curbing fiscal competition, forcing it to halt at the threshold where it becomes economically damaging; the Council of Ministers of the European Union adopted a series of measures to that end in 1997, while an OECD Recommendation echoed those measures in 1998.[68]

The alternative lies in the common adoption of measures to restrict competition by establishing ties between the various systems. These can be harmonisation measures: in that spirit, for instance, the OECD adopted model double tax treaties, of which some—for example, the Model Tax Treaty on Income and on Capital—have been extremely successful.[69] Other common strategies could be envisaged, which would for instance serve to establish common control activities or forms of mutual recognition.[70]

---

[67] Jean-Philippe Robé, 'Multinational Enterprises: The Constitution of a Pluralistic Legal Order' in Gunther Teubner (ed), *Global Law without a State* (Aldershot, Dartmouth, 1997), 45.

[68] Xavier Oberson, 'L'impact de la mondialisation sur le droit fiscal suisse' in Morand, *Le droit saisi par la mondialisation* (n 5), 429.

[69] ibid.

[70] Harald Baum, 'Globalizing Capital Markets and Possible Regulatory Responses' in Jürgen Basedow and Toshiynki Kono (eds), *Legal Aspects of Globalization* (The Hague, Kluwer Law International, 2000), 77.

b. Competition between Legal Traditions

One of the most significant aspects of global competition between legal systems lies in the competition between legal traditions.

The issue arises currently, for instance, as to whether some legal systems are better equipped than others in the context of the competition between legal systems fostered by globalisation, for example because they are a more favourable 'legal petri dish' for establishing and developing economic activities. This leads to the opinion often voiced that common-law systems are supposedly particularly well suited to economic globalisation, owing to their natural tendency to make economically efficient rules.[71] Contrast this with civil-law systems, which are allegedly more cumbersome in this field. The debate lies at the heart of discussions that have developed over a number of years concerning the World Bank's *Doing Business* reports,[72] mainly juxtaposing English-speaking countries with those in continental Europe.[73]

In any case, it is clear that common-law systems, and particularly American law, are increasingly important in international business law. It must also be pointed out, however, that the continental legal influence is just as strong in other spheres of globalisation. This is the case for certain areas of public law: administrative law, for instance, or techniques for the protection of human rights.[74] It would also appear to be the case for environmental law.

C. Harmonising Legal Systems

Another essential characteristic of legal globalisation is its tendency to foster a trend towards the harmonisation of legal systems. The phenomenon encompasses two main aspects. By various means, legal globalisation drives

---

[71] Ugo Mattei, *Comparative Law and Economics* (Ann Arbor, The University of Michigan Press, 2000), ch 5; Anthony Ogus, 'Competition Between National Legal Systems: a Contribution of Economic Analysis of Comparative Law' (1999) *International and Comparative Law Quarterly* 48, 405.

[72] Published annually since 2004, the *Doing Business* reports are intended to classify countries depending on the aptitude of their respective laws for facilitating the creation and expansion of companies. They are therefore based on a benchmarking system relating to the various economic regulations, together with the procedures and formalities that make up the framework for the life of companies: visit www.doingbusiness.org. The philosophy and methodology of these reports are hotly disputed by some countries, the controversy being especially lively in France: Bertrand du Marais (ed), *Des indicateurs pour mesurer le droit? Les limites des rapports. Doing Business de la Banque Mondiale* (Paris, Editions Société de Législation Comparée, 2006).

[73] Which furthermore have their own legal influence strategies, eg French influence in Africa through the *Organisation pour l'Harmonisation du Droit des Affaires en Afrique* (OHADA— Organisation for the Harmonisation of Business Law in Africa): Paul Dima Ehongo, 'L'intégration juridiques des économies africaines à l'échelle régionale et mondiale' in Mireille Delmas-Marty (ed), *Critique de l'intégration normative* (Paris, PUF, 2004), 179.

[74] Jean-Bernard Auby (2004) 'Quand la *common law* perd du terrain devant le droit continental', *Droit administratif*, April, 3.

legal systems towards a relative approximation; a relative convergence. At the same time, however, we can see that this convergence more often takes the form of harmonisation rather than a submission to common rules—harmonisation rather than a unification (even in part). Some clarification should be given on this phenomenon, the importance of which we have already glimpsed here and there; the factors contributing to it; the ways in which it operates; and the results that it yields.

i. Towards a 'Common' Law?

That legal globalisation is a driving force behind the approximation of legal systems is perfectly clear. Not only the interpenetration of legal systems that brought about and is driven by legal globalisation—an increasing number of transnational players struggle with the transaction costs that the plurality of laws imposes on them—but also the tensions that it causes in relations between legal systems incite them to co-operate in seeking out buffers. The proliferation of conflicts of laws leads to the development of a 'uniform law', 'model laws', etc, which will render the management of such situations less complex and costly.[75] States often realise that competition between legislation generates significant economic distortions and, sooner or later, they generally agree to establish some kind of framework.[76]

At the same time, the development of a genuinely 'common' law is often impossible to achieve, bearing in mind cultural and political issues, and the diversity of legal cultures.[77]

ii. Aspects of Legal Harmonisation

The harmonisation process itself encompasses two main aspects: the incubation of harmonisation norms and standards; and the dissemination of those norms and standards within legal systems.

a. Towards Legal Harmonisation

It has been noted that one of the essential functions of international law in the modern era was to work towards the harmonisation of domestic laws.[78]

---

[75] Jürgen Basedow, 'The Effects of Globalization on Private International Law' in Basedow and Kono, *Legal Aspects of Globalization* (n 70), 1.

[76] Roger van den Bergh (1998) 'Subsidiarity as an Economic Demarcation Principle and the Emergence of European Private Law' 5 *Maastricht Journal of European and Comparative Law* 2, 129.

[77] On the significance of this obstacle to the unification of laws, see particularly the work by Pierre Legrand, eg: (1996) 'European Legal Systems are not Converging' *International and Comparative Law Quarterly* 45, 52; (1996) 'Sens et non-sens d'un Code Civil Européen' *Revue international de droit comparé*, 779.

[78] Slim Laghmani, 'Droit international et droits internes: vers un renouveau du *jus gentium*?' in Achour and Laghmani, *Droit international et droit interne* (n 42) 23.

We have seen that the globalisation of trade law operates particularly through traditional international agreements—'uniform law', in particular, such as environmental law or the law on human rights.

However, the sources of norms and standards of harmonisation are sometimes more informal: we can think of the 'doctrines' circulated by the World Bank and the IMF in the governance sphere.

We can also think of the dissemination of standards and concepts which operates through imitation or reference, which national law-makers source in other systems,[79] particularly in the context of 'judicial dialogue' to which we shall return later.

Occasionally, harmonisation is paradoxical in origin, in the sense that it is brought about by legal measures which in themselves are intended to safeguard national sovereignty. We have already highlighted the way in which the legal autonomy exceptions that the major treaties on economic globalisation or human rights grant, for example to public order or public health concerns, allowing the keepers of those treaties to become involved in processes that define public order, public health requirements, etc, thereby harmonising national conceptions of such notions.[80]

b. Dissemination within Legal Systems

As for the dissemination of norms and standards of harmonisation within legal systems, it must above all be said that it does not solely operate in an organised and voluntary way.

It doubtless does operate thus in part. For instance, international agreements containing 'model laws' in the trade sphere are transposed by national laws. However, it also operates through a spillover effect,[81] of which two examples now follow.

As we have already recalled, under pressure from EU law—specifically the decision in *Factortame*—English law had to accept that the courts could sometimes grant injunctions against the Crown. This outcome was initially confined to decisions likely to affect the application of Community law, but the courts soon felt bound to generalise it as it proved impossible to justify

---

[79] See, eg Fabrice Melleray (ed), *L'argument de droit comparé en droit administrative français*, coll 'Droit Administratif/Administrative Law' (Brussels, Bruylant, 2007).

[80] See above, this chapter, 'Public order exceptions, states and legal globalisation'.

[81] Sophie Robin-Olivier and Daniel Fasquelle (eds), *Les échanges entre les droits, l'expérience communautaire. Une lecture des phénomènes de régionalisation et de mondialisation du droit* (Brussels, Bruylant, 2008); Paul Beaumont, Carole Lyons and Neil Walker (eds), *Convergence and Divergence in European Public Law* (Oxford, Hart Publishing, 2002); Roberto Mastroianni (1999) 'On the Distinction between Vertical and Horizontal Direct Effects of Community Directives: What Role for the Principle of Equality?' *European Public Law* issue 3, 417; Jack Beatson and Takis Tridimas (eds), *New Directions in European Public Law* (Oxford, Hart Publishing, 1998).

that this new guarantee of citizens' rights—the possibility of rapidly halting an unlawful prosecution—should be limited to compliance with EU law.[82]

Another very good example is the way in which the requirements under Article 6(1) of the European Convention on Human Rights regarding the impartiality of judicial or quasi-judicial bodies have been disseminated in such a way as to apply to scenarios otherwise not governed by the same Article. This is how, under French law, case law has extended these same requirements to certain proceedings before the courts responsible for controlling public finances—the *Cour des comptes*, the *chambres régionales des comptes*—which otherwise did not fall within the remit of Article 6(1).[83]

iii. Levels of Approximation

The level of approximation between systems brought about by these harmonisation processes varies greatly from one field to the next, and we can only sketch the following broad lines.

Firstly, it is not impossible for the harmonisation of laws that operates under globalisation to affect procedures more readily and more profoundly than it does content. The globalisation of public contract law, which we have mentioned previously, approximates national laws around transparency and competition mechanisms. The European Convention on Human Rights has developed its most remarkable effects within domestic laws where the right to a fair trial is at issue. In some way, it may be considered that the strongest effects that EU law has produced within European legal systems are procedural in nature, be it administrative procedures (competition in the field of public contracts, information for citizens and inquiries in the environmental sphere, immigration proceedings) or judicial procedures (with the case law in *Zuckerfabrick*, *Francovich*, and *Brasserie du Pêcheur*).[84]

Secondly, as we have seen on several occasions, globalisation sometimes approximates legal systems in terms of the understanding of important concepts, playing a more or less strategic role: the ECHR contributes in stating what constitutes a fair trial or a penalty, EU law making its own special contribution to the definition of public service, each having its own approach to the concept of public order, etc. Clearly, in some of these scenarios, substantive factors are at stake.

Thirdly, it would appear that one of the most interesting aspects of the phenomenon resides in that which links the harmonisation of systems and

---

[82] Craig, *Administrative Law* (n 51) 837 ff.

[83] CE, Ass., 27 February 2000, *Société Labor Métal*.

[84] Ton Heukels and Jamila Tib, 'Towards Homogeneity in the Field of Legal Remedies: Convergence and Divergence' in Paul Beaumont, Carole Lyons and Neil Walker (eds), *Convergence and Divergence in European Public Law* (n 81), 111.

their respective balances, in the dialogue between that which approximates legal systems and the mass of mechanisms, institutions, usage, etc that make up their respective balances. The margins of appreciation and of subsidiarity that the mechanics of legal globalisation generate are at stake, together with the way in which each system accommodates whatever impacts its particularity. We do not have to look too far in order to see that not all reactions are the same: amongst European legal systems, some have a tendency to view the contributions made by legal globalisation as useful, while others experience the same contributions as akin to an assault.

4

Power and Legitimacy in the Global Legal Sphere

CURRENTLY, IT WOULD perhaps be adventurous to speak of a global 'legal system'. The law influenced by globalisation is far from constituting a system, with a formalised apparatus of bodies, its own normative structure, etc. We will therefore avoid using such a premature phrasing.

However, we can accept that there now exists a global legal sphere, in the sense of a legal stage produced by identifiable social, economic and political phenomena, with a specific range of players and normative processes, and developing particular inter-systemic relations.

On this legal stage, in this new—or at least partly new—legal sphere, the legal information on power and legitimacy are out of step with the world's new structure. The players involved not being quite the same, the legal configuration of power is changing: the place of the state has been altered (see 'I. The State and Legal Globalisation'); the legal forms of international governance have been transformed (see 'II. The Development of New Legal Forms of International Governance under Globalisation'); the government of the world is increasingly based on models of multilevel governance, which naturally have legal implications (see 'IV. The Legal Dimension of Multi-layered Governance').

This more or less significant discordance within the organisation of institutions and powers reveals a number of issues relative to legitimacy, in terms of values: the linked issues of citizenship, democracy and constitutionalisation in the global legal sphere (see 'V. Citizenship, Democracy and Constitutionalisation in the Global Legal Space'); the problem of the subjugation of new powers to the requirements of the rule of law (see 'VI. Legal Globalisation and the Imperatives of the Rule of Law'); and, lastly, the issue of how public affairs, the general interest and public goods can be legally defined and served in the context of globalisation (see 'VI. Legal Globalisation and the Imperatives of the Rule of Law').

I. THE STATE AND LEGAL GLOBALISATION

Today, there are numerous studies examining the fate of the state in a globalisation context from an economic, political or international relations point of view.[1] We shall use certain elements thereof, but our own analysis differs in that it seeks to identify the legal dimension of globalisation; to establish the place occupied by the state, as it is legally conceived, in the sphere of legal globalisation. The situation can be summed up as follows: an undeniable decline in the state's legal power does not prevent its regulatory functions being maintained at a high level, but nevertheless requires that a new definition of sovereignty be considered.

A. Decline of the State's Legal Power

i. Decline of Economic and Political Power

There is no doubt that globalisation brings with it a decline in the economic and political power of states. Decisions made by the latter are increasingly fenced in by international constraints, be they global or regional. Their economic might is challenged by that of big business. In terms of legitimacy, they have to compete with various other entities dedicated to seeking the public interest, from NGOs to local authorities. Transnational situations, mechanisms and entities are flourishing, and increasingly tend to elude state control.

Globalisation is, of course, only one of many factors in this decline, and finds itself challenged by other factors. For instance, contrary to what is sometimes asserted, globalisation is not the root cause of the privatisation policies, particularly in the industrialised world, which have significantly reduced the scope for state intervention in economic matters. Globalisation has simply supported and disseminated those policies: for instance, in the funding provided by the World Bank, which is particularly in favour of public–private partnerships, a growing proportion thereof has in recent decades been devoted to schemes associating governments with private-sector partners.

ii. Decline in Legal Power

In those areas where its influence is most strongly felt, globalisation also brings with it—partly as a corollary, partly through a separate trend—a decline in the state's legal power. This decline, which we have come across

---

[1] See, eg, the enlightening work of Pierre de Senarclens, *La mondialisation. Théories, enjeux et débats*, 4th edn (Paris, Armand Colin, 2005).

previously, may be characterised by two factors, which may be linked to the common idea of the state's loss of legal centrality.[2]

a. Forms of Legal Divestment

The first aspect of legal divestment takes a number of forms.

The most extreme concern scenarios in which states have consented to genuine surrenders of sovereignty to international bodies. The most advanced example of such situations is the European Union (EU), in which sovereignty is actually shared between the Union and Member States.[3]

Next, reference must be made to the fact that, under globalisation, states are competing with other law-makers, both public and private. State legal systems have found themselves circumvented insofar as arbitration has expanded.[4]

In addition to the above, there is the fact that, in the sphere of legal globalisation, states have increasingly agreed to the creation of 'sources' of norms that are theoretically under their remit, but which operate largely independently of states. A more accentuated form of the phenomenon can be found in those cases where states afford international institutions the possibility of making secondary laws. The EU is clearly the main example here. Naturally, one objection is that Community secondary legislation retains its ties with states, as it exists only with their permission, and it is made by authorities in which the states are represented. However, the permission granted by the treaties is unlikely to be challenged (except in the event of a major crisis) and, in a certain number of spheres, secondary legislation is adopted by a majority, not unanimously. The link with the state's willingness would appear to be severely restricted.

To a lesser extent, ECHR law, together with WTO law,[5] present the same characteristics as legal entities that have largely broken ties with the legal power of the states to which they apply and which originally created them.

---

[2] Neil Walker (ed), *Sovereignty in Transition* (Oxford, Hart Publishing, 2002).

[3] Jean-Paul Jacqué, *Droit institutionnel de l'Union européenne*, 3rd edn (Paris, Dalloz, 2004) 90 ff.

[4] As Horatia Muir Watt points out, 'the buffer that they retain with the possibility of asserting their police laws when appeals can be made to their judges in order to ensure the enforcement of their arbitral awards has, it would seem, been weakened: the imperative nature of national police rules has been undermined by the acceptance of choice of court clauses in areas that are subject to police regulations' ((2003) 'Globalisation des marchés et économie politique du droit international privé' *Archives de Philosophie du Droit*, 243).

[5] David J Bederman (2007–2008) 'Diversity and Permeability in Transnational Governance', 57 *Emory Law Journal* 201: 'What distinguishes the WTO and a handful of other international organizations is the extent to which they have diverged from their original state-centered modes of operation and have, instead, sought legitimacy from, and accountability to, a wide variety of international stakeholders, while also pursuing goals and embracing values that might be divergent from many (if not most) states. Another distinguishing factor for these international entities is the degree to which they can compel states to obey their decisions without recourse to domestic enforcement mechanisms' (215).

Naturally, in all of these scenarios, states can theoretically still retain the option of refusing, of leaving such organisations, of withdrawing from agreements, etc. At the very least, such an action would generally appear to be quite out of proportion.

b. Forms of Legal Constraint

Globalisation inflicts a kind of legal divestment on the state. It also exposes its legal power which, owing to various factors, often finds itself subject to external legal constraints.

As we have seen above, one of the effects of legal globalisation is the intrusion of external norms into national legal systems, those norms increasingly coming into contact with legal rules and mechanisms situated near the top of the hierarchy within those systems. EU law—like ECHR law, for that matter—comes into contact with constitutional principles. In *Sirdar* and *Kreil*, decisions to which we have already referred, the Court of Justice states that the Community rule on equal treatment of men and women in the context of their professional activities applies to access to military posts; this directly contradicts German constitutional law, which excludes women from the armed forces—the combat units, at least.[6]

As previously stated, democracy may be considered as having become a norm under international law,[7] which means that states no longer have full control over the traditionally central attribute of state sovereignty that it is the right to choose a political system.

Various classic sovereignty instruments are framed by external legal constraints. A state's power to intervene in economic matters has been altered by the limits imposed on the provision of public financial aid by WTO rules, or EU rules on state aid. Their power to levy and collect taxes is limited by a number of agreements, particularly those adopted at the behest of the OECD, and by Community constraints for EU Member States.[8] States are sometimes legally framed by the combination of internal and external forces that can 'sandwich' them. This is the case for environment protection groups relying on international conventions to combat inertia in ecological matters on the part of their home states. It is also the case for national courts relying on international norms in order to extend their margin for review, where they consider it too narrow.

---

[6] Jürgen Schwartze (2002) 'Constitutional Perspectives in the European Union with Regard to the Next Intergovernmental Conference in 2004' 8 *European Public Law* 2, 241.

[7] See above, chapter 2, 'Global law on governance, state organisation and state institutions'; David J Bederman 'Diversity and Permeability' (n 5).

[8] Michel Bouvier, *Introduction au droit fiscal général et à la théorie de l'impôt*, 5th edn (Paris, LGDJ, 2003) 158 ff.

A short time ago, domestic legal players generally pulled more in the direction of safeguarding the national system—through greater awareness, as a minimum—and it was often the state that forced them to adapt to international legal innovations. Nowadays, those same players often use international norms—including, on occasion, decisions handed down by international courts—in order to gain greater independence vis-à-vis the state. Furthermore, where necessary, the latter has responded by inciting the creation of new international instruments,[9] which simply maintains the cycle.

B. Maintaining the State's Regulatory Functions

i. Economic Influence

In economic and political terms, state institutions, whilst finding themselves increasingly confined by external constraints and competing with other players, nevertheless retain considerable influence.

Contrary to what is sometimes believed, the place occupied by states in economic terms continues to grow. In the 1980s, the share of public expenditure in global GDP rose on average from 36 per cent to 40 per cent. Studies conducted by the OECD have shown that, between 1990 and 1995, state power grew significantly in industrialised countries, owing to the increase in transfers and subsidies.[10]

In a sense, the state has made something of a comeback over the last 20 years or so, international institutions having convinced themselves that there remained a degree of essential balance in the complex tangle of economic and political relations created by globalisation. The UN subscribed to that idea.[11] More strikingly, the World Bank, which had been a proponent of small government, also rallied to the cause, as was shown in its 1997 Annual Report, which emphasised the importance of state institutions whilst pointing out ways to increase credibility and efficiency.[12]

Whatever the developments, it would appear that the state remains by far the most—and occasionally the only—appropriate entity for performing a number of essential functions. Peace and collective security rest with

[9] Patrick Daillier, 'Monisme et dualisme: un débat dépassé?' in Rafâa Ben Achour and Slim Laghmani (eds), *Droit international et droit interne. Développements récents* (Paris, Pedone, 1998) 9.

[10] de Senarclens *La mondialisation* (n 1) 82; see also Robert Gilpin, *Global Political Economy. Understanding the International Economic Order* (Princeton, NJ, Princeton University Press, 2001) 362 ff.

[11] Yves Daudet (ed), *Les Nations unies et la restauration de l'Etat* (Paris, Pedone, 1995) 79.

[12] Ibrahim Shihata (1999) 'The Changing Role of the State and Some Related Governance Issues' 4 *Revue européenne de droit public* 4, 1459.

the state. It remains the 'indispensable focal point of political debate'.[13] It decides national structural policies on competitiveness; and it is the state that ensures, for the most part, economic and social regulation and risk management in our open economies.[14] It is the state that is able to manage the links between the economic sphere of flows and the social sphere of locations, between economic functions and social experience, as Jürgen Neyer points out.[15]

ii. Regulatory Influence

Equally, the decline in the state's legal power, quite aside from the fact that it varies depending on the area concerned, and depending on the states considered, in no way has any decrease in the regulatory functions of state institutions as its corollary. The ever fundamental nature of the state's position in this regard can be summed up by three main points.

All in all, the state remains responsible—or at least mainly responsible—for the legal constitution of society or the market; in this sense, it plays an essential role in regulating the global economy.

The state is also very much responsible for defining the rules in the context of which individuals and companies operate in society or in the market. Specifically, the state is, as it has been since at least the nineteenth century,[16] a 'market builder', ie it continues to establish legal frameworks in the absence of which the market cannot function and without which there is no market.

Admittedly, part of this market regulation is undertaken by non-state bodies—corporate structures, for instance—and globalisation has given rise to a not inconsiderable proportion of self-regulation in a number of spheres.[17] However, this is never full self-regulation: at best, it is tantamount to co-regulation.

The state remains the regulator—or, at the very least, the main regulator, of legal relationships between internal and external systems. Whatever

---

[13] François Crépeau, 'Introduction', in François Crépeau (ed), *Mondialisation des échanges et fonctions de l'Etat* (Brussels, Bruylant, 1997) 12.

[14] Nicolas Baverez, 'A l'épreuve de la mondialisation' in Roger Fauroux and Bernard Spitz (eds), *Notre Etat. Le livre-vérité sur la fonction publique* (Paris, Robert Laffont, 2000) 607.

[15] Jürgen Neyer, 'Binding Territoriality and Functionality? Globalization Meets the Law' in Volkam Gessner and Ali Cem Budak (eds), *Emerging Legal Certainty: Empirical Studies on the Globalization of Law (Onati International Series in Law and Society)* (Aldershot, Ashgate, 1998) 401.

[16] John Gray, *False Dawn: The Delusion of Global Capitalism* (London, Granta, 1998).

[17] See above, chapter 3, 'A. Creating Norms' ff.

the scale of transnational legal relations, whatever the scale of the 'permeabilisation' of legal systems, states continue to control the majority of legal flows between internal and external systems.

International law always leaves them a great deal of freedom in deciding who can enter their territory.[18]

As a general rule, states retain the power freely to designate the legal realities that they consider as falling within the remit of their system: nationality, legal personality, etc.

The state continues to perform—and does so primarily on the global stage—a third, absolutely essential regulatory function, consisting in guaranteeing legal certainty.[19]

It also falls to the state to establish and manage a legal and institutional framework favourable to internal security, social and economic wellbeing, and environmental protection.[20]

As we have already seen, the state's legal resources are also counted upon, in the main, for guaranteeing compliance with legal rules and the enforcement of dispute-resolution decisions. In the EU sphere, Member States are the quasi-exclusive custodians of these enforcement powers.[21]

There are other considerations. Brigitte Stern[22] points out that states remain the principal arbiters between the market and society, guardians of non-market values, purveyors of solidarity and identity.

In continuing to perform these essential functions, states emerge in truth as pillars of globalisation, as the craftsmen of globalisation: they allow it to function.[23]

C. Towards a Redefinition of Sovereignty?

From the position briefly described above, it is difficult not to conclude that the very concept of sovereignty must be re-examined. Indeed, it is a situation

---

[18] Catherine Dauvergne, 'Illegal Migration and Sovereignty' in Catherine Dauvergne (ed), *Jurisprudence for an Interconnected Globe* (Aldershot, Ashgate, 2003) 187.

[19] Gessner and Budak *Emerging Legal Certainty* (n 15) introduction, 4.

[20] de Senarclens *La mondialisation* (n 1) 82 ff.

[21] Jeanne Scott, 'Member States and Regions in Community Law: Convergence and Divergence' in Paul Beaumont, Carole Lyons and Neil Walker (eds), *Convergence and Divergence in European Public Law* (Oxford, Hart Publishing, 2000) 19; Jan Jans, Roel de Lange, Sacha Prechal and Rob Widershoven (eds), *Europeanisation of Public Law* (Europa Law Publishing, 2007).

[22] 'How to Regulate Globalization?' in Michael Byers (ed), *The Role of Law in International Politics. Essays in International Relations and International Law* (Oxford, Oxford University Press, 2000) 249.

[23] Sassia Sassen, *A Sociology of Globalization*, (New York, WW Norton & Company, Inc, 2007) 45 ff; Juan-Cruz Alli Aranguren, *Derecho administrativo y globalización*, (Madrid, Thomson-Civitas, 2004) 305 ff.

full of contrasts, in which legal theory generally[24] maintains the notion that the state remains the alpha and omega of its legal system, when there are significant symptoms of a decline in its actual legal power.

Certainly, if we settle for a formal view of this notion, we may consider that nothing has really changed. As stated by Lord Bridge in one of the decisions handed down by the House of Lords in *Factortame*, '[w]hatever limitation of its sovereignty Parliament accepted when it enacted the European Communities Act 1972 was entirely voluntary'.[25] From the same formal perspective, we may accept that 'international law is a law made by states, even where they are divested of their power, as such divestment is an act of sovereignty'.[26]

Thus conceived, the concept can accommodate extreme forms of decline in the state's legal power; all that is required is that the latter should appear to have consented to the same in principle, at some point or other. But one cannot help but feel that it does not account adequately for realities arising from globalisation, in which the state's legal powers are reduced, challenged or transferred; nor does it account for these other than in a purely formal way.

This is why a concept has emerged here and there whereby, without renouncing the notion of sovereignty altogether—which would not be realistic[27]—it should be altered in terms of how it is understood. Three different avenues are put forward by a number of authors.[28]

i. The State as Mediator

The first focuses on the essential mediation functions that the state performs under globalisation: functions involving the regulation of legal flows, guaranteeing legal certainty, or as the legal authority over the market, etc, which have already been mentioned above.

From this point of view, sovereignty would appear to be as much a responsibility as a right. In the world of legal globalisation, the state performs a

---

[24] The main opponents of the theory of sovereignty—Georges Scelle, Kelsen—have few followers (at least on this issue).

[25] See Paul Craig, 'The Impact of Community Law on Public Law', in Peter Leylands and Terry Woods, *Administrative Law Facing the Future: Old Constraints and New Horizons* (Oxford, Blackstone, 1999) 271.

[26] Denys de Béchillon (1999) 'La structure des normes juridiques à l'épreuve de la post-modernité' *Revue interdisciplinaire d'études juridiques* 43, 1.

[27] Prosper Weil (1992) 'Toujours le même et toujours recommencé: les thèmes contrastés du changement et de la permanence du droit international' *Recueil des cours de l'Académie du Droit International* 237, reproduced in Prosper Weil, *Ecrits de droit international* (Paris, PUF, 2000).

[28] In addition to the references given below: Trudy Jacobsen et al (eds), *Re-envisioning Sovereignty* (Aldershot, Ashgate, 2008); Wenhau Shan, Penelope Simons, Dalvinder Singh (eds), *Redefining Sovereignty in International Economic Law* (Oxford, Hart Publishing, 2008).

number of essential intermediary functions in the service of global public interest,[29] whilst also guaranteeing its domestic equilibrium.

It may be that the state holds such a position owing to the fact that, although it is not so much 'master of territories', it broadly remains 'master of time', to paraphrase Habermas.

ii. Shared Sovereignty

The second path focuses on the fact that, to an increasing extent, sovereignty appears to be shared.

Obviously, this is especially apparent in the relations between the EU and its Member States. In that context, sovereignty is indeed clearly shared: the EU evidently has certain attributes of sovereignty, while Member States themselves have also retained part of their sovereignty. In the context of the EU, sovereignty is therefore shared: Member States have kept one part exclusively, but exercise the other part in conjunction with the Union, ie with the states as a collective whole.[30] One author talks of the 'unbundling'[31] of state attributes of sovereignty, part of which is entrusted to the Union to be exercised collectively.

But it is a more widespread phenomenon. In various areas impacted by globalisation, we may also see the growing obligation incumbent on states jointly to exercise their attributes of sovereignty: one study demonstrates the increasingly divided nature of state sovereignty with regard to nationality.[32] Sovereignty is 'mutualised' to an ever increasing extent.[33]

iii. Towards 'Co-operative' Sovereignty

This naturally leads us to consider a conception of 'inclusive' or 'co-operative' sovereignty, which corresponds to the following notions.

Bearing in mind the scale of transnational legal realities, the extent of the 'permeabilisation' of legal systems, as well as the powerful phenomena associated with multilevel governance which we shall soon discuss, the traditional definitions of sovereignty, which conceive it as an exclusive power, are not really tenable—whence the position, defended by Ulrich Beck,[34]

---

[29] Peter Penhaler (2000) 'The New Function of Small states in a World that Gets Connected' 12 *Revue européenne de droit public* 1, 63.

[30] Florence Chaltiel, *La souveraineté de l'Etat et l'Union européenne. L'exemple français. Recherches sur la souveraineté de l'Etat membre* (Paris, LGDJ, 2000).

[31] Paul Taylor, *International Organization in the Age of Globalization* (London, Continuum, 2001).

[32] Linda Bosniak (2002) 'Multiple Nationality and the Postnational Transformation of Citizenship', *Virginia Journal of International Law* 42, 979.

[33] Jean-François Bayart, *Le gouvernement du monde. Une critique politique de la globalisation* (Paris, Grasset, 2004) 53 ff.

[34] Ulrich Beck, *What is Globalization* (Cambridge, Polity Press, 2000) 132 ff.

whereby a concept of inclusive sovereignty is emerging, in which the state's power is not defined independently of its transnational confines.

Indeed, sovereignty must increasingly be conceived as a relational resource rather than a sphere of autonomy. According to Robert Keohane, '[s]overeignty is less a territorially defined barrier than a bargaining resource for a politics characterised by complex transnational networks'.[35]

In other words, in the context of interpenetration between systems which characterises globalisation, in a sense sovereignty is internationally instituted and can only, therefore, be understood as part of the international environment in which it is organisationally inserted.[36]

It may also be suggested that modern sovereignty must be defined as co-operative. It would cease to be little more than a negative principle in relation to the state's independence and its freedom to act, in order to become a positive principle reflecting the state's membership of the international community and its duty to make an active contribution to its development.[37]

It can be argued that, turned inside out, one might wonder whether the concept genuinely continues to have actual meaning: if we take an 'exclusivist' approach, the answer is certainly negative. It is clear, however, that the legal interaction aspect must be included in a modern definition of sovereignty, which can no longer be conceived nowadays as that kind of subjective, indefinite, inviolate and sacred law to which it tends to be compared in the more classical conception.

The Dutch sociologist Saskia Sassen[38] expresses the above reality in enthralling fashion when she explains that, in light of the interdependence of public institutions, and the integration of their respective roles, the state finds itself 'denationalised' in a sense. In fulfilling its functions, the state serves purposes that lay beyond its remit. By exercising its sovereignty, it also serves interests that lie beyond its remit.

II. THE DEVELOPMENT OF NEW LEGAL FORMS OF INTERNATIONAL GOVERNANCE UNDER GLOBALISATION

Globalisation processes, whilst impacting on national governance,[39] quite naturally bring about changes in the legal forms and institutional

---

[35] 'Hobbes' Dilemma and Institutional Change in World Politics: Sovereignty in International Society' in Hans-Henrik Kolm and G Sorensen (eds), *Whose World Orders?* (Boulder, Colorado, Westview Press, 1995) 165. See also Anthony McGrew, 'Global Legal Interaction and Present-Day Patterns of Globalization' in Gessner and Budak, *Emerging Legal Certainty* (n 15) 325.

[36] Ryan Goodman and Derek Jinks (2003) 'Towards an Institutional Theory of Sovereignty' *Stanford Law Review* 55, 1479.

[37] Franz Xavier Perez, *Cooperative Sovereignty. From Independence to Interdependence in the Structure of International Law* (The Hague, Kluwer Law International, 2000).

[38] Sassen, *A Sociology of Globalization* (n 23) 32 ff.

[39] See above, chapter 2, '(National) Governance'.

mechanisms of international governance. Amongst the new phenomena that have emerged, there has been a striking expansion of networks, which merits much closer examination.

A. General Points[40]

The effects that globalisation has on the various forms of international governance can only be understood if one bears in mind three concepts discussed above. The first is that the effects of globalisation are not entirely confined to the international—and, necessarily, global—plane: they also affect national public systems. The second is that globalisation has both vertical and horizontal effects: it affects relations between international and domestic matters vertically, whilst having transnational effects horizontally. The third is that international or transnational non-state players play an increasingly significant role in the conduct of public affairs under globalisation. By considering these three concepts together,[41] we can highlight the following phenomena in particular.

i. Public International Systems

Two public international systems are especially striking.

The first is derived from the fact that international institutions increasingly fulfil traditionally national functions: they concern themselves more and more with issues traditionally related to domestic public systems, be they environmental, sanitary, transport or communications related, etc. As a corollary, entities have developed therein which increasingly resemble national administrative bodies, in terms of both their composition—their members are experts as opposed to diplomats or politicians—and their functions—they settle very specific implementation issues. In certain cases, alongside these administrative bodies, there have emerged a variety of administrative 'courts'—the International Tribunal for the Law of the Sea, for instance. Globalisation encompasses a trend towards judicialisation, to which we shall return later.

The second is related to the proliferation of global bodies, be it within or on the fringes of international institutions, which take the form of or rely on networks. We shall return to these below.

---

[40] See Karl-Heinz Ladeur (ed), *Public Governance in the Age of Globalization* (Aldershot, Ashgate, 2004).

[41] As we have done previously in chapter 1. See boxed text 'Conducting public affairs in a globalised context'.

ii. International or Transnational Non-state Players

As we have seen, it is increasingly common for international or transnational non-state players to take on functions linked to the conduct of public affairs: regulatory functions, for example, or the operational implementation of public policies, which are sometimes explicitly entrusted to them by public institutions in a context of outsourcing, and have sometimes been developed by them with a kind of tacit consent on the part of public institutions.

iii. National Public Institutions

Globalisation also alters the way in which national public systems are positioned with regard to the management of public affairs on an international level.

We must remember here both the fact that national public institutions increasingly take on international functions (implementing public policies defined internationally; taking part in international public missions (eg in the context of international humanitarian or military operations)) and the expansion witnessed in transnational co-operation between national institutions (administrative networks or arrangements, etc) and subnational institutions—co-operation between local authorities, etc.

B. The Proliferation of Networks

One of the main phenomena that impact on the legal forms of international governance under globalisation is the proliferation of networks. This development has been studied in particular by Anne-Marie Slaughter, in a number of well-known publications.[42]

Public affairs on an international level are increasingly conducted by networks of institutions, bodies and persons, and not by entities wholly located within a given international organisation; nor are traditional diplomatic paths followed.

These networks are especially varied. Some connect public institutions, which may be classic national administrations, or independent administrative

---

[42] Anne-Marie Slaughter, *A New World Order* (Princeton, NJ, Princeton University Press, 2004); 'Government Networks: the Heart of the Liberal Democratic Order' in Gregory H Fox and Brad R Roth (eds), *Democratic Governance and International Law* (Cambridge, Cambridge University Press, 2000) 199. See also: Patrick le Galès and Mark Thatcher, *Les réseaux de politique publique. Débat autour des policy networks* (Paris, L'Harmattan, 1995).

authorities.[43] Court networks feature amongst these government networks.[44] Some of these networks are attached to an international organisation, while others operate independently on the basis of simple administrative arrangements,[45] for instance, or even without any legal formalisation of their existence.

Others are semi-public—one example being the Basel Committee—or private, but all play a part in conducting public affairs. This is the case, for example, for those networks of private organisations which, for a time, led the fight against apartheid in South Africa,[46] or those monitoring the implementation of norms established by the International Labour Organisation.[47] These are sometimes referred to as 'issue networks'.[48]

It is also the case for the international arbitration community, which is made up of arbitration centres, recognised arbiters and specialist lawyers.[49]

To conclude, we would add that the presence of networks contributing to the conduct of public affairs internationally is not seen solely worldwide, but also on a European level. This is reflected particularly in the existence of a considerable number of commissions and transnational bodies, which bring together either government experts only, or government experts and non-governmental stakeholders (scientists, trade unions, etc).[50] Naturally, there are also issue networks on a European level; transnational lobby groups concerned, for instance, by environmental or social issues.

III. GLOBALISATION AND TERRITORIAL PLURALISM: THE GLOBAL–LOCAL DIALOGUE

In the reality of legal globalisation, there is quite a particular dialectic between global and local, globalisation and decentralisation; this is a highly unusual and interesting phenomenon which can be described as follows.[51]

---

[43] For example, as regards the regulation of financial markets: Dimitry Kingsford Smith, 'Networks, Norms and the Nation-state: Thoughts on Pluralism and Globalized Securities Regulation' in Dauvergne, 'Illegal Migration and Sovereignty' (n 18) 93.

[44] Julie Allard and Antoine Garapon, *Les juges dans la mondialisation* (Paris, Le Seuil, 2005).

[45] Sassen, *A Sociology of Globalization* (n 23) 138 ff.

[46] Slaughter, *A New World Order* (n 42).

[47] Jill Murray, 'Relabelling the International Labour Problem: Globalization and Ideology', in Dauvergne, 'Illegal Migration and Sovereignty' (n 18) 129.

[48] Margaret Keck and Kathryn Sikking, *Activists Beyond Borders: Advocacy Networks in International Politics* (Ithaca, Cornell University Press, 1998).

[49] Sassen, *A Sociology of Globalization* (n 23) 130 ff.

[50] Mario Savino (2006) 'Le rôle des comités transnationaux au niveau européen et mondial' 6 *Global Jurist* 3.

[51] Jean-Bernard Auby, 'Globalisation et décentralisation', in *Mélanges offerts au président Benoît Jeanneau* (Paris, Dalloz, 2002).

A. Territories

There are two interfaces between the phenomenon that is globalisation and decentralisation: the first is linked to the impact of globalisation on territories, while the second relates to its effects on public systems.

As we have seen, there is in the nature of the globalisation trend a kind of 'erasure' of territories. Many activities no longer have any spatial connections, or freely choose their spatial connections.

Add to that the fact that globalisation tends, as Jacques Chevallier puts it, 'to shift the relevant level of decision-making towards more extended areas', and thereby distances some realities from the potential area of influence of local power and local democracy.[52]

Nevertheless, such deterritorialisation phenomena are compensated by others which, conversely, point in the direction of a natural promotion of the local.

The globalised world is a universe of territorial competition and, correlatively, of competition between institutions responsible for of those territories. This is due to the fact that economic activities are increasingly mobile and more likely, therefore, to move from one territory to another which appears to offer a more comfortable setting in terms of their costs (social, fiscal, etc) and from the point of view of their physical and social environment.[53]

In reality, within the results of globalisation (beyond that which leads to the abolition of territories and local particularisms), we can find a dialogue; a dialectic between the global and the local. This dialectic, already often referred to as 'glocalisation',[54] relates above all to the following realities.

The global economy is not indifferent to territorial anchoring. Its standardisation effects are more limited than is widely believed. It often uses local particularisms, and indeed depends on them: in branches of McDonalds in India, the usual beef 'Big Mac' has been replaced by the lamb-based 'Maharaja Mac'.[55]

Furthermore, globalisation has allowed the emergence of local entities which, largely outside the scope of the state within whose jurisdiction they fall, directly achieve global status, directly develop relations and activities

---

[52] Jacques Chevallier, 'Synthèse' in *La démocratie locale. Représentation, participation et espace public* (Paris, PUF, 1999) 414.

[53] Pierre Veltz, 'Le développement local face à la mondialisation' in *Comment améliorer la performance économique des territoires?* (Paris, Caisse des Dépôts et des Consignations, 2000) 19.

[54] Ulrich Beck, *What is globalization?* (Cambridge, Polity Press, 2000) 42 ff. Jan Aart Scholte, *Globalization. A critical introduction* (London and New York, Macmillan, 2000) 59 ff.

[55] ibid.

located on the international plane. This quite specifically concerns (particularly since Saskia Sassen's ground-breaking work) that which can now be characterised as 'global cities'.

The emergence of local governments and cities under legal globalisation

Traditionally, local governments—sub-state territorial authorities—and cities (with the exception of those that accidents of history have endowed with an international status, such as Danzig or Jerusalem) have no international legal status: their relations with the international legal sphere exist through the intermediary of the state.

This is not the case nowadays, and we can see a growing international legal emergence of local governments and cities, which is reflected in the following phenomena.

1. Sub-state authorities increasingly have, to a greater or lesser extent, the possibility of directly establishing international legal relations. This is in addition to the case (of which there are classic examples) of federated states authorised to form international legal relations; they are entities that share the same nature as states.

   Particularly in the European sphere, such a possibility is broadly accepted in the context of mechanisms for decentralised co-operation, which is encouraged by the EU, the framework for which was established by the 1980 European Outline Convention on Transfrontier Co-operation between Territorial Communities or Authorities.

2. It is also increasingly common for international legal mechanisms to encourage, or even require, a certain level of decentralisation or local self-government within national systems.

   The UN has such a policy as part of its Human Settlements Programme (UN-Habitat), which notably drafted a World Charter on Local Self-Government, adopted in 1998.

   As part of its aid policy, the World Bank encourages decentralisation, and particularly the financial autonomy of local governments, which it considers a factor in reinforcing accountability.

   In the European context, the 1985 European Charter of Local Self-Government genuinely imposes a requirement on the 30 or so ratifying states to comply with a number of principles concerning decentralisation.

   In addition to its support for decentralised co-operation, the EU includes an institution the role of which is to promote the interests of the local authorities that make it up: the Committee of the Regions.

> 3. Linked in part to the realities described above, local authorities
> are increasingly subject to rights and obligations arising under
> international law. Rights include those granted by a treaty such
> as the European Charter of Local Self-Government. Obligations
> include those imposed by EU law regarding public procurement, the
> environment, etc.
>
>   See, eg, Jean-Bernard Auby, *La décentralisation et le droit* (Paris,
> LGDJ, 2006); Yishai Blank (2005–2006) 'The City and the World'
> *Columbia Journal of Transnational Law* 875, and (2006) 'Localism
> in the New Global Legal Order' *Harvard International Law Journal*,
> 263; Gerald Frug and David Barron (2006) 'International Local
> Government Law' *Urban Law*, 38, 1; Nicolas Levrat, *L'Europe et
> ses collectivités territoriales* (Brussels, Bern, Berlin, PIE-Peter Land,
> 2005).

In addition, faced with the effects of remoteness caused by globalisation, an attachment to the local serves as a counterweight or as compensation. In a globalising world which appears to attach importance only to functional identities, individuals are rediscovering a taste for their territorial identities. Moreover, the observation that we can all make as to the difficulties encountered by states in controlling the effects of globalisation naturally leads us to wish for a strengthening of local levels of government, which seem to provide greater stability.[56]

B. Public Systems

The second interface between globalisation and decentralisation can be found in the effects that the former generally has on public systems.

Globalisation has imposed—and indeed continues to impose—constraints in terms of adaptation on the various national public systems. As we have seen, national governance is far from being impervious to its effects. To this may be added the fact that globalisation compels public systems to allow more room for citizens, who draw greater autonomy and power from the cultural and political openness on a planetary scale; such independence and power must be accommodated.

Above all, globalisation leads to greater complexity and flattened hierarchies within public systems.

---

[56] Jürgen Neyer, 'Binding Territoriality and Functionality? Globalization Meets the Law' in Gessner and Budak, *Emerging Legal Certainty* (n 15) 420: 'the regulatory deficits of modern states are leading to a growing demand for local levels of governance to provide substitutes'.

Local levels have a part to play in this two-fold phenomenon, which we shall examine more closely below. The hierarchy of public spaces is disrupted, inter alia, by the fact that local levels of government have greater freedom to communicate and co-operate between themselves or with various international players, going over the head of states often operating as a network.[57] Our regions, for instance, have increasingly close relations with their foreign counterparts and the EU, over which the state exercises ever more limited control. One way of describing this situation is to say that they are no longer wholly contained within the state.[58] What is at stake here, inter alia, is the above-mentioned phenomenon of global cities.

C. Decentralisation

Under the influence of the phenomena described above, some connections can be made between the globalisation trend and decentralisation, ie the existence, within public systems, of institutions in charge, more or less independently and under citizen control, of local affairs.

The main aspect of this is the fact that legal constraints arising directly from legal globalisation are imposed on local institutions.

There is no need to place too much emphasis on the obligations imposed by EU law (the phenomenon having been quite widely studied) on local governments with a view to opening their operation to the free movement of persons, services, goods, capital and to Community competition. EU law on public procurement and works concessions fully applies to local contracts falling within either of those two categories. Local government aid for businesses is fully subject to the rules on state aid. The free movement of workers requires that citizens of other EU Member States be allowed to join the local civil service.

Local authorities have also begun to receive similar constraints in terms of openness, transparency and competition from the global level. The WTO Agreement on Government Procurement, which seeks to open public procurement up globally, also applies to contracts awarded by local governments.[59]

That said, the legal repercussions of globalisation for local institutions cannot be summed up simply as the imposition of constraints or requirements. On occasion, globalisation is also synonymous with new opportunities for such institutions.

---

[57] Alain Bourdin, *La question locale* (Paris, PUF, 2000) 53 ff.

[58] Beck, *What is globalization?* (n 54) 108.

[59] Thiébaut Flory, *L'Organisation mondiale du commerce. Droit institutionnel et substantiel* (Brussels, Bruylant, 1999) 194; Sue Arrowsmith and Arwel Davies (eds), *Public Procurement: Global Revolution* (The Hague, Kluwer Law International, 1998) 13.

i. Improved International Relations

Local governments sometimes clearly benefit from the economic, social and cultural opportunities presented by globalisation.[60]

Local governments have, like many others, drawn considerable advantages from the liberalisation of international financial markets, which gave them access to more favourable lending terms. The duty incumbent upon them to open their public contracts to European, or even wider, competition is not just a burden: it also offers the chance of benefiting from the expertise of a greater number of companies.

It is no accident that the rise of globalisation is accompanied by an expansion in the international relations of local institutions. This trend, which is specific neither to a particular country nor to Europe,[61] was strongly supported in the European context (as recalled above), especially on the part of the Council of Europe and the EU.

ii. Increased Decentralisation

Beyond these phenomena, we can also see that globalisation produces relative, but real, pressure towards a general increase in decentralisation. This is because the state, which often appears to be too small a scale for controlling public affairs, sometimes and conversely proves to be too high a level for settling them properly.[62]

Amongst the various recipes for good governance advocated by the World Bank in its 1997 Report on the state,[63] which we have already seen,[64] decentralisation is often put forward (at least in those contexts where it is possible) as a way to bring the state and citizens closer together, which the World Bank views as a springboard for economic efficiency. In practice, the World Bank will sometimes propose decentralisation reforms for some countries with a view to circumventing completely ineffectual state institutions, for example because these are heavily affected by corruption.

In the European sphere, decentralisation is encouraged by both the Council of Europe with the European Charter of Local Self-Government 1985 and the European Charter for Regional or Minority Languages 1992 and,

---

[60] Stéphane Paquin, *Paradiplomatie et relations internationales. Théorie des stratégies internationales des régions* (Brussels, Bern, Berlin, PIE-Peter Lang, 2004).

[61] Société française de droit international, *Les collectivités territoriales non-étatiques dans le système juridique international* (Paris, Pedone, 2002).

[62] Ann Peters, 'The Globalization of State Constitutions', in Janne Nijman and André Nollkaemper (eds), *New Perspectives in the Divide Between National and International Law* (Oxford, Oxford University Press, 2007) 251.

[63] World Bank, *World Development Report 1997: The State in a Changing World* (New York: Oxford University Press, 1997).

[64] See above, 'Maintaining the State's Regulatory Functions', and Shihata, 'The Changing Role of the State' (n 12) 1459.

although with a greater degree of caution, by the EU. While it ensures that it does not circumvent states too much as its institutional structure depends on them, the Union still has a natural tendency to promote decentralisation.[65] This is demonstrated by the Committee of the Regions, the insistence on the involvement of regions of Member States in the implementation of the Union's regional policy (the partnerships doctrine), etc, not to mention the emphasis placed on the principle of subsidiarity by the Maastricht Treaty and the possibility, currently open to Member States, of being represented on the Council by regional officials on condition that they are duly authorised to represent their respective national government (Article 16 of the Treaty on European Union).[66]

D. The Primacy of EU Laws

It is also apparent that the primacy of EU law compels local authorities to ensure that the legal rules prevail over national law; in other words, it sometimes forces them to disobey the laws of the state, to set the latter aside in favour, for example of EU law on public procurement in the event of conflict.[67]

Here is an example, taken from the *Périphérique Nord de Lyon* case, on which the French *Conseil d'Etat* ruled in *Tête* on 6 February 1998.[68] The provisions on works concessions featuring in the Council Directive 89/665/EEC of 21 December 1989 on the co-ordination of the laws, regulations and administrative provisions relating to the application of review procedures to the award of public supply and public works contracts not having been transposed into national law in time, the *communauté urbaine* of Lyons had believed that it could award the contract for the construction and operation of the city's northern ring-road without prior European publicity. The *Conseil* annulled the decision to award the concession, on grounds of failure to comply with the Directive. The local authority ought to have ignored national law and relied on the Directive that had not been transposed.

---

[65] Nicolas Levrat, *L'Europe et les collectivités territoriales. Réflexions sur l'organisation et l'exercice du pouvoir territorialisé dans un monde globalisé* (Brussels, Bern, Berlin, PIE-Peter Lang, 2005); Jean-Bernard Auby (1995) 'L'Europe et la décentralisation' *Revue française de la décentralisation* 1, 16.

[66] On the latter point: Rainer Arnold (1997) 'Federalism and European Community Law—A Study on the Mechanisms of Internal Participation in European Decision-Making in Germany, Austria and Belgium' Tulasne European Civil Forum, 12, 159; Andrew Evans (2000) 'Regionalist Challenge to the EU Decision-Making System' 6 *European Public Law* 3, 377; Graham Pearce (2000) 'British Sub-National Government Engagement in Europe 6 *European Public Law* 4, 595.

[67] Jean-Claude Bonichot, in Bertrand Faure and Jean-Bernard Auby (eds.), *Les collectivités locales et le droit. Les mutations actuelles* (Paris, Dalloz, « Actes », 2001), 212.

[68] *Recueil*, 30, conclusions by Henri Savoie.

Such a decision is an illustration of local law directly impacted by EU law—by that aspect of global law that is EU law—where national law is silent. In other words, local law sometimes serves as a vector for global law to penetrate national law.

There are similarities between the respective natures of globalisation and decentralisation. Not only are they both tensions to which our public systems are jointly subject, but they are linked to a certain extent. In pushing forward transnational realities and mechanisms, globalisation encounters (inter alia) local institutions which, in turn, view it as a vector for emancipation even if they are subsequently subject to a number of constraints as a result.

This complicity between global and local is one of the more interesting paradoxes under globalisation.

IV. THE LEGAL DIMENSION OF MULTI-LAYERED GOVERNANCE

Globalisation has a profound impact on the formations of public spaces. Not only does it lead to a proliferation of public spaces implicated in and impacted by globalisation (ie from local to global), but it also creates highly unusual relations between those various public spaces, which break with accepted hierarchical lines. This is multi-layered or multilevel governance.[69] It can be described in general terms and in terms of its legal dimensions—which are of particular interest to us here—as follows.

Globalisation creates interactions and interconnections, and overlaps between legal and political public spaces, affecting them both horizontally and vertically.[70]

Public spaces intertwine horizontally. This is illustrated, for instance, by the development of international relations between local governments, discussed above.

Equally, if not more, significant on this level is the densification of inter-administrative networks linking different segments of national governments in order to ensure the co-ordination of various policies. We have already seen an example of this 'transgovernmentalism'[71] with the Basel Committee, which brings together the governors of the leading central banks and plays a very important role in regulating the world's financial and banking system.[72] These administrative interconnections are clearly particularly

---

[69] See, eg, Scholte *Globalization. A critical introduction* (n 54) 143 ff.

[70] Dominique Leydet, 'Mondialisation et démocratie: la notion de société civile globale' in François Crépeau (ed), *Mondialisation des échanges et fonctions de l'Etat* (Brussels, Bruylant, 1997) 264; Anthony McGrew 'Global Legal Interaction' (n 35).

[71] As per the phrase coined by Shihata: 'The Changing Role of the State' (n 12).

[72] See above, chapter 2, 'A Financial Markets Law—ii Global Regulation'.

strong within the EU, but they are also especially dense in the wider context of the OECD.[73]

Inter-judicial networks tend to be added to these inter-administrative networks, eg the regular meetings held between judges of the Supreme Courts of the EU, or the Association of Superior Court Judges on the American continent.[74]

Globalisation adds vertical overlaps to these horizontal connections between public spaces.

In all sorts of scenarios, legal and political relations pass through various levels in the organisation of public spaces. Local authorities enter into dialogue with the EU. Citizens assert their rights directly before Community institutions. National groups directly lobby Community authorities, even global institutions, etc.

This permeability of levels of governance is spiced up by the fact that the division of powers between the various levels often appears to be quite unclear. Community powers are shared with Member States, if only because as an indirect administrative system demands, the latter are for the most part responsible for the implementation of the policies and acts produced by the exercise of those powers.

The result is that the overlay of levels of governance looks less and less like a hierarchical interlocking.[75] Relations have become increasingly reciprocal or circular. They are moving away from the pyramid model towards that of the network; we shall return to this below.

V. CITIZENSHIP, DEMOCRACY AND CONSTITUTIONALISATION IN THE GLOBAL LEGAL SPACE

Under the influence of globalisation, the forms and the legal configuration of power change on the international stage, as we seen above. This being the case, the issue of the legitimacy of powerful new entities and the altered workings of power naturally arises. Can what is currently developing be deemed acceptable from the perspective of requirements under the rule of law, or from the perspective of what can be considered the right conditions for defining and implementing the general interest?

One author perfectly described the situation, writing that the fundamental question that we face is this: how to build a global legal and political

---

[73] de Senarclens, *La mondialisation* (n 1) 185.

[74] Anne-Marie Slaughter, 'Government networks: the heart of liberal democratic order', in Fox and Roth, *Democratic Governance* (n 42), 199.

[75] Veltz 'Le développement local face à la mondialisation' (n 53); Patrice Duran, 'Action publique, action politique' in Jean-Philippe Leresche (ed), *Gouvernance territoriale et citoyenneté urbaine* (Paris, Pedone, 2001) 369.

order without having to build a global state.[76] There lies the rub. A realistic agenda cannot include the creation of a global state, which would undoubtedly not be desirable in any case. It is therefore in the composite space established under globalisation that issues of legitimacy must be raised, beginning with that of citizenship, democracy and the additional, related issue of the constitutionalisation of major global players.

A. The Challenge of Global Citizenship and Democracy[77]

i. Globalisation and Democracy

The essential question raised here is an easy one to set out.

From a democratic perspective, it is difficult to accept that legal norms can, at least on some significant level, be produced or enshrined by authorities that are not more or less under citizen control.

Naturally, the dispersal of normative sources under globalisation is a problem in this respect. It obviously raises issues in any case where it allows the development of forms of self-regulation by private players, or co-regulation with private players; from a democratic perspective, that can only be accepted within strict limits. However, it also raises issues in any case where it allows the development of normative sources in public spaces other than the national space, which remains the meeting point for the mechanisms of democracy. It also raises issues where decision-making power within international organisations moves away from intergovernmental bodies and towards administrative entities, comitology bodies, etc.

This does not mean that globalisation has no positive effects on democracy; it does, being linked, for instance, to the fact that international public opinion can supplement the weight of national public opinion on a given issue.[78] Nevertheless, there are signs of a democratic deficit, which may be viewed as all the more problematic in that the erosion of sovereignty renders states less effective as guarantors of democratic control over public affairs.[79]

ii. Growing Democratisation

It is true that the problem has now been identified, and efforts have been made in the recent past to establish connections between various international

---

[76] Stéphane Chauvier, *Justice et droits à l'échelle globale* (Paris, Vrin-Ehess, 2006).

[77] Alfred Aman, *The Democracy Deficit. Taming Globalization through Law Reform* (New York, New York University Press, 2004).

[78] Peters 'The Globalization of State Constitutions' (n 62) 251.

[79] Pierre de Senarclens, and Ali Kazancigil (eds), *Regulating Globalization: Critical Approaches to Global Governance* (United Nations, United Nations University Press, 2007).

organisations and, if not directly with citizens, then at least representative organisations of those who may be considered to be stakeholders, depending on the focus of the given organisation. In the sphere of the EU, democratisation efforts literally take the form of relations with citizens.

In the context of its 'Global Compact' initiative,[80] the UN has establishes close and regular links with a number of non-governmental organisations that it consults on a variety of topics.

The WTO, long criticised for its indifference to the issue, eventually also adopted a policy of establishing contacts with non-governmental organisations. Furthermore, proceedings before the Panels and the Appellate Body were opened up to allow the involvement of such organisations as *amicus curiae*, as well as broadcasting hearings (subject to consent from the states parties, but it would appear that such consent has never been withheld).[81]

Many highly unusual aspects combine to ensure a direct connection between citizens and EU institutions. First, elections for the European Parliament, of course. Next, the fact that EU law vests citizens with various prerogatives that they can assert directly.[82] The fact that, having a double allegiance, EU citizens can sometimes establish triangular relations with EU and national institutions, and play one off against the other if necessary.[83] The fact that European institutions should themselves be surrounded by various NGOs. Quite simply, 'voting with their feet', which allows free movement and free establishment.[84]

The oft-decried 'democratic deficit' nonetheless remains, even on an EU level.

iii. The Democratisation of Globalisation

The truth is that the issue of the democratisation of globalisation appears, on closer examination, to be particularly complex. It encompasses at least three lines of questioning, each more complex than the last.

a. A Global Civil Society

The first is that of whether there exists such a thing as a global civil society and global citizens—on an EU level, whether there exists a European civil society, with European citizens living and behaving as such.

---

[80] See above, chapter 3, 'Self-regulation'.

[81] Peter van den Bossche (2008) 'NGO Involvement in the WTO: a Comparative Perspective' *Journal of International Economic Law* 4, 717–749.

[82] Sybilla Fries and Jo Shaw (1998) 'Citizenship of the Union: First Steps in the European Court of Justice' 4 *European Public Law* 4, 533.

[83] Sabino Cassese, *La crisi dello Stato* (Bari, Editori Laterza, 2002) 67.

[84] Deirdre Curtin, *Postnational democracy* (The Hague, Kluwer Law International, 1997).

According to this notion, there is a global civil society, under the gaze of which globalisation and its resulting law develop. According to Ulrich Beck,[85] a transnational civil society is emerging, one of its initial signs being the episode in the summer of 1995 when Greenpeace succeeded in forcing Shell to dismantle an oil platform on land which the company had been considering sinking in the North Atlantic.

This global civil society is made up of all movements (NGOs, environmental or humanitarian groups, 'anti-globalisation' movements, etc) that strive to voice, on a global level—or through local activities aimed at global public opinion—the concerns of citizens who consider that they have a contribution to make to the understanding and conduct of world affairs.[86]

As appealing as it may be, the concept of a 'global civil society' nevertheless appears to be far from operational. It refers instead to a plurality of highly varied sub-groups and disparate entities.[87] Furthermore, the democratic legitimacy of such entities is generally weak, while their transparency is sometimes extremely limited.

Add to that the fact that 'global civil society' may only be considered an acceptable vector for the legitimisation of globalisation and its law if it were connected to institutions themselves responsible for globalisation and its law. Where NGOs have close ties with the UN, they traditionally have very few—and then strikingly hostile—relations with the WTO, which is nevertheless the organisation most likely to become a kind of governmental apparatus for economic globalisation worldwide.[88]

In the context of the EU, things are certainly more advanced, and the fact that there are European citizens is indisputable: the law of the Union has given rise directly to that reality. Nonetheless, as has been shown by the EU's various guises since the constitutional treaty episode, everything points to the fact there is no European political body yet capable of forming the full basis for the democratisation of the Union's institutions.

---

[85] Beck, *What is Globalization?* (n 58) 64 ff. See also: Jan Aart Scholte, 'Global Civil Society' in Ngaire Woods (ed), *The Political Economy of Globalization* (London and New York, Macmillan, 2000).

[86] *cf* Sassen, *A Sociology of Globalization* (n 23) 190 ff, Peter Fitzpatrick and Patricia Tuitt, *Critical Beings, Law, Nation and the Global Subject* (Cambridge, Cambridge University Press, 2004); Kenneth Anderson (2000) 'The Ottawa Convention Banning Landmines: the Role of International Non-Governmental Organizations and the Idea of International Civil Society' *European Journal of International Law* 11, 91.

[87] Gunther Teubner, 'Un droit spontané dans la société mondiale?' in Charles-Albert Morand (ed), *Le droit saisi par la globalisation* (Brussels, Bruylant, 2001) 225; Leydet, 'Mondialisation et démocratie' (n 70) 264.

[88] Charles-Albert Morand, 'Le droit saisi par la mondialisation: définitions, enjeux et transformations' in Charles-Albert Morand (ed), ibid 81. See also Francis Snyder (ed), *Regional and Global Regulation of International Trade* (Oxford, Hart Publishing, 2002).

b. Which Institutions to Democratise?

The second line of questioning raised by the programme for the democrati-sation of globalisation is a two-fold question: for which institutions must a democratic link be sought, and how to go about it?

Which international players must be democratised? The answer to this question is far from obvious. All international institutions suffer to a greater or lesser extent from a democratic deficit in their functioning—quite aside from the fact that they also sometimes include states that are not democracies.[89] Should the main concern be the UN, which may be consid-ered as a pillar of the world's legal and political organisation? This would be to forget that other organisations, be they global or regional, play a much more significant, practical role, which ought to make them the main priority in terms of democratisation.

Moreover, are international bodies the only problem? Some argue, for example, that leading multinational corporations having become major players under globalisation, so the issue of the representation of interests within their decision-making structures must also be raised.[90]

When the decision as to which institutions are to be democratised has been made, a number of questions naturally arise concerning the ways in which that democratisation must be implemented,[91] including the following. Improving the democratic basis for the representation of states within inter-national organisations: can this be implemented, for example, by granting specific mandates to state representatives, discussed with national assemblies, as is current practice with regard to US representation in the WTO?[92] The International Labour Organization gives the example of an extreme formula which consists in ensuring direct representation of civil society—through employers' organisations and trade unions—in the organisation's various bodies.[93] When choosing to forge links with stakeholder organisations, how are the latter to be selected and how can their representativeness be ascertained? Where the organisation has judicial or quasi-judicial mecha-nisms, can the possibility of opening these to individuals affected by its decisions be envisaged? Such openings are, in practice, quite rare.[94]

---

[89] Marc Plattner (2006) 'Internationalisme et démocratie' *Commentaire* 113, 43.

[90] Kim Rubenstein, 'Globalization and Citizenship and Nationality', in Dauvergne (n 18).

[91] Rainer Nickell, 'Participatory Transnational Governance', in Christian Joerges and Ernst-Ulrich Petersmann (eds), *Constitutionalism, Multilevel Trade Governance and Social Regulation* (Oxford, Hart Publishing, 2006) 157.

[92] Ernst-Ulrich Petersmann, 'Multilevel Governance in the WTO Requires Multilevel Constitutionalism', in Joerges and Petersmann (ibid) 5.

[93] Jill Murray, 'Relabelling the International Labour Problem: Globalization and Ideology' in Dauvergne *Jurisprudence for an Interconnected Globe* (n 18) 129.

[94] José E Alvarez (2003) 'The New Dispute Settlers: (Half) Truths and Consequences' *Texas International Law Journal* 38, 405.

c. Which View of Democracy?

The third line of questioning is that of knowing which view of democracy forms the basis of the quest to democratise legal globalisation.

Clearly, if the focus is on a classic conception of representative democracy, there is a high risk of never finding a solution to the problem: the organisation of circuits of representativeness connecting the world's citizens to so many centres of law-making in the global legal sphere is a conundrum.

The objective becomes more readily achievable if other conceptions are endorsed (which can only be done accessorily): 'deliberative' democracy or 'procedural' democracy, depending on the conceptualisation given by Jürgen Habermas.[95] Thus the issue becomes one of representing interests—how to involve the various stakeholders—and organising sufficiently robust control, participation, concertation and accountability mechanisms.[96] This is much easier to accomplish, as it does not assume the existence of a global civil society presenting the same characteristics as national political bodies.

B. The Challenge of Constitutionalising Global Players

The issue to be discussed here concerns whether and how global players must be subject to constitutionalisation processes, ie equipped with bodies of fundamental regulations which clearly stipulate the relationship between the various powers therein, their ties with institutions and persons affected by their activities, and the essential principles and values with which they are asked to comply. Naturally, this is linked to that of democracy and citizenship, in that one of the problems that constitutionalisation necessarily encounters is the connection with civil society and the guarantees for individual rights; but it is separate in that it also raises problems concerning the balance of powers, review and compliance with the law that are beyond its scope.

In order to tackle the issue of constitutionalisation properly, it must be remembered that alongside public—state or inter-state—players, globalisation reserves a special place for non-state players; so this question must be asked for the latter as well as the former[97,98].

---

[95] Patricia Nanz, 'Democratic Legitimacy and Constitutionalization of Transnational Trade Governance: A View from Political Theory' in Joerges and Petersmann *Constitutionalism* (n 91) 59.

[96] Nickell 'Participatory Transnational Governance' (n 91).

[97] The issue of theoretical paradigms to which the reflections discussed here lead will be examined later: see below, chapter 7, 'C. Globalisation and Constitutional Law'.

[98] David Schneiderman, in *Constitutionalizing Economic Globalization* (Cambridge, Cambridge University Press, 2008), suggests an approach to constitutionalisation applied to international investment protection schemes, which have implications for the national constitutions on which they are incumbent, for instance as regards the issue of property and expropriation (which international agreements in this sphere strive to restrict). It is a different approach with a constitutional purpose in substantive terms, but not on an organic or formal level.

C. The Issue of Constitutionalising Global Public Bodies[99]

i. Why Constitutionalise?

The first question to be asked is why there is a need to constitutionalise under globalisation those public players that do not already have that kind of framework.

One might doubt that such an operation is even necessary, insofar as international institutions have statutes that are akin to constitutions, in the sense that they define the main principles to be obeyed, together with the respective competence of their various bodies and the relationships between them. If there remains room for constitutionalisation, it is for reasons which can be called both organic and substantive. While they structure relationships between the institutions concerned and their member states, these international statutes are not generally concerned with forging links with the citizens concerned—or more widely with stakeholder groups—on the one hand; and, on the other hand, they are generally not concerned with specifying the fundamental values or principles that the institution's various bodies must observe, in terms of human rights, compliance with principles of the rule of law, accountability, etc.

A second objection may be made on the grounds that the reflection on the constitutionalisation of international institutions is not useful where member states themselves have constitutions, and that is enough. However, this objection is no more acceptable than the last, for two reasons. The first is that member state control over certain international institutions is limited: where decisions are made by a majority vote, they can come up against a constitutionally recognised norm in a given member state. The second is that everything indicates that, in the global legal sphere, national constitutions have increasingly become only *partial* constitutions.[100] Like the states themselves, they are not up to the task of dealing with certain problems, and they can guarantee human rights protection and the production of public goods outside state borders only with an international complement.[101]

---

[99] See in particular: Joerges and Petersmann, *Constitutionalism* (n 91); Jan Klabbers, Anne Peters and Geir Ulfstein, *The Constitutionalization of International Law* (Oxford, Oxford University Press, 2009); Bruce Ackerman (1997) 'The Rise of World Constitutionalism', 83 *Virginia Law Review* 771; Deborah Z Cass (2001) 'The 'Constitutionalization' of International Trade Law: Judicial Norm-Generation as the Engine of Constitutional Development in International Trade' 12 *European Journal of International Law* 1, 39; Zaki Laidi, *La norme sans la force. L'énigme de la puissance européenne* (Paris, Presses de Sciences Po, 2005), 247 ff.

[100] Peters, 'The Globalization of State Constitutions' (n 62).

[101] Ernst-Ulrich Petersmann, 'Multilevel Governance in the WTO Requires Multilevel Constitutionalism', in Joerges and Petersmann *Constitutionalism* (n 91) 5.

ii. What is Constitutionalisation?

Some elements of what 'to constitutionalise' means are incontrovertible, but others are open to different interpretations.

Constititionalisation is a matter of equipping a global public body with fundamental norms that: determine its structure; isolate legislative, executive and judicial functions therein; and organise its relations with those members of the community for whom its activities are intended, at the same time defining those rights that are recognised to them. It is also a matter of setting down these norms for the long term, and in a general, abstract form that guarantees that all their intended recipients are bound thereby, and draw benefit therefrom, on a non-discriminatory basis.[102]

Beyond this, it goes without saying that options present themselves as, while constitutionalism has a constant framework of inspiration, constitutional forms and contents inspired thereby can vary. Naturally there is variation in the ways in which decision-making and review models can be organised, as well as the mechanisms through which the institution can be linked with its stakeholders. There is also variation in the view that may be taken of the institution's involvement in the sphere assigned to it, depending on whether such involvement is considered as subsidiary in a sense—in relation to the market, or the 'natural' functioning of society—in a view connected to the constitutional political economy, or that the institution is bound to be more proactive, in a perspective which promotes its possible action to deliver public goods.[103]

As regards essential principles, and particularly those concerning the protection afforded to the rights of the intended recipients of the institution's activities, there is a sort of core, of broadly common heritage, resulting from general mechanisms under international law, and the large corpus of international law on human rights: this body of 'public interest norms' established in an international law which had once been made up of norms intended to harmonise relations between states and therefore were, in that sense, 'private interest norms'.[104]

iii. The Targets and Methods of Constitutionalisation

A third series of questions relates to the issue of which institutions are the main targets of the constitutionalisation process, and which methods ought to be used.

As to the first question, we can only offer an answer similar to that relating to citizenship and democratisation. All global public players suffer from

---

[102] ibid.
[103] Schneiderman, *Constitutionalizing Economic Globalization* (n 98).
[104] Giuliana Ziccardi Capaldo, *The Pillars of Global Law* (Aldershot, Ashgate, 2008), 45 ff.

a constitutionalisation deficit as we understand it, as their charters have always been conceived in a different spirit that is essentially functional, in order to produce collective public actions in an inter-state sphere. However, naturally, attention must be paid primarily to those institutions that have the most significant powers or the most strategic functions: the UN, the WTO, the EU, etc.

As regards methods, it must be stressed that the approach to be taken is necessarily multilevel, in the sense that any constitution for a global public body must be conceived as being a piece of a whole, as being in alignment with other constitutional levels, in a model of multilevel constitutionalism.[105] It is essentially a matter of making the multiple partial state constitutions respond to, complete and connect to each other, together with that which may be forged for global institutions.

D. Constitutionalising Non-state Players[106]

Considering the growing importance of certain non-state players under globalisation, we cannot help but wonder whether constitutionalisation efforts ought not also to extend to them—and all the more so given that they are as removed as possible from the constitutional model, as their legal status is in practice simply that of a private entity, or that of a non-profit private body, immersed in the ordinary rules of national law.[107]

As we have seen, just as we may potentially concern ourselves with the means for 'democratising' those entities, we may also strive to constitution-alise them. In what sense? The essence of the problem for them is ensuring that their actions are in keeping with the fundamental values and princi-ples that govern public activities—of which they are part—and particularly those relative to the protection of individual rights.[108]

There are only a small number of solutions, but they are potentially linked to two sources of inspiration. They may relate to an effort to extend the principles and values governing public bodies to non-state entities involved

---

[105] Petersmann, *Constitutionalism* (n 91).

[106] Gavin Anderson, *Constitutional Rights after Globalization* (Oxford, Hart Publishing, 2005).

[107] Wilfried Bolewski, *Diplomacy and International Law in Globalized Relations* (Berlin, Heidelberg, Springer, 2007) 53 ff.

[108] As regards entities responsible for outsourced public services, see Laura Dickinson, 'Public Law Values in a Privatized World' (2006) *Yale Journal of International Law* 383; Jean-Bernard Auby, 'Contracting Out and Public Values' in Susan Rose-Ackerman and Peter Lindseth (eds), *Comparative Administrative Law* (Aldershot, Ashgate, 2010).

in the conduct of public affairs, and this through a process of assimilation which leads to the conclusion that, in such a position, they may be compared to public bodies and must consequently be regulated by those same disciplines.[109] They may set the target of inducing the non-state entity to include within its own rules, within its corporate governance, compliance with values and principles similar to those governing public activities—all in all, to internalise the corresponding disciplines. This is essentially the approach taken by the UN from 2000 onwards as part of its Global Compact policy, which encourages multinational corporations to declare their commitment to human rights protection, and particularly the protection of workers' rights, in those developing countries where they make purchases or have subsidiaries.[110]

VI. LEGAL GLOBALISATION AND THE IMPERATIVES OF THE RULE OF LAW

The question to be examined here is both broader and narrower than those discussed in the preceding section. It consists of understanding the extent to which the imperatives of the rule of law are observed in a global legal space characterised by the plurality and diversity of lawmakers and normative processes, together with the common informality of those lawmakers and processes. It is narrower than the issues of democracy and constitutionalisation, as the principles that form the basis of the issue raised here do not necessarily assume democracy and constitutionalisation. It is also broader, in that it does not relate solely to the operation and organisation of legal globalisation's main players, but also to all of its mechanisms.

A. Essential Values Under Globalisation

When put in the latter, more general sense, the above question amounts to asking what fate awaits the essential values of the rule of law—legal certainty; equality before the law; the existence of mechanisms to remind public authorities to act in accordance with the law; transparency; the separation of powers; judicial independence, etc— under legal globalisation.[111]

---

[109] This is what happens when a public institution which outsources a given service or task expressly requires compliance with a certain number of principles (eg transparency, non-discrimination, etc) on the part of the entity to which it delegates said task or service, for example through express provisions contained in the contract between the two parties.

[110] Bolewski, *Diplomacy and International Law* (n 107).

[111] On the issue of legal certainty: Volkmar Gessner, 'Globalization and Legal Certainty' in Gessner and Budak, *Emerging Legal Certainty* (n 15): see the concluding article.

As Anne Peters explains particularly well,[112] the effects of those principles in this area are partly positive, partly negative. Legal globalisation contributes to the strengthening of the rule of law within national systems, through the development of its human rights component.[113] The rules that it produces in order to foster free trade strengthen more classic citizen rights *vis-à-vis* public authorities. Multilevel global governance thus creates a kind of 'vertical' separation of powers. Globalisation opens the way to new means of obtaining and sharing information.

Conversely, globalisation generates situations in which legal guarantees are diminished: for example, the acts of global institutions cannot generally be brought before the courts. The complexity of the processes of making and applying laws damages the clarity and transparency of those laws. Globalisation's norms are often part of a 'soft law' which tends to grant fewer guarantees to its intended recipients. Controls of all kinds—not only judicial—on globalisation's main protagonists are often lacking.

In this very general field, there is little more left to say, and perhaps even the question perhaps lacks meaning at that level. The global legal space no doubt has its regulations—and we will come back to this point—but it is certainly insufficiently organised for it to fulfil the tenets of the rule of law on a general level.

B. Compliance with the Rule of Law Under Globalisation

What does have specific meaning and is very much a live issue in the development of legal globalisation is to assess the extent to which legal globalisation's players, viewed individually, are (or indeed are not) caught in a legal web which demands that they comply with the basic requirements of the rule of law.

Like democracy and constitutionalisation, this issue deserves to be put forward with regard to global public bodies and non-state players under globalisation.

The decision in *Kadi* and judgments handed down on the subject by the European Court of First Instance and the Court of Justice[114] have made it quite apparent that certain global bodies (and in *Kadi*, it was no less than the United Nations Security Council) sometimes make decisions that impact

---

[112] n 52.

[113] Eric Carpano, *Etat de droit et droits européens* (Paris, L'Harmattan, 2008).

[114] See above, chapter 1, 'b. A Forum in which Globalisation is Co-produced'.

dramatically on individual rights without any kind of appeal against such decisions being possible.

This merely relaunches discussions conducted for some time—inter alia, in the context of the theory of global administrative law, to which we shall return below[115]—on ways to improve levels of accountability within global public bodies, ie mechanisms which drive them to account to those who may be affected by their activities and decisions, to inform them, to afford them the possibility of challenging their choices, etc.

The problem of accountability has been raised in respect of various classic international bodies—as demonstrated by *Kadi*—and takes on even greater significance with regard to administrative bodies, such as those of a public-private nature, because traditional international bodies—depending as they do on governments—are indirectly subject to the controls incumbent on the latter. As Anne-Marie Slaughter explains,[116] this particularly concerns those taking the form of networks.

The most significant issues that it encompasses include transparency and the appeal process. As the heirs of the habits of secrecy traditionally associated with diplomacy, global public bodies are rarely constrained by rules requiring them to provide to disclose information in their possession.[117] The decisions made by global public bodies are rarely likely to be subject to appeal; there are notable exceptions, naturally, including that embodied by the WTO's appeals mechanism.[118]

The problem of the accountability of non-state players under legal globalisation is even more difficult, in that these players are immersed in legal melting-pots—national corporate law or the law on non-profit organisations—which generally include only minimal requirements in terms of transparency, appeals processes, etc.[119] This deficit has been observed in the case of various non-state regulators, for example those involved in the financial markets sphere.[120] It has also been observed in relation to non-governmental organisations, although some of their number have voluntarily instituted an

---

[115] See, specifically: Benedict Kingbury, Nico Krisch and Richard B Stewart (2005) 'The Emergence of Global Administrative Law' 68 *Law and Contemporary Problems* 3–4: see 37 ff.

[116] Anne-Marie Slaughter (2001) 'The Accountability of Government Networks' *Indiana Journal of Global Legal Studies* 8, 347.

[117] Peters 'The Globalization of State Constitutions' (n 62).

[118] Achim Heldemach and Bernhard Zangi, 'Dispute Settlement Under GATT and WTO: an Empirical Enquiry into a Regime Change', in Joerges and Petersmann *Constitutionalism* (n 91).

[119] Sorcha MacLeod and John Parkinson (eds), *Global Governance and the Quest for Justice*, vol II, *Corporate Governance* (Oxford, Hart Publishing, 2004).

[120] Janet Koven Levit (2005) 'A Bottom-Up Approach to International Law-Making: the Take of Three Trade Finance Instruments' *Yale Journal of International Law* 30, 125.

internal governance system which maintains strict control over their directors; Amnesty International is a prime example.[121]

VII. PUBLIC AFFAIRS, GENERAL INTEREST AND PUBLIC GOODS UNDER LEGAL GLOBALISATION

The question to be examined here is, all in all, that of whether, under legal globalisation, there could be mechanisms allowing the identification and implementation, on a level not too far removed from that traditionally reached in the state sphere, of 'public affairs', of functions and tasks of general interest or, to employ a concept that is quite prominent nowadays, of 'public goods'.

In practical terms, the key issues to consider are that of defining public affairs and general interest, and that of the production of public goods.[122]

A. Defining 'Public Affairs' and the General Interest under Legal Globalisation

There is an oft-voiced suspicion that globalisation systematically sows confusion with regard to the understanding of the values of the general interest, and the quest for the fulfilment thereof, either because, having a purely economic rationale, globalisation could only be indifferent to such values; or because it would naturally destroy national mechanisms for defining and implementing the general interest, and this without bringing with it any kind of substitute or equivalent.

Such warnings are not entirely without basis insofar as globalising law often confuses the issue of identifying the public interest, if only because it amalgamates and forces into coexistence very different ways of proceeding with that identification. In any event, it generates a kind of fragmentation of authorities and mechanisms through which public affairs and the general interest are identified and shaped; it is difficult to perceive such fragmentation as anything other than a vector of uncertainty.

There are however essentially two categories of argument against such a view.

---

[121] Peter J Spiro (2002) 'Accounting for NGOs', *Chicago Journal of International Law* 3, 161.

[122] Jean-Bernard Auby, 'Global Public Goods and Global Administrative Law', in Gordon Anthony, Jean-Bernard Auby, Jon Morison and Tom Zwart (eds), *Values in Global Administrative Law* (Oxford, Hart Publishing, 2010).

First, we must return yet again to the notion that states today are no longer up to the task of certain public problems: the environment, communications, the regulation of financial activities, for example. Consequently, defining these as public policy issues (as falling within the scope of 'public affairs'); defining certain values connected to those issues as being public goods; and identifying general interest purposes linked thereto is not done purely on a state level, but instead must increasingly be accomplished on a global level. The task of defining the public interest under globalisation is inevitably complex.

A phenomenon that is all too often underestimated is that within the very mechanisms of legal globalisation, elements of a definition for the characteristic values of public affairs can nevertheless be found. How can that be?

It sometimes comes about directly and formally when the imperatives of environmental protection, freedom of trade, health protection, the fight against hunger, the rule of law and many others are expressed in globalising law. One of the major developments in international law of the modern era is that, where it was once the law of co-existence between states, with characteristics similar to those of private law in the domestic legal sphere, it has since increasingly taken on a public aspect, concerning itself with issues of direct interest for the international community as a whole and conveying public interest norms applied to those issues.[123]

However, it also comes about indirectly, through mechanisms by which global law grants self-governance exceptions to states, allowing them to hide behind the requirements of public order, public security, the protection of public health, etc.

As has already been pointed out,[124] quite naturally through the technique of public order reservations, the definition of the corresponding imperatives ceases at some point to be left to states—who use it all too readily as a loophole—and is instead placed under the control of authorities that stand as the guardians of global norms. Where a state applies to the WTO in order to enforce the Agreement on Technical Barriers to Trade, the Dispute Settlement Body may find itself having to rule on arguments relating to national security, or the protection of public health, submitted by the reluctant respondent state. Where a Member State invokes public order requirements as grounds for a measure restricting free movement, the Court of Justice is likely to check whether the situation argued does indeed

---

[123] Giuliana Zaccardi Cappaldo, *The Pillars of Global Law* (Aldershot, Ashgate, 2008); Jean d'Aspremont, 'Contemporary International Rulemaking and the Public Character of International Law', IILJ Working Paper (New York, New York University, 2006/12).

[124] See above, chapter 3, 'Public order exceptions, states and legal globalisation'.

correspond to public order imperatives, as the Court itself has defined them.[125]

What does all that engender? It produces a partial and gradual global definition of public affairs, of the public interest, of public goods.[126] This is how, for example, the IMF increasingly sees itself as an institution charged with the general interest function of guaranteeing the stability of the international financial system,[127] while the World Intellectual Property Organisation aims to develop a kind of global public scientific and technical information service.[128]

It also produces a more or less marked or extensive rapprochement in the ways in which interests and values, as encompassed by the search for these 'public goods', may be conceived.

This obviously also has implications for national definitions of public affairs and the public interest. Indeed, this requires states to strive to elucidate public interest considerations[129] when, quite often, such considerations are contained in the law as the trace of a political postulation on which there is not very much to say—except that judges are left to adapt to the lack of clarity that is sometimes their lot.

B. Producing Public Goods under Legal Globalisation[130]

The concept of global public goods has now taken on great importance in the discussion surrounding international public issues, and in particular those related to the environment, health, and education. It is the extension of a concept drawn from economic theory, and which serves in understanding and characterising major areas of public action.

---

[125] Thomas Hamoniaux, *L'intérêt général et le juge communautaire* (Paris, LGDJ, 2001) 105 ff; Abdelkhalek Berramdane, 'L'ordre public et les droits fondamentaux en droit communautaire et de l'Union européenne', in *Territoires et libertés, Mélanges offerts à Yves Madiot* (Brussels, Bruylant, 2000) 157.

[126] It may be argued that, in any case, in our complex societies, the definition of 'public goods' is inescapably undermined and proceduralised: Daniel Innerarity, *El nuevo espacio publico* (Madrid, Espasa, 2006) 171 ff. While this may be true on a national level, then it is all the more so in the global sphere.

[127] Geneviève Burdeau, 'Le FMI et la surveillance de l'espace monétaire et financier mondial' in Eric Loquin and Catherine Kessedjian (eds), *La mondialisation du droit* (Paris, Litec, 2000) 261.

[128] Martine Barré, 'L'OMPI et la mondialisation du droit de la propriété intellectuelle' in Loquin and Kessedjian (ibid) 277.

[129] 'A vital function of revealing collective preferences', according to Zaki Laidi and Pascal Lamy, 'L'Europe au défi de la gouvernance mondiale', in Olivier Delas and Christian Deblock (eds), *Le bien commun comme réponse politique à la globalisation* (Brussels, Bruylant, 2003) 115.

[130] Olivier Delas and Christian Deblock (eds), *Le bien commun comme réponse politique à la globalisation*, ibid.

The concept of global public goods

1. Born out of the economic analysis of market failures, the concept of 'public good' refers to certain goods or services, the hallmark of which is that of being either 'non-excludable' (ie it is impossible to prevent a person from using them), 'non-rival' (ie when a person uses one, this does not reduce the quantity available to others), or both 'non-excludable' and 'rival'. Those goods and services that combine both characteristics are pure public goods: national defence or public health, for instance. Those that are 'non-excludable' but also 'rival' goods or services are common goods, such a shoal of fish, for instance: people cannot be prevented from fishing, but whatever fish are caught by one person reduces the number available for others. Those which are 'excludable' but 'non-rival' goods or services are club goods, such as a television programme: access can be restricted by the use of a code, but the fact that another viewer has tuned in does nothing to diminish the amount of entertainment or information, etc available to others.

   Public goods are an example of market failure in that, were their production left to the market, it would deviate from the economic optimum. The main reason—which applies in any event to pure public goods—is that it is difficult to charge for them because it is all too easy for 'free riders' to use them and that, consequently, if it is left to the market, their production will necessarily be sub-optimal.

   As a result, it is necessary for public authorities to concern themselves with the production of these goods and services. This does not mean to say that they deal with them directly, but rather they must ensure that said goods and services are made available in sufficient quantities (through state aid, or by delegating the corresponding public service, to employ the same language used by some laws, or via other avenues).

2. Since the late 1990s, various authors and institutions—including the UN—have given rise to the concept of 'global public good' to describe public interest tasks that must be taken on by the international community because states have become too narrow a framework for their performance.

   These 'common concerns of humanity' are, for example, the fight against climate change, the search for more effective regulation of financial markets, or the fight against international corruption, but also more traditional concerns such as the fight against world hunger or the eradication of certain diseases. These are all public goods in that they combat global problems, fights which can only be led internationally.

The question is obvious: that of how the international community is organised in order to ensure the production of goods and services recognised as global public goods. This poses both substantive problems, in terms of the identification by the international community of values that it intends to serve, and organisational problems, in view above all of the fact that the corresponding tasks will often necessarily involve multiple global, regional, state and sub-state players. See, in addition to the UN's Global Public Goods website:

On the concept of public goods: Ejan Mackaay and Stéphane Rousseau, *Analyse économique du droit* (Paris, Dalloz, 2008); François Lévêque, *Economie de la réglementation* (Paris, La Découverte, 2004); Giulio Napolitano and Michele Brescia, *Ananlisi economica del diritto pubblico* (Bologna, Il Mulino, 2009) Philippe Simonnot, *L'invention de l'Etat. Economie du droit* (Paris, Les Belles Lettres, 2003).

On the concept of global public goods: Jean-Bernard Auby, 'Public Goods and Global Administrative Law' in Gordon Anthony, Jean-Bernard Auby, John Morison and Tom Zwart (eds), *Values in Global Administrative Law* (Oxford, Hart Publishing, 2010); Scott Barrett, *Why Cooperate? The Incentive to Supply Global Public Goods* (Oxford, Oxford University Press, 2010); François Constantin, *Le bien commun comme réponse politique à la globalisation* (Paris, L'Harmattan, 2003); Olivier Delas and Christian Deblock (eds), *Le bien commun comme réponse politique à la globalisation* (Brussels, Bruylant, 2003); Inge Kaul, Isabelle Gurndberg and Marc Stern (eds), *Global Public Goods: International Cooperation in the 21st Century* (Oxford, Oxford University Press, 1999); Inge Kaul and Pedro Conceição (eds), *Providing Global Public Goods: Managing Globalization* (Oxford, Oxford University Press, 2003); Marie-Claire Amouts, *Forêt tropicale, jungle international* (Paris, Presses de Sciences Po, 2001); John Vogler, *The Global Commons. Environmental and Technological Governance* (Chichester, John Wiley, 2000).

Public goods are services and values, the provision of which must be guaranteed by governments—either by producing them themselves or by ensuring that they are produced by the private sector; we will come back to this—as the market is not naturally inclined to provide them, owing essentially to the fact that it is not possible, in practical terms, to reserve the benefits thereof purely for those who are prepared to pay for them.

The concept has been raised on an international and a global level, and it has been recognised as an appropriate intellectual tool for describing a number of public interest issues that can no longer be, or are less suited than ever to being, handled on a national level.[131] Emblematically, the fight against climate change has been described as such.[132]

The concept of global public goods is of interest in that it is the right tool for reflecting on ways in which the public interest and those concerns constituting 'public affairs' could be implemented in the interconnected, multi-level universe that is globalisation.[133]

Global public goods may be natural or cultural resources, corresponding to the idea of 'common heritage of humanity'[134]—space, the spectrum of radio-electrical frequencies, the biological resources of the sea, the sea beds, etc—or values or objectives, such as education or environmental protection. It goes without saying that it is no easy task for global players to agree on a definition for public goods and the methods for their production. To give but one example, the recognition of such a qualification to plant genetic resources has long been and will always be debated.[135] International discussions demonstrate that northern and southern countries do not always agree on the identification of global public goods.[136]

Quite naturally, there remains the issue of finding mechanisms to ensure that such multilevel production is effective. It must not be forgotten here that, in economic theory, while public authorities must concern themselves with the production of public goods, that does not mean to say that they must produce those goods themselves: ensuring that there is an effective education system does not necessarily mean having an entirely public education system.

Expressed in the global sphere, this concept reminds us that public issues are, to a significant extent, taken on by non-state players: NGOs, various non-state regulators, etc.[137] The problem is that of how to ensure that such non-state producers of public goods do indeed perform the corresponding tasks. This is essentially an issue of defining those tasks and of supervision. It is, moreover, a well-known issue in the national sphere. It calls into

---

[131] Mattias Kumm (2005) 'The Legitimacy of International Law: A Constitutional Framework of Analysis' 15 *European Journal of International Law* 5, 923.

[132] See the Global Public Goods website, linked to that of the UN Development Programme.

[133] Ernst-Ulrich Petersmann, 'Multilevel Trade Governance in the WTO Requires Multilevel Constitutionalism' in Joerges and Petersmann *Constitutionalism* (n 91).

[134] Monique Chemiller-Gendreau, 'Le bien commun universel, quels outils juridiques? quelle pensée politique?', in Delas and Deblock *Le bien commun comme réponse politique à la globalisation* (n 129).

[135] Geneviève Bastid Burdeaux, 'Le principle de souveraineté permanent sur les ressources naturelles à l'épreuve de la mondialisation', in *Mélanges Puissochet* (Paris, Pedone, 2008).

[136] Laidi and Lamy, 'L'Europe au défi de la gouvernance mondiale' (n 129).

[137] See above, chapter 3, 'Non-state players and regulators under globalisation'.

question control over 'contracting out'[138] and the services sector, ie over those entities which, from their inception, are in charge of public goods—spontaneously, as it were—without having been entrusted with the task in question by a public authority; without, therefore, any specific act of devolution defining the methods for their activities and oversight.[139]

Naturally, the corresponding difficulties are all the greater in the global sphere where, as we have seen, non-state entities in charge of public issues lack a legal framework, their nature generally being that of a private entity subject to any national law.

---

[138] Michael Dowdle (ed), *Public Accountability* (Cambridge, Cambridge University Press, 2006).

[139] Martk Freedland and Silvana Sciarra (eds), *Public Services and Citizenship in European Law* (Oxford, Oxford University Press, 1998).

5

How the Global Legal Sphere Operates

MANY QUESTIONS MAY be asked as to the ways in which the global legal sphere operates and how it is structured, the forces at work therein and the various balances that it encompasses. We will discuss four of those factors in this chapter: firstly, the role played by the law under globalisation (see 'I. The Role Played by the Law in Globalisation'); secondly, the changes that globalisation causes in legal practices (see 'II. Globalisation and Legal Practice'); thirdly, whether there are mechanisms for regulating legal globalisation; and, lastly—and we will only skim over this—how best to understand the overall operation of the global legal sphere (see 'IV. Theories on the General Operation of Global Law').

I. THE ROLE PLAYED BY THE LAW IN GLOBALISATION

A word on this first question, for the following reason: an examination of globalisation, of the 'global society', sometimes gives the impression that the law somehow occupies a privileged place therein; that the regulation of globalisation and of the 'global society' rests on the law in a particularly intense way. This hypothesis has been described by some as 'the Empire of Law'. While it is an interesting hypothesis, its shortcomings cannot be ignored.

A. The 'Empire of Law' Hypothesis

The idea that, in the age of globalisation, the law has been substituted for power relations in the regulation of international relations, has been expressed in particular by Jarrod Weiner:[1]

> the regulation of transnational communities of civil society actors engaged in particular practices governed by more or less undifferentiated laws administered by different state authorities can be conceived as no less than an Empire of Law.

[1] Jarrod Wiener, *Globalization and the Harmonization of Law* (London and New York, Pinter, 1999) 190.

That idea can be put differently. Our societies dovetail with each other as a result of increasingly close economic, cultural or social ties. Governments have only limited control over those ties. It is therefore perhaps primarily through the law, rather than through power relations, that the system emerging from those ties can be regulated.

This view is acceptable only to a certain extent, as follows.

i. The Judicialisation of Social Relations

It is doubtless true that, in the globalisation sphere, there is a growing proportion of social relations that are governed by the law.

What is likely at stake, within the working of globalisation, is a process of judicialisation of social relations similar to that which can be seen in more traditional internal spheres. Just as, on a domestic level, law increasingly emerges as an essential moderating power in a democracy,[2] it doubtless appears in the context of globalisation as an often useful substitute for purely economic and political confrontations.

More prosaically, the reality of relations produced by globalisation sometimes leads to a natural search for a legal mechanism. As Martin Shapiro points out,[3] long-distance business relationships are difficult to regulate other than by the law. To this may be added the fact that a number of players in globalisation are wary of political intervention and will therefore prefer to establish a legal structure for the relationships into which they enter.

This holds true in the economic sphere: in the regulation of financial markets, for example, which we have already discussed.[4] However, it is also true in the area of fundamental rights where, frequently, NGOs will in fact seek to overwhelm governments through the law: law is the principal policy tool in the 'global civil society'.[5]

This is reflected particularly in the proliferation of judicial or quasi-judicial structures and mechanisms.[6]

---

[2] eg Pierre Bouretz (ed), *La force du droit. Panorama des débats contemporain* (Paris, Editions Esprit, 1991) 11 ff.

[3] Martin Shapiro (1993) 'The Globalization of Law' *Indiana Journal of Global Legal Studies* 1.

[4] See above, chapter 2, 'Financial Markets Law' ff. See also: Klaus Frick, 'Third Cultures versus Regulators: Cross-Border Legal Relations of Banks' in Volkam Gessner and Ali Cem Budak (eds), *Emerging Legal Certainty: Empirical Studies on the Globalization of Law (Onati International Series in Law and Society)* (Aldershot, Ashgate, 1998) 93.

[5] Richard Falk, *Law in an Emerging Global Village. A Post-Westphalian Perspective* (Ardsley, NY, Transnational Publishers Inc, 1998).

[6] José E Alvarez (2003) 'The New Dispute Settlers: (Half) Truths and Consequences' *Texas International Law Journal* 38, 405.

ii. Maintaining Balance through the Law

One even gets the impression that, in the context of globalisation, important balances are sometimes maintained by the law or legal regulation.

The transition from the GATT to the WTO system brought with it a strengthening of the part played by the law in the workings of the organisation of world trade.[7] Wide-reaching economic issues—eg regarding genetically modified organisms—depend nowadays on the decisions of the WTO's authorities, and in particular its Dispute Settlement Body.

In the EU sphere, the judicialisation of major economic, social or political choices is naturally and especially marked. Its full implications become apparent in the Court of Justice's leading case law options, which are in turn a response to particularly weighty issues: we need only look, once again, at *Cassis de Dijon*.

As the Court itself stated, the EU constitutes a 'Community based on the rule of law'.[8]

B. The Limits of the Hypothesis

The 'Empire of Law' thesis must be considered with some circumspection, like any sociological theory based around the idea of the end of politics, or any legal theory proclaiming that peace prevails through the law.[9]

As Martin Shapiro again points out:

> when we speak of the globalization of law, we must be conscious that we are speaking of an extremely narrow, limited and specialised set of legal phenomena set into a globe in which it is not at all clear whether the total quantum of legal relationship governed by law has increased or decreased over the last century.[10]

Moreover, we must not shy away from the fact that, behind the law, there lie power relations, which are sometimes more than just a driving force. With the extraterritorial laws intended to penalise companies—be they

---

[7] Hélène Ruiz-Fabri, 'La contribution de l'organisation mondiale du commerce à la gestion de l'espace juridique mondial' in Eric Loquin and Catherine Kessedjian (eds), *La mondialisation du droit* (Paris, Litec, 2000) 347.

[8] In Case 294/83 *Parti écologiste 'Les Verts' v Parliament* [1986] ECR 01339 and in its opinion of 14 December 1991 on the Agreement on the European Economic Area. See Joël Rideau (ed), *De la Communauté de Droit à l'Union de Droit. Continuités et avatars européens* (Paris, LGDJ, 2000). See also Thomas AJA Vandamme and Jan-Herman Reestman (eds), *Ambiguity in the Rule of Law. The Interface Between National and International Systems* (Groningen, Europa Law Publishing, 2001).

[9] Prosper Weil (1992) 'Toujours le même et toujours recommencé: les thèmes contrastés du changement et de la permanence du droit international', *Recueil des cours de l'Académie du Droit International*, t 237, reproduced in Prosper Weil, *Écrits de droit international* (Paris, PUF, 2000).

[10] n 4.

American or otherwise—trading with Cuba (Holmes-Burton Act 1996) or Libya (Amato-Kennedy Act 1996), the USA gave legal globalisation a characteristic aspect of a-territorial or extraterritorial law reflecting nothing but its political will.

All in all, owing to the indisputable fact that legal globalisation increasingly judicialises transnational relations which develop due to economic, political, and social globalisation, it would be foolhardy to conclude that the regulation of international relations is slowly drifting towards generalised judicialisation.[11] This would be to ignore the limits of legal globalisation, to ignore that it varies in intensity—being at its maximum level in the Community sphere, while producing quite limited effects in relations between developed and developing societies, for example. It is also to confuse legal globalisation and the judicialisation of globalisation.

II. GLOBALISATION AND LEGAL PRACTICE

The functional transformations wrought upon the law by globalisation have had and continue quite naturally to have consequences for legal practice. There follow a number of observations that may be made on the subject, concerning the legal professions and comparative law.

A. The Legal Professions under Globalisation[12]

It is quite clear that legal globalisation has already had a marked influence on the ways in which the legal professions are organised and on their activities on a global scale.

i. The Internationalisation of the Business Law Market

The most obvious point here relates to the considerable internationalisation of the market for business law.

---

[11] For some, economic globalisation even goes so far as to erode legal regulation: André-Jean Arnaud, *Critique de la raison juridique. 2. Gouvernants sans frontières. Entre mondialisation et post-mondialisation* (Paris, LGDJ, 2003). It may be thought that globalisation changes such regulation more than it restricts it.

[12] See William D Henderson (2007) 'The Globalization of the Legal Profession' 14 *Indiana Journal of Global Legal Studies* 1; Tom Zwart, 'The Reflection of Cross-Border Law Practice in the Organization and Regulation of the Legal Profession', Séminaire de Droit Administratif Comparé, Européen et Global de la Chaire 'Mutations de l'Action Publique et du Droit Public' de Sciences Po (8 Feburary 2008). http://www.sciencespo.fr/chaire-madp/sites/sciencespo.fr.chaire-madp/files/tom_zwart.pdf. On the outsourcing of legal services to India by Western companies, see *Le Monde*, 3 April 2009, 3.

The driving force behind this phenomenon, to which the legal professions have adapted, is the internationalisation of the legal market that has gradually emerged since the Second World War. What, then, brought about that trend? The answer would appear to be the following factors, in succession:[13] the expansion of American investments in Europe after the war; the emergence of the Eurodollar market in the 1970; the UK's accession to the EEC in 1973; and the globalisation of financial markets in the 1980s.

Be that as it may, the result is that legal services are now highly internationalised. Several years ago, an OECD study showed that the balance of legal services between the USA and the UK stood at around US $2 billion.[14]

The legal professions adapted to this development through the creation of major international firms, which include not only the leading accountancy and auditing companies (ie the Big 8, now the Big 4: PriceWaterhouse Coopers, Deloitte & Touche, etc)—which may, in some countries, also offer legal services—but above all, major and mainly British and American law firms: Clifford Chance, Freshfields Bruckhaus Deringer, Shearman & Sterling, etc.[15] The latter expanded particularly following the UK's entry into the Common Market in 1973 and the globalisation of financial markets in the 1980s; from their bases in London or New York they have spread, establishing especially important offices in Paris, Frankfurt, Tokyo, Singapore, etc.[16]

These international firms control a significant share of the business law market. For the remainder, they are in fierce competition—depending on the country—with local firms.[17]

It is important to add that the internationalisation of accountancy and law firms does not mean that national systems opened up to transnational practices—in the sense of the possibility for practitioners from a given legal system of practising in another system. On this point, the EU alone has developed any genuine option for practitioners from a given Member State to practise in another Member State. On a global level, the 1995 WTO General Agreement on Trade in Services ought in theory to allow such an opening, although no such breakthrough has been made to date.[18] It is understandable that law firms can become global firms without the lawyers

---

[13] Francis Neate, 'The Lawyer's Role in International Business Practice', in J Ross-Harper (ed), *Global Law in Practice* (The Hague, Kluwer Law International, 1997).

[14] Peter Goldsmith, 'Globalization of Laws, Tearing Down the Walls', in Ross-Harper (ibid) 139.

[15] Henri Nallet, *Les réseaux pluridisciplinaires et les professions du droit* (Paris, La documentation française, 2000), 19 ff, 87 ff.

[16] Francis Neate, 'The Lawyer's Role in International Business Practice', in Ross-Harper, *Global Law in Practice* (n 13).

[17] Jens Drolshammer and Michael Pfeifer, *The Internationalization of the Practice of Law* (The Hague, Kluwer Law International, 2001).

[18] Zwart, 'Reflection of Cross-Border Law Practice' (n 12).

practising therein necessarily being authorised to draft legal documents in legal systems other than their own.

Lastly, while the legal and business professions have been transformed by the legal globalisation trend, they have also had a hand in producing that trend and continue to do so. British law firms importing American techniques with regard to loans has been a significant factor driving the globalisation of financial markets.[19] The contractual 'engineering' performed by international law firms generally occupies a central place in the creation of practices under global trade law.[20]

ii. The Further Development of Global Legal Practices

It would be wrong to reduce the internationalisation of legal practices to the mere internationalisation of the market for company law. Global legal practices are currently being developed beyond the bounds of that particular market.

Aside from the clear multiplication of lawyers within international organisations—as their administrative-type functions have multiplied—various communities of international lawyers have developed; for instance, within non-governmental organisations which, as we have seen, are often the custodians of high-quality legal expertise.

Moreover, transnational advocacy networks have been established in a number of areas, being international networks of practitioners fighting for the protection of labour law, human rights, environmental law, etc.[21]

B. Globalisation and Comparative Law[22]

It is easy to understand, on brief reflection, how the practice of comparative law has been transformed by legal globalisation, the latter calling both the issues and the methods into question.

i. The Raison d'Etre of Comparative Law

Confusingly, at first glance there is the immediate suspicion that legal globalisation must generate a need for comparative law. An increasing number

---

[19] Francis Neate, 'The Lawyer's Role in International Business Practice', in Ross-Harper, *Global Law in Practice* (n 13).

[20] Volkmar Gessner, 'Globalization and Legal Certainty', in Gessner and Budak, *Emerging Legal Certainty* (n 4), 429.

[21] Boaventura da Sousa Santos, *Law and Globalization from Below* (Cambridge, Cambridge University Press, 2005), 64 ff.

[22] Ian Edge (ed), *Comparative Law in Global Perspective* (New York, Transnational Publishers, 2000); Jean-Bernard Auby (2006) 'Globalisation et droit comparé' 8 *European Journal of Law Reform* 1, 43.

of legal situations are governed by measures that rest on the interlacing of international systems of rules and various national solutions; an examination of such situations necessarily requires work in the field of comparative law.[23] As William Twining writes, 'in an increasingly interdependent world, nearly all legal studies are inevitably more or less cosmopolitan'.[24]

In addition, the complex structure of measures under global law—in which domestic laws and international law, general international law and laws on regional integration, public law and private law are mingled—calls for wholesale comparative legal research here, there and everywhere, not just along the traditional lines that lead from one national law to another.[25]

However, the main point lays in the fact that comparative law is currently witnessing genuine upheaval in terms of its challenges. Traditionally, the *raison d'être* of comparative legal inquiries was essentially theoretical: it was a matter of learning about other legal systems the better to understand one's own, and to discover the secret of the very essence of law. At most, the exercise occasionally served to identify 'recipes' within other legal systems for improving one's own. However, this practical challenge remained limited, with the exception of those cases where a state, compelled to conduct sweeping reforms of its legal system, decided to draw on foreign examples. This was the case for Japan at the turn of the nineteenth and twentieth centuries.[26] A more recent example of such situations was presented by Eastern European states after 1989: they picked and chose amongst the various Western legal traditions in order to rebuild their constitutional law, civil law, commercial law, etc.

In the world of globalisation, the challenges tend to become constantly and immediately real. The practice of comparative law takes on an operational dimension that it did not have before, or to any great extent. Other legal systems are no longer mere models to be considered, or possible sources of inspiration. They are both partners and competitors in the legal cross-fertilisation that globalisation brings about. It is a straightforward task to explain this mechanism in the Community sphere, for instance: national legal systems therein are competitors in inspiring EU law solutions,[27] enmeshed

---

[23] Olivier Dubos, 'Le droit administratif et les situations transnationales: des droits étrangers au droit comparé' in Fabrice Melleray (ed), *L'argument de droit comparé en droit administratif français* (Brussels, Bruylant, 2008); Bénédicte Fauvarque Cosson, 'Le droit comparé et le droit international', *Revue internationale de droit comparé* (2003-530).

[24] William Twining (1999) 'Globalisation and Comparative Law' 6 *Maastricht Journal of European and Comparative Law* 3, 217. See also, by the same author: *Globalization and Legal Theory* (London, Butterworths, 20000; 'The Province of Jurisprudence Re-examined', in Catherine Dauvergne (ed), *Jurisprudence for an Interconnected Globe* (Aldershot, Ashgate, 2003) 53.

[25] Walter van Gerven (1998) 'Mutual Permeation of Public and Private Law at the National and Supranational Level', *Maastricht Journal of European and Comparative Law* 1, 7.

[26] See, eg, Eric Agostini, *Droit comparé* (Paris, PUF, 1988), 310 ff.

[27] Koen Lenaerts (2001) 'Le droit comparé dans le travail du juge communautaire' *RTD européen*, July–September, 488.

in those solutions (which are often compromises between national mechanisms, or a common denominator thereof)[28], jointly called upon to ensure the application thereof (given the share falling to national law in the implementation of EU law), bound to accept each other reciprocally through the mechanisms of mutual recognition, etc.

In such circumstances, knowledge of other legal systems becomes politically and economically strategic. Other systems are, in effect, partner–rivals, the evolution of which must be monitored.

ii. Transforming Comparative Law Methods

It would appear that this transformation of the challenges faced by comparative law necessarily brings with it a transformation in its methods.

Comparative law has increasingly become an analysis of influences between legal systems. What is increasingly of capital importance is an understanding of how they are interlinked, or how phenomena of legal transplantation[29] or cross-fertilisation are produced—be it horizontally, or through an international system such as EU or ECHR law; in other words, how the many meeting points between legal systems, brought about by globalisation, unfold. Comparisons, in the traditional sense, must be powerfully combined with an examination of the various fluctuations of legal globalisation.

Correlatively, comparative law focuses its interest on competition between laws, between legal systems, between legal traditions. It is a matter of understanding by which avenues, by which precise channels, for example, common law acquired the significant places it now occupies in the globalisation of trade;[30] or the ways in which various legal traditions competed to inspire the private and public laws of former Eastern bloc states.

In the sphere of economic globalisation at least, an economic analysis of law provides tools here, which serve in evaluating the solutions furnished by various legal systems in this or that area, and particularly in terms of economic efficiency. There is a significant field of research in which an important place is occupied—for the time being—by studies showing that common law may be better adapted than other legal traditions to produce economically efficient rules.[31] This same field of research also encompasses the controversial World Bank 'Doing Business' reports.[32]

---

[28] Such as instances when the Court of Justice must remedy the damage caused by the Community, referring to those principles common to all Member States regarding extra-contractual liability: Article 288 of the Treaty.

[29] Ugo Mattei, *Comparative Law and Economics* (Ann Arbor, The University of Michigan Press, 2000) 123 ff.

[30] On this point, see all contributions to Ross-Harper, *Global Law in Practice* (n 13).

[31] See in particular the work of Mattei, *Comparative Law* (n 29) 147 ff.

[32] See above, chapter 3, 'B Competition between legal Systems—iii Consequences'.

The Community sphere has witnessed an already considerable development of analyses that may be termed 'omnicomparative', ie which compare solutions provided by European national laws, assess their respective influence on Community law or, conversely, the influence that the latter may have, the influence that each has on the others,[33] etc.

It may be added that in the age of legal globalisation, the task that may be fulfilled by comparative law is by no means insignificant—on the contrary, it is essential. Knowing the substance of legal systems, it is even better equipped to understand the ways in which they interact.

Comparative law may also contribute to the reflection on the complex regulations of the globalised world. This also includes the normative level, ie by making proposals as to what those regulations ought to be, the values that they ought to maintain (be they fundamental rights, values linked to the rule of law, or something else).

III. REGULATING LEGAL GLOBALISATION[34]

The issue discussed here is to be understood in the most straightforward sense. It concerns the question of whether, in its complex and apparently highly disordered configuration, legal globalisation encompasses regulation mechanisms, in the sense of mechanisms that—in the medium term, at least—maintain a level of coherence therein and are likely, in the event of a crisis, to re-establish balance in its structure and operation.

The reality would appear to be that legal globalisation is far from devoid of regulation. Having established this, we will then go on to consider the mechanisms that ensure that regulation.

A. Legal Globalisation is not Devoid of Regulation

An observation of globalisation readily gives the impression that where it is driving the legal sphere is extremely disordered and does not contain any credible regulation mechanisms. Normative processes are increasingly scattered, the capacity to create norms is granted to a growing number of highly varied players, institutions proliferate by taking on increasingly diverse forms, and the norms themselves take on unprecedented forms and content. As we have seen, all of this gives the sense of extreme fragmentation and a lack of discipline.

---

[33] Sophie Robin-Olivier and Daniel Fasquelle (eds), *Les échanges entre les droits, l'expérience communautaire. Une lecture des phénomènes de régionalisation et de mondialisation du droit* (Brussels, Bruylant, 2008).

[34] Jean-Bernard Auby (2008) 'Is Globalization Regulated? Memling and the Business of Baking Camels' 4 *Utrecht Law Review* 3.

As has been emphasised previously, at times some essential values of dem-ocratic legal systems would appear to be difficult to guarantee in a globalisa-tion context: the rule of law and legal certainty, in particular.

It even emerges that some of the key operations of legal techniques some-times become difficult in that context, in particular those that revolve around the allocation of acts and situations. Indeed, it sometimes becomes difficult to determine exactly who does what and on behalf of whom. European laws—both national and Community—had to determine on whose behalf national administrations act when they implement Community norms and policies. Under French law, for example, it was not until 1981[35] that the *Conseil d'Etat* clearly stated that national administrations, when devoted to the implementation of Community policies and law, do not for all that cease to act as national authorities. While this may now be fairly well defined in national and Community case law, the question of who is liable when dam-age is caused in the context of the national implementation of Community acts nevertheless raises significant practical problems.[36]

Equally, the WTO's various bodies had to decide whether states had acted on behalf of the EU when breaching WTO rules.[37] As is becoming increas-ingly common, where national military units take part in humanitarian operations and peacekeeping missions, for whom do their soldiers act? Who is liable when they cause or suffer damage? And to which courts, be they national or otherwise, should applications for compensation be made?[38]

And yet, legal globalisation does indeed appear to be regulated. It can simply be said that, were it pure anarchy, it would not have endured for several decades. However, the argument is above all that it appears capable of adapting to particularly delicate situations, which could cause crises that are fatal to legal globalisation. European law, which is at the crossroads of so many of globalisation's mechanisms and flows, has often displayed that capacity to maintain a balance under serious threat. With the assistance of the European Court of Human Rights in Strasbourg, the Court of Justice has succeeded in avoiding the looming conflict through the mechanism of the European Convention of Human Rights, by placing it high up in the hierarchy of the Community's norms, as one of the sources of its general principles of law. In *Yusuf* and *Kadi*, the General Court, then the Court of Justice, succeeded with a great deal of ingenuity in combining the respect that all international institutions owe to the Charter of the United Nations

---

[35] CE, 2 April 1981, *GIE Vipal*, Dalloz 1981-209, concl B Genevois.

[36] eg Guy Isaac, *Droit communautaire général*, 7th edn (Paris, Armand Colin, 1999) 280 ff.

[37] They replied in the positive: Panel Report, 15 March 2005, European Communities—Protection of Trademarks and Geographic Indication for Agricultural Products and Foodstuffs, WTO Doc, WT/DS174/R.

[38] The *Conseil d'Etat* found itself facing the same problem in 2007: Jean-Bernard Auby, 'La police, la PESC, le juge administratif'(2007) *Droit administratif* March, 3.

('the mother of all treaties'), with the principles of European law which require that all decisions made by EU authorities be subject to a minimum level of judicial review, even where these are quite simply the implementation of decisions made by UN bodies.[39]

Legal globalisation encompasses resources and mechanisms likely to allow it to manage any possible major inconsistencies. The question now is one of knowing precisely what those resources and mechanisms are.

B. Mechanisms for Regulating Legal Globalisation

On the subject of what the mechanisms for regulating legal globalisation are, several series of observations can be made.

i. New Mechanisms and Traditional Ones

It may be asserted, first of all, that legal globalisation is regulated through mechanisms that are, in part, new mechanisms and, in part, traditional mechanisms transformed by the context in which they operate.

Evidently, the tensions generated by legal globalisation often find their solution in some of the traditional means by which law is regulated in its international dimension since the emergence of the latter. If, suddenly, trade relations between two countries become strained owing to difficulties of a legal nature—which may relate, for instance, to the non-enforcement of court decisions that are transnational in scope—a solution will eventually be found at some point through traditional diplomatic avenues, in the form of a legal agreement. Cross-border co-operation between local authorities sometimes raises thorny legal issues, the solution to which is to be found in a combination of traditional devices under public international and private international law.

It must be understood, however, that these traditional means for settling difficulties arising from legal globalisation tend to be transformed by the context in which the latter places them. While many problems are now resolved through the traditional intergovernmental method, it is often through new configurations related to networks[40] or to comitology. A significant proportion of the regulation of legal globalisation is performed by international— intergovernmental—organisations; however, amongst their number, the leading roles are no longer played by global political organisations, but

---

[39] See above, chapter 1, The Contradictions and Limits of Legal Globalisation.

[40] Anne-Marie Slaughter, *A New World Order* (Princeton, NJ, Princeton University Press, 2004); Juan-Cruz Alli Aranguen, *Derecho administrativo y globalización* (Madrid, Thomson-Civitas, 2004) 351 ff.

rather by economic and regional bodies. Moreover, within international institutions, a significant share of the real power tends to be placed in the hands of bodies that are more of an administrative nature rather than more classic international political organisations.[41]

No one can deny that private international law plays a significant role in regulating legal globalisation—a point to which we shall return below. However, its substance would appear to be quite transformed by its growing significance. Not only does the corpus of laws, which is traditionally national, become increasingly international—and increasingly European-ised, in the corresponding sphere—but it would also appear that its very function is undergoing a similar transformation: where once it was designed to settle issues arising under private law, it has become a field in which national regulations compete with each other.[42]

Legal globalisation is also regulated by new means, or at least by mechanisms that contributed only very little to international regulation in the modern world.[43] An essential role is now played by national institutions, and particularly by national courts. An examination of national case law reveals just how frequently national courts have to apply international and European norms; thereby, they mechanically take on part of the regulation of legal globalisation.

Consideration must also be given to the existence of regulation provided outside the scope of state institutions, through those non-state entities with regulatory powers, which we have discussed on several occasions in this book. It is trite to say that the Internet is largely self-regulating, the discipline thereof being broadly ensured by operators themselves, through internal processes, as well as by ICANN which, as we know, is not a state entity.[44] We also know that non-state regulation is sometimes performed by non-state networks, illustrated, as we have seen, by the case of standardisation and the role played by the International Standardization Organization (ISO) in that field.[45]

ii. The Means of Regulating Globalisation

These classic-yet-transformed means for regulating legal globalisation can be described further around three thematic axes. Their unusualness lies in what they encompass in terms of regulatory operators, regulatory norms and regulatory processes.

---

[41] See above, chapter 4, 'II. The Development of New Legal Forms of International Governance under Globalisation'.

[42] Horatia Muir Watt (2003) 'Globalisation des marchés et économie politique du droit international privé' *Archives de philosophie du droit*, 47, 243.

[43] Gessner and Budak, *Emerging Legal Certainty* (n 4).

[44] See above, chapter 2, 'ICANN (Internet Corporation of Assigned Names and Numbers)'.

[45] As regards finance, see Dimitry Kingsford Smith,'Networks, Norms and the Nation State: Thoughts on Pluralism and Globalised Securities Regulation' in Dauvergne (n 24), 93.

a. Regulatory Operators

Two points must be made regarding operators in the regulation of legal globalisation. The part played by international institutions is undeniable but, as pointed out above, the main role is assigned nowadays both to major economic organisations (WTO, World Bank, IMF) which are at the very head of the regulatory system for legal globalisation although they obviously do not cover all aspects, and to regional bodies. In particular, the EU[46]—which, on its own level, is both an area for and an operator in globalisation—thus clearly emerges as a regulator of the latter because it both regulates flows in its sphere (striving to influence them in line with its own set of values), and takes on a constitutional function of legitimisation *vis-à-vis* globalisation by ensuring that, on its own sphere, public action—being multilevel by its very nature, complies with certain principles.

Undoubtedly the most interesting phenomenon is the growing roles played by the courts, which tend to be essential regulators of legal globalisation whereas their influence on international legal life was previously traditionally quite limited. This concerns international courts, which proliferate within international institutions,[47] and domestic courts, the influence of which (as we have highlighted above) in the practical implementation of international norms continues to grow. One especially important phenomenon here is *judicial dialogue*, ie the increasingly common practice on the part of national and international courts—and their judges, taken individually—of establishing a dialogue across national and institutional borders in order to compare their respective solutions; this practice naturally has a 'smoothing' effect on legal globalisation, the scope of which cannot be underestimated.

Judicial dialogue and legal globalisation

There is today constant expansion in the international dialogue between national and international courts. It is a dialogue that may be described as vertical (in the sense that it sometimes takes place between national and international courts—for example, the respective positions adopted by national courts, the European Court of Justice and the European Court of Human Rights on the issues that they are jointly called upon to settle) and horizontal (in the sense that it sometimes takes place between international courts, or between national courts inspired by their

---

[46] Jean-Bernard Auby, 'The EU and Global Administrative Law', in Patrick Birkinshaw and Mike Varney (eds), *The European Legal Order after Lisbon* (The Hague, Kluwer Law International, 2010) 57.

[47] José E Alvarez (2003) 'The New Dispute-Settlers: (Half) Truths and Consequences' *Texas International Law Journal* 38, 405.

counterparts. In the text cited below, Sophie Robin-Olivier mentions the House of Lords decisions in *Director General of Fair Trading v First National Bank* [2001] UKHL 52 and *Macfarlane & Another v Tayside Health Board* [1999] All ER (D) 1325, together with the French Court of Cassation's 2000 decision in *Perruche*.[48] It sometimes takes personal or corporate avenues—court associations, clubs, or periodic meetings between, for instance, constitutional judges—and institutional paths—use of other case law in proceedings or even in decisions.

Nevertheless, this dialogue does not come naturally, each court legitimately feeling that it is responsible for a unique legal corpus and that it should draw inspiration only from the will of those with the power to legislate thereon. The issue of whether it is acceptable is sometimes the subject of lively debate, the best example of which emerged in the USA where, following the decision in *Lawrence v Texas*[49]—a case in which the Supreme Court referred to ECHR case law—the House of Representatives passed a resolution in 2004 condemning the reference to foreign legal inspiration (except whether these could shed light on the 'original meaning' of American laws); the Supreme Court itself remains split on the subject.

Nonetheless, international dialogue between courts continues to develop inexorably. Two essential characteristics of legal globalisation contribute thereto: the growing interdependence between systems and the increasing fragmentation of rules. The combination of those factors makes it absolutely necessary for judges, as Sabino Cassese explains, to build bridges, to nurture connections that help the system hold together.

All in all, this leads to judges performing a sort of constitutional function in the global legal space, by identifying and disseminating common basic values and principles. Again, as Sabino Cassese points out, the process has its advantages and disadvantages. A global legal system developed by the courts necessarily remains incomplete and unequal. Conversely, the development of global law led by the courts is incremental and procedural, which is a fairly good gauge for flexibility and efficiency.

See: Julie Allard and Antoine Garapon, *Les juges dans la mondialisation. La nouvelle révolution du droit* (Paris, Le Seuil, 2005); Sabino Cassese, *La fonction constitutionnelle des juges non nationaux. De l'espace juridique global à l'ordre juridique global*, speech to the Court of Cassation (11 June 2007); by the same author: *Il diritto globale. Giustizia e democrazia oltre lo stato* (Milan, Einaudi, 2009); Jean-Paul Jacqué (2007) 'Droit constitutionnel national, droit communautaire,

---

[48] C Cass, Ass. plen, 17 November 2000, *Perruche*, Application no 99-13701.
[49] 539 US 558 (2003).

CEDH, Charte des Nations unies. L'instabilité des rapports entre ordres juridiques' *Revue française de droit constitutionnel*, 69; Charles Koch (2002) 'Judicial Review and Global Federalism' *Administrative Law Review* 54, 491; Fabrice Melleray (ed), *L'argument de droit comparé en droit administratif français* (Brussels, Bruylant, 2007); Sophie Robin-Olivier, 'La référence (non imposée) à d'autres droits par les juges des Etats membres de l'Union européenne' in Sophie Robin-Olivier and Daniel Fasquelle (eds), *Les échanges entre les droits, l'expérience communautaire* (Brussels, Bruylant, 2008), 141; Anne-Marie Slaughter (2003) 'A Global Community of Courts' *Harvard International Law Journal* 44, 141.

b. The Importance of Normative Links

The fragmentation of law-making and lawmakers under globalisation confers an especially crucial role to normative links, links between distinct legal corpuses that the same fragmentation keeps separate. Whence the particular importance of 'network nodes', as Jean-Paul Jacqué[50] describes them; whence the importance of these networks of norms, of these reciprocal connections between regulatory systems that can be identified through close examination in all sorts of areas, particularly those concerned by the theory of 'global administrative law';[51] whence the importance also of processes by which those who find themselves at the 'network nodes' of legal globalisation can reconcile the norms to which it gives rise in such varied spheres—the same processes and concepts that serve in making all sorts of trade-offs between norms, such as the principle of proportionality (some authors have established that it plays that same role in WTO law)[52] or the principle of consistent interpretation.[53]

c. A Multilevel Regulation

As regards the processes that it brings into play, it is accepted that the regulation of legal globalisation stands out primarily owing to the fact that it

---

[50] 'Droit constitutionnel national, droit communautaire, CEDH, Charte des Nations unies. L'instabilité des rapports entre ordres juridiques' (2007) *Revue française de droit constitutionnel* 69.

[51] Sabino Cassese (2007) 'Le droit administratif global: une introduction' *Droit administratif* May, 15.

[52] Mads Andenas and Stefan Zleptnig (2007) 'Proportionality and Balancing in WTO Law: A Comparative Study' 20 *Cambridge Review of International Affairs* 1, 71.

[53] Which leads, for instance, to the European Court of Human Rights accepting that the European Convention must be interpreted in line with other principles of international law, of which it is part: *Öcalan v Turkey*, Application no 46221/99, ECHR 2005-IV.

frequently mobilises several levels and multiple institutions. The regulation of globalisation is multilevel, as is legal globalisation itself.

This can be seen particularly if we focus on the issue of national or international judicial or quasi-judicial review of acts involving globalisation. Indeed, we discover that national and international mechanisms converge in order more frequently to submit public acts concerning international life to judicial or quasi-judicial review. Globalisation disperses the power of the law, but that diffuse power can be concentrated on certain targets.

The regulation of legal globalisation: the (national and international) review of (national and international) acts

Considering the crossover of the various levels and the interchangeability of functions under legal globalisation, one of the important questions raised by the regulation of legal globalisation is the extent to which situations where national or international acts relating to globalisation are subject to review by national or international authorities.

It would appear that the situation can be summed up according to the table below:

Review	International	National
National acts (concerning international relations)	International judicial or quasi-judicial authorities sometimes have the power to rule on national acts (European Court of Human Rights, European Court of Justice in the context of proceedings for failure to fulfil obligations but also, eg, the WTO Appellate Body on occasion). International commercial arbitrators must sometimes review the legality of state actions in light of international law (Emmanuel Gaillard, *La jurisprudence du CIRDI* (Paris, Pedone, 2004) 767).	Traditionally, the majority of national public acts concerning international relations fall outside the scope of the usual judicial review of public acts owing to theories such as that of government acts under French law, acts of state in the UK, and political questions in the USA. The current historical trend tends, however, to reduce the impact of those theories, either because some acts concerning international relations cease to be considered as falling with the scope thereof (eg extradition cases under French law) or through the concept of unconnected act (see Bolewski, cited below).
International acts	International institutions are rarely equipped with judicial or quasi-judicial mechanisms applicable to acts issued by their authorities. *Kadi* showed, for example, that no appeals may be brought against acts of the UN Security Council, even those likely to cause serious harm to private interests.	

Review	International	National
	As we know, there are exceptions, the most notable being that of the EU, whereby the acts of EU bodies can be referred to the Court of Justice.	In theory, national courts cannot rule on international acts. However, some constitutional courts reserve the right to rule on any potential breach of their constitution by the acts of international organisations: this is the case for Spain, Denmark and Ireland (see Peters, cited below). In 2000, the Bosnian Constitutional Court ruled that it had jurisdiction to review decisions made by the UN High Commissioner in Bosnia (see Kingsbury et al, below).

See: Stefano Battini, *Amministrazioni nazionali e controversie globale* (Milan, Giuffrè, 2007); Wilfried Bolewski, *Diplomacy and International Law in Globalized Relations* (Springer, 2007) 95 ff; Benedict Kingsbury, Nico Krisch, Richard Stewart and Jonathan Wiener (special eds) (2005) *The Emergence of Global Administrative Law, Law and Contemporary Problems*, 68, 3–4; Anne Peters, 'The Globalization of State Constitutions' in Janne Nijman and André Nollkaemper (eds), *New Perspectives on the Divide Between National and International Law* (Oxford, Oxford University Press, 2007) 251.

IV. THEORIES ON THE GENERAL OPERATION OF GLOBAL LAW

In light of the elements above, this section will give an overview of two of the main theories put forward to describe the general operation of legal globalisation and the global law to which it gradually gives rise. We will present them briefly, as the scope of this book does not allow for much in-depth discussion. These theories centre on two complementary concepts: the global legal space and global law can be described as marked by a pluralist structure and operating in a network.

A. Pluralism in the Structure

From a structural perspective, everything indicates that legal globalisation may be understood in terms of its overall logic only by borrowing from one or other of the theories of legal pluralism.

i. Conceptions of Pluralism

We say one or other of the theories as there is no one conception of legal pluralism.[54] The associated theories share a common trait in that they tend, as Charles Leben puts it, to accept 'the existence of sub-state or trans-state (also described as transnational) legal orders that are established on the fringe of States'.[55] Another way of expressing the same notion is to say that we can speak of legal pluralism where two or more legal systems co-exist in the same social field.[56]

Roughly speaking, there are three types of legal pluralism, each of which is based on a different explanation for the existence of such pluralism.

The basis of legal pluralism may be normative: in this hypothesis, the independence of partial or transnational legal orders will be the result of whether it is accepted, favoured or tolerated by the state order. Charles Leben[57] shows that such a pluralist view can even be accepted in Kelsenian theory.

The basis for legal pluralism may be institutional: in this hypothesis, institutions are held to constitute legal orders as and of themselves, as encompassing partial legal orders by their very nature; pluralism is quite simply born out of the plurality of institutions. This is the view taken by Santi Romano,[58] the best-known theoretician in the field of legal pluralism. In truth, the intuition could already be seen in the writings of Maurice Hauriou, to whom Romano pays homage whilst differing therefrom through a broader conception of institutions.[59]

Lastly, the basis for legal pluralism may be sociological: in this hypothesis, pluralism arises from the legal practices of specific social groups that have forged—or retained, despite their inclusion in a state whole—particular ways of organising their legal relations. This approach to legal pluralism was developed by Georges Gurvitch in his *L'idée du droit social*, published in 1932.[60]

---

[54] A table is provided by Jean-Guy Belley in André-Jean Arnaud (ed), *Dictionnaire encyclopédique de théorie et de sociologie du droit* (Paris, LGDJ, 1993), V Pluralisme juridique.

[55] Charles Leben (2001) 'De quelques doctrines de l'ordre juridique' 33, 19.

[56] Sally Engle Merry (1998) 'Legal Pluralism', *Law and Society Review* 22, 869.

[57] Leben (2001) 'De quelques doctrines de l'ordre juridique' (n 55).

[58] Santi Romano, *L'ordre juridique* (Dalloz, 2002).

[59] ibid, 21 ff.

[60] *L'idée du droit social* (Paris, Sirey, 1932)

ii. Pluralism in the Global Legal Space and Global Law

Resorting to theories of pluralism is essential to set out precisely the structure of the global legal space and global law.[61]

One of the most obvious and compelling aspects of legal globalisation is a 'proliferation of sources of juridicality', to paraphrase Antoine Garapon.[62] As we have seen, these sources of juridicality sometimes develop quite independently of states—although ties between the two are never completely severed—if only because various forms of 'self-regulation' need to be able to rely on the state's enforcement powers.

It is clear that pluralist theories are particularly well suited to accounting for this situation. Indeed, this has already been argued by various authors, including Gunther Teubner[63] and William Twining.[64]

Which type of pluralist theory is especially adapted to shed light on legal globalisation?

The form of pluralism advocated by Santi Romano is no more than a key to the institutionalist perspective: indeed, the legal ties that fuel the globalisation of law are as broadly inter-institutional and lateral as they are related to the internal legal operation of institutions. However, there is a great deal to be drawn, in order to shed light on the operation of the global legal space, from the examinations developed by Romano regarding links of 'relevance' that may connect partial legal orders. A conception of legal pluralism can only be defended if it also sheds light on the links between the plural legal orders that it identifies, and this is key to the line of thought developed by Santi Romano in *L'ordre juridique*.

Legal pluralism under globalisation may also be viewed as normative pluralism. It has developed on the basis—be it direct or tacit—of state consent to plurality, as long as 'transnational orders can exist as a last resort, only because states accept, foster, tolerate or even are unaware of their existence';[65] it is a pluralism that, at the very least, is merely tolerated.

It is undoubtedly and above all a sociological pluralism. It is driven only formally by the will of states; what truly drives it is the existence and density of transnational economic, social and cultural ties which continue to grow day by day in the modern world, and the plurality of players and normative processes that are woven into the corresponding social, economic and political fabric. Gunther Teubner describes it as 'the emergence of a multiplicity

---

[61] Gavin Anderson, *Constitutional Rights after Globalization* (Oxford, Hart Publishing, 2005) 44 ff.

[62] In Pierre Bouretz (ed), *La force du droit. Panorama des débats contemporains* (Paris, Editions Esprit, 1991), 222.

[63] 'Global Bukowina: Legal Pluralism in World Society' in Gunther Teubner (ed), *Global Law without a State*, (Aldershot, Dartmouth, 1997) 3.

[64] William Twining, *Globalization and Legal Theory* (London, Butterworths, 2000).

[65] Leben (2001) 'De quelques doctrines de l'ordre juridique' (n 55).

of civil constitutions gradually born out of the constitutionalisation of a multiplicity of independent sub-systems within global society'.[66]

B. Operating in a Network

Pluralism, the existence of multiple sources of juridicality that often enjoy a great deal of autonomy, is not the only fundamental aspect by which the global legal space and global law may be described.

Another is that of operating in a network. Global law and the global legal space would appear to function typically in the fashion that is characteristic of modern law, as François Ost and Michel van der Kerchove have theorised[67] They explain that modern law is no longer organised according to the classic pyramidal model—according to the 'Jupiterian' model—but rather according to that of the network—the 'Hermes'[68] model—that is characterised in particular by the multiplicity of legal players, the imbrication of legal spaces and functions, the multiplication and flattening of power hierarchies.

This view is especially useful in understanding the operation of globalising law.

There is no need to embark on another examination of the multiplicity of players under a law which constantly causes internal and external, public and private players, democratically vested or otherwise, to interact.

The imbrication of legal spaces and functions is also inherent to globalisation: not only do the realities therein transcend borders and often ignore the distinction between domestic and international, but also where regulations are often furnished by complexes of mechanisms involving both private and public players, national and international, in an often disconcerting distribution of roles.

The flattening of power hierarchies and, correlatively, of normative architectures, are one of the most remarkable attributes of legal globalisation. We have seen how public spheres tend to be linked according to the flattened hierarchies of multi-layered governance. We have seen the extent to which the hierarchy of norms is affected by the uncertainties of global law.[69]

Globalisation's legal operation is assuredly not pyramidal; rather, it is an operation in a network. Relations based on mutual legitimisation have

---

[66] 'Societal Constitutionalism: Alternatives to State-Centred Constitutional Theory', in Christian Joerges, Inger-Johanne Sand and Gunther Teubner (eds), *Transnational Governance and Constitutionalism* (Oxford, Hart Publishing, 2004) 3.

[67] *De la pyramide au réseau. Pour un théorie dialectique du droit*, Bruxelles, Publications des Facultés Universitaires Saint-Louis, 2002.

[68] François Ost, 'Jupiter, Hercule, Hermès: trois modèles du juge', in Pierre Bouretz (ed), *La force du droit. Panorama des débats contemporains* (Editions Esprit, 1991)—see conclusion.

[69] See above, chapter 3, 'Relations between Norms under Legal Globalisation: Models of the "Double Mirror Effect"'.

come to replace hierarchical relations; it is only in these terms that relations between the European treaties and Member State constitutions, for example, can realistically be read.[70] In additional, with horizontal legal relations being developed powerfully across national borders, and in circumstances over which states—the vertical lines of the pyramid—have less and less control, a circular network operation is becoming the mode of being for legal relations seized upon by globalisation.

This operation in a network has as a corollary an interpenetration of legal systems that is not without its difficulties. Ultimately, it may indeed blur the identity of those legal systems, complicate the process of imputation itself, as has been highlighted. It is easier to take snapshots of a pyramid than a network, but it appears to describe the various strands that make up the fabric of legal globalisation.

---

[70] As is accepted in theories of multilevel constitutionalism, or the 'new constitutionalism': Sabino Cassese, *La crisi dello Stato*, (Bari, Editori Laterza, 2002), 67 ff; Ingulf Pernice (1999) 'Multilevel Constitutionalism and the Treaty of Amsterdam: European Constitution-Making Revisited' *Common Market Law Review*, 703.

6

The Structure of the Global Law Under Construction

SOMETHING AKIN TO a global law is being built on the various foundations discussed in preceding chapters: a fabric of legal relations, institutions and norms which do not fit into the more classic frameworks, and which make up the legal operation of that interconnected (vertically and horizontally) set of state, inter-state, non-state players; this is the world engaged in the globalisation process.

We do not yet know a great deal about this global law under construction. More exactly, we have only begun to be familiar with how it is constructed; we still know relatively little about the end product or what the stable form of what is currently developing will be.

We can, however, put forward a number of theories. The next chapter will hazard several on the substance of global law. This chapter will seek to mention other, more structural ones, simply by wondering—if we may call it that, as it is easy to ask questions; answers are harder to come by—about what happens to the distinction between international law and domestic law (see 'I Globalisation and the Distinction between International Law and Domestic Law'), and the public–private divide (see 'II Globalisation and the Public–Private Divide') in the globalisation process.

I. GLOBALISATION AND THE DISTINCTION BETWEEN INTERNATIONAL LAW AND DOMESTIC LAW

The developments mentioned above have already allowed us to identify a number of symptoms of globalisation's effects in transforming the relationship between international law and domestic law.

This transformation would appear to be quite significant, but complex in terms of meaning and content. Here are some avenues for further reflexion, derived from the notion that legal globalisation affects not only the functional relations between the two spheres, but also their conceptual relationship.

A. Changes in Functional Relations

i. Interpenetration

The most obvious change is the fact that significant trends affect the functional relations between international law and domestic law.

What is at issue here is the clear and growing interpenetration of the two spheres.[1]

International norms increasingly and more readily penetrate national legal systems—and indeed to such an extent that, as Denis Alland points out, they can be 'applied within a domestic legal system to situations that present no international aspect other than (their) own intervention'.[2] We have already seen examples of this phenomenon in the context of public contracts, for example.[3]

Conversely, in their very content, international norms relate increasingly to domestic issues: issues of taxation law, administrative law, even constitutional law.

This is true of treaties, a growing number of which are concerned with this kind of issue—one example being international law-making on environmental matters—but it is also true on various other levels of international law-making. For instance, international judicial or quasi-judicial bodies commonly have to examine situations typical of domestic administrative law, as was the case for the World Bank's Inspection Panel in the 'Mumbai Urban Transport Project' case.[4]

ii. Allocation of Roles

What would also appear to be transformed correlatively is the allocation of roles between international law and domestic law in regulating international society.

That said, things are not as straightforward here as they seem at first glance. The most glaringly obvious is the various signs from all sides that a growing number of legal relationships are regulated by international norms where once they were governed by domestic law.

---

[1] Giuliana Ziccardi Capaldo, *The Pillars of Global Law* (Aldershot, Ashgate, 2008) 171 ff; Walter van Gerven (1998) 'Mutual Permeation of Public and Private Law at the National and Supranational Level', *Maastricht Journal of European and Comparative Law* 1, 7.

[2] Denis Alland (2000) *Droit international public* (Paris, PUF, coll 'Droit fondamental', 2000), 19.

[3] See above, chapter 2, 'C. Public Contract Law' ff.

[4] 21 December 2005, report no 34725: in this case, the Inspection Panel had to examine claims concerning a local project, supported by the World Bank, to restructure public transport.

For example, the classic issues of conflicts of laws and courts raised by private 'international' law—which are, as we know, traditionally settled by stances adopted by national laws—are increasingly resolved by rules set down in international agreements, such as the 1968 Brussels Convention on jurisdiction and the enforcement of judgments in civil and commercial matters, or the 1980 Rome Convention on the law applicable to contractual obligations.[5]

The same trend can be seen in the case of state contracts: as we have noted above, the rules applicable to those contracts are increasingly determined by multilateral agreements or bilateral investment treaties, where once they were traditionally immersed in the law of the host state.[6]

Nevertheless, conversely, it is in seeking to harmonise domestic laws—in relying on domestic laws—that the globalisation of law often operates. As we have seen previously, it is mainly through national laws that international regulation is instituted with regard to financial markets, for instance, or the Internet. It is mainly through national laws, and particularly through domestic courts, that international human rights law has found an avenue for its practical implementation.[7] A further example may be added: the fight against money laundering. The international fight against money laundering was structured around principles jointly set down in 1985 during a Congress held by the United Nations and, in 1988, at a meeting of the Basel Committee which, as we have seen, brings together the governors of the various leading central banks. However, those guidelines were made enforceable through national legislations, harmonised with regard to money laundering and banking supervision.[8]

There are evidently new conjunctions in the relations between international law and domestic law, cases where the traditional roles have been reversed; a sort of unprecedented intermingling between the two.

Developments in the allocation of roles between international law and domestic law

The developments in the allocation of roles between international and domestic law, as described here, can be summarised by using the concept of relevance, so dear to Santi Romano.

---

[5] Aside from the references above, see Pierre Mayer, *Droit international privé*, 6th edn (Paris, Montchrestien, 1998), 15 ff.

[6] See Prosper Weil, 'L'Etat, l'investisseur étranger et le droit international: la relation désormais apaisée d'un ménage à trois' in *Liber Amicorum Ibrahim F.I. Shihata* (The Hague, Kluwer Law International, 2000), reproduced in Prosper Weil, *Ecrits de droit international* (Paris, PUF 2000) 64 ff.

[7] Harold Hongju Koh (1999) 'How is International Human Rights Law Enforced?' *Indiana Law Journal* 34, 1397.

[8] Jarrod Wiener, *Globalization and the Harmonization of Law* (London and New York, Pinter, 1999).

The point to remember here is that international law has become increasingly relevant on a national level, while national law has become increasingly relevant in the international sphere.

National relevance of international law	International law increasingly regulates domestic situations.	International law increasingly regulates relationships between national systems.
International relevance of national law	The main aspects of the application of international law are performed by domestic legal mechanisms.	Situations in which national laws produce extraterritorial effects continue to proliferate (see chapter 1, 'Extraterritoriality in a context of legal globalisation' above). Conflict of laws rules tend to apply to situations governed by public law (see below, this chapter, 'A Symptoms of a Loss of Meaning').

See Stefano Battini (2006) 'The Globalization of Public Law' 18 *European Review of Public Law*, 1, 27; Paul Schiff Berman (ed), *The Globalization of International Law* (Aldershot, Ashgate, 2005), Introduction; Slim Laghani, 'Droit international et droits internes: vers un renouveau du *jus gentium*?' in Rafâa Ben Achour and Slim Laghmani (eds), *Droit international et droit interne. Développements récents* (Paris, Pedone, 1998) 23; Horatia Muir Watt (2003) 'Globalisation des marchés et économie politique du droit international privé', *Archives de Philosophie du Droit* 47, 243.

There is, moreover, a sense that these overlaps can only lead to uncertainty in the conceptual relationships between the two spheres.

B. Changes in Conceptual Relations

i. Blurring Distinctions

It is quite apparent that the clear-cut distinction between international law and domestic law has been altered.

As we have seen, the theoretical guarantee on sovereignty and home affairs afforded by Article 2(7) of the UN Charter no longer prevents purely internal political events from being considered as being international affairs: where human rights breaches reach a particular gravity threshold, the United

Nations tends to consider that the matter ceases to be an internal one.[9] As one political scientist puts it, the dividing line between internal and external affairs is increasingly blurred.[10]

In a register similar to that of human rights, as Frédéric Sudre points out,[11] there comes a point where there is a genuine 'denial of the theory of two spheres on which classic international law was built'. When a domestic court applies Article 6(1) of the European Convention on Human Rights, is it applying international law or domestic law? It is impossible to tell anymore.

EU law is naturally the ultimate illustration of the changes in the above distinction. International law by its origins, it is now fully part of domestic laws; the distinction between international and domestic law is practically cancelled out.[12]

ii. Respective Maturity

A more in-depth reflection on the conceptual relations between international law and domestic law leads to a further line of questioning.

Up until now, there existed a certain stereotypical relationship between international and domestic law, which viewed the former as being in a sort of state of infancy, of immaturity, waiting for its accession to the status of legal system, embodied in theory by domestic law.

Can these respective images endure in a context of legal globalisation? It is uncertain if only because, in its more advanced forms—EU law, ECHR law, etc—international law proves to be suited to governing extremely complex situations, where state legal systems often struggle to master the complexity of the societies for which they are responsible.

Globalisation appears here to contribute to developments in the relations between different models, even a reversal of paradigms.

II. GLOBALISATION AND THE PUBLIC–PRIVATE DIVIDE[13]

Let us look now at how to comprehend the consequences that may be brought about by globalisation as regards the distinction between public law and private law.

---

[9] Gérard Cohen-Jonathan, 'Droits et devoirs internationaux des individus', in Denis Alland (ed), *Droit international public* (Paris, PUF, 2000).

[10] Philippe Moreau Defarges, *L'ordre mondial* (Paris, Armand Colin, 2000) 155.

[11] Frédéric Sudre, *Droit international et européen des droits de l'homme*, 9th edn (Paris, PUF, 2008) 43.

[12] Société française pour le Droit international, *Droit international et droit communautaire. Perspectives actuelles* (Paris, Pedone, 2000) 108 ff.

[13] Jean-Bernard Auby, 'Three Questions Concerning the Public–Private Divide in Legal Globalization', report to the Law of the Future Conference, The Hague, 8–9 October 2009.

There are various avenues that may be followed. While, in some respects, the law of globalisation contributes to a loss of relevance of this divide, it is more likely that, in the end, it causes a shift in meaning. This then raises the question of which roles are played by public law and private law respectively in the current structure of legal globalisation.

A. Symptoms of a Loss of Meaning

i. A Distinction Contested in Some Traditions

Various reasons could lead us to believe that the legal world under globalisation is not particularly open to the divide between public law and private law.

Globalisation sparks an intermingling of legal cultures, in which Anglo-American legal culture is increasingly influential, at least in the field of economic relations. As is well known, since the writings of William Dicey in the second half of the twentieth century, common law has displayed a marked reticence with regard to that divide.[14] In the modern era, it is less systematically hostile to that same divide than is generally believed by continental lawyers: the House of Lords has expressly relied on it in a number of famous decisions.[15] It nevertheless remains reluctant; in any event, where the divide is used, in the modern era, by Anglo-American lawyers, it is either for purely didactic purposes—administrative law or constitutional law will be classed under public law, without that classification carrying any legal consequences—or specific judicial review mechanisms. It goes no further, and the idea that there may be a public law of contract or a law of public assets, etc, is not accepted. It is generally from the perspective of a lack of differentiation between public law and private law that the common law presents itself in the face of legal globalisation and exerts its own influence therein.

Under EU law, as has been noted on numerous occasions, the separation of public and private law is not enshrined anywhere; nor is it under WTO law, etc.

ii. State Law Tends to Be Less Specific

To this may be added regular signs that, in the globalised world, state-made law tends all too easily to be unimaginative. The decline of sovereignty,

---

[14] John Allison, *A Continental Distinction in the Common Law. A Historical and Comparative Perspective on English Public Law* (Oxford, Clarendon Press, 1996); Dawn Oliver, *Common Values and the Public–Private Divide* (London, Butterworths, 1999).

[15] Particularly in *O'Reilly v Mackman* [1983] 2 AC 237.

and therefore of the state's specific legal essence, naturally acts in that way, but there are also other very practical avenues, such as the decline of state immunities; and that fact that states more readily agree to submit to international arbitration. As we have seen, the consequences of such agreement is all the greater as international arbitrators are reluctant to apply rules specific to public law when examining State contracts.[16]

iii. The Allocation of Roles Between Public and Private Actors
Becomes More Complex

Ultimately, the changes wrought by globalisation on the role of the state and its law, the transformations that it imposes on the architecture of public spheres, the important role that it allows to be played by various non-state entities, and the uncertainty that is now part of the distinction between public and private entities,[17] are such that what is currently under construction is difficult to read in terms of the public–private divide.

The distinction between public international law and private international law is also increasingly blurred. Traditionally, it is based on a distinction between subjects: public international law governs relationships between states—not to mention international organisations—while private international law governs relations between private individuals and legal persons where those relations involve a foreign element.[18] In the context of the globalisation of law, private individuals and legal persons are increasingly the intended recipients of rules of public international law, which recognises rights that they can assert directly. Conversely, as we have recalled previously, legal relations involving states—contractual relations in any event—tend to be increasingly drawn to private international law.[19]

B. A Shift in Meaning?

In spite of the various elements above, it can be argued that, in reality, the public–private divide has not lost its relevance. Rather, a kind of shift in meaning affects it and will continue to do so.

---

[16] See above, chapter 2, 'Lessons to be drawn from the globalisation of public contract law' and Gérard Marcou, 'La sentence arbitrale relative à la convention d'utilisation du tunnel sous la Manche par la SNCF et British Rail' (*AFDI*, 1997).

[17] Sabino Cassese even talks of a public-private bipolarism: *La crisi dello stato* (Bari, Editori Laterza, 2000) 130. See also Claire Cutler, *Private Power and Global Authority* (Oxford, Oxford University Press, 2003).

[18] Patrick Daillier and Alain Pellet, *Droit international public*, 6th edn (Paris, LGDJ, 1999) 36; Pierre Mayer, *Droit international privé*, 6th edn (Paris, Montchrestien, 1998) 4 ff.

[19] Paul Schiff Berman (ed), *The Globalization of International Law*: '*conflicts law and international business transactions have become a staple of state-to-state relations*' (Aldershot, Ashgate, 2005), Introduction.

i. Globalisation Sometimes Increases the Specificity of
Public Legal Relations

First of all, it would be wrong to believe that, while it influences domestic laws, globalising law always tends to result in the trivialisation of public law.

Indeed, it can on the contrary render public legal relations subject to special rules.

Thus, EU law has compelled states to submit public procurement to special rules where traditionally public contracts are considered as being purely and simply governed by ordinary law; one German author, for instance, explains how, on its own terms, EU public procurement law has 'publicised' German law in the same field.[20]

In the same vein, the transposition of the European Convention on Human Rights into English law by the Human Rights Act 1998 has essentially resulted in the enhancement of judicial review, a strengthening of specific forms of judicial oversight of the administration.[21]

To this we may add a collection of symptoms indicating that international law itself tends to be 'publicised'. We have already noted a number of instances thereof with regard to private international law.[22] However, the same may be argued for public international law on the following grounds. Traditionally, it is a co-ordinating law—between states—and not a law that by its essence is intended to serve the public interest; in that sense, it resembles private law on the national plane. While it is now increasingly influenced by public interest concerns, it often becomes a guardian of the greater good, creator of public goods; in that sense it is closer to public law on the national plane.[23]

ii. Global Law Sometimes Fully Embraces the Divide

We must understand, moreover, that while they sometimes undermine the concept of a state-specific law, there are others instances in which globalisation's norms themselves fully accept that same concept and are involved in its implementation.

---

[20] Peter Huber (2001) 'The Europeanization of Public Procurement in Germany' 7 *European Public Law* 1, 33.

[21] Paul Craig, 'The Impact of Community Law on Public Law', in Peter Leylands and Terry Woods, *Administrative Law Facing the Future: Old Constraints and New Horizons* (Oxford, Blackstone, 1999) 552 ff.

[22] See Horatia Muir Watt (1997), 'Droit public et droit privé dans les rapports internationaux (vers la publicisation des conflits des lois)' *Archives de philosophie du droit* 41, 207.

[23] See above, chapter 4, 'Defining "Public Affairs" and the General Interest under Legal Globalisation' and Capaldo, *Pillars* (n 1) 48 ff.

As has been identified above on a number of occasions, the majority of the legal mechanisms structuring economic globalisation or the globalisation of human rights protection, consent here and there to exceptions to the rules that they set down, where certain public realities demand it.

For example, WTO law and EU law both accept the mitigation of various rules where the following are concerned: public health, public order, public authority, general interest services, etc.

The same applies in the field of human rights. Wherever they proclaim a given right, all the major international protection mechanisms contain the same kind of acceptance that, under certain circumstances, the right will be restricted in the face of public order or public health concerns, for instance. They sometimes accept that this or that right ends at the threshold of the realities of public authority. This is the case, for example, of the right to a fair trial, guaranteed by Article 6 of the European Convention on Human Rights, which stumbles in the face of proceedings concerning political asylum, or civil servants involved in the exercise of public authority; as Frédéric Sudre points out, a distinction is made between '*jus imperii* and *jus gestionis*' in the application of Article 6 to public bodies.[24]

As has already been suggested, the most interesting aspect is not only the fact that these various legal mechanisms accept the notion of a special legal status where 'public affairs' are concerned in different forms. It also lays in that fact that, having seized upon it, they have a say in its definition. As, generally, it tends to attach specific legal consequences only to nodal public realities, the most regalian public concerns, it may even be a 'redefinition' for those legal traditions in which the scope of public law is especially broad. Globalising law thus contributes, in its own way, to a kind of re-creation of public law.

C. The Respective Shares of Public Law and Private Law in Structuring Global Law

Next, the question may be asked as to what is—and what ought to be in future—the respective share of public law and private law in the management of the globalised legal sphere.

The initial impression is that private law is relentlessly gaining ground. International standardisation has increasingly followed the various pathways of private law.[25] The development of international arbitration is heading, as

---

[24] Frédéric Sudre (2001) 'A propos du dynamisme interprétatif de la Cour européenne des droits de l'homme' 1 *JCP* 335.

[25] See Katia Boustany and Normend Halder, 'Mondialisation et mutations normatives: quelques réflexions en droit international', in François Crépeau (ed), *Mondialisation des échanges et fonctions de l'Etat* (Brussels, Bruylant, 1997) 41.

we have seen, in the same direction. Legal harmonisation, which has set-tled a number of issues and particularly under economic globalisation, is brought about by means of national laws private law rules (commercial, civil, etc): we are moving 'from public to private governance', according to Jarrod Wiener.[26] Private international law plays a growing regulatory role: specifically, it is becoming a sort of constitutional law for global private governance systems, as Gunter Teubner writes.[27]

Nevertheless, aside from the trend (which must be recalled here) towards the 'publicisation' of private international law,[28] it is clear that many deter-mining aspects of legal globalisation are regulated by public law mecha-nisms: through inter-governmental institutions, or classic international treaties, or judicial techniques clearly drawn from public law (constitution-ality review, judicial review of the lawfulness of administrative decisions), or implementation methods that are undoubtedly part of the public law arsenal (use of state coercion). Ultimately, if one asks whether it is through public law or private law processes that those areas that strike us as being the essential sectors of legal globalisation—trade, the environment, human rights, national governance[29]—one is clearly forced to conclude that public law plays a leading role; this holds true for international trade, which is by its essence the one amongst those various sectors which is most strikingly self-regulating.

On a different note, let us look at another example by asking what are cur-rently the essential driving forces behind the EU legal construct. Although the latter now concerns itself with private law mechanisms on which its development depends—the development of rules under private interna-tional law made by the EU legislature, the quest to harmonise civil law concepts, etc—these mechanisms play only a limited role in the legal edi-fice which, all told, is essentially composed of constitutional law (in terms of substantive principles, the organisation of European powers and their relations with national powers) and administrative law. Within the mass of legal mechanisms that make up the European construct, those contributing to the implementation of legislative norms play an increasingly important role—and administrative law measures twice over: on the one hand, on the

---

[26] Wiener, *Globalization* (n 8) 20; in the field of intellectual property: Graeme Dinwoodic (2001) 'The Development and Incorporation of International Norms in the Formation of Cop-yright Law' *Ohio State Law Journal* 62, 733.

[27] Gunter Teubner (2000) 'Contracting Worlds: The Many Autonomies of Private Law' 9 *Social & Legal Studies* 3, 399. See also: Robert Wai (2002) 'Transnational Liftoff and Juridical Touchdowns. The Regulatory Function of Private International Law in an Era of Globaliza-tion' 40 *Columbia J Transnational Law*, 209.

[28] And of international arbitration, in which public interest concerns—the environment, for example—now have a place: Julie Allard and Antoine Garapon, *Les juges dans la mondialisa-tion* (Paris, Le Seuil, 2005) 22 ff.

[29] See above, chapter 2, 'The Key Areas of Legal Globalisation' ff.

side of EU law, the proportion of which that may be deemed as composed of administrative law is constantly expanding; and, on the other hand, on the side of domestic laws, within which the implementation of EU law is broadly ensured by administrative laws. Indeed, their common contribution to that task drives their convergence. As Mario Chiti contends, the EU is a community founded on administrative law.[30]

The notion that globalisation leads to a privatisation of the legal relations that it concerns, and therefore works towards a privatisation of international—or rather, transnational—legal relations, is thus false; as false as that (to which the latter idea is often linked) which equates globalisation with the globalisation of trade.

---

[30] *Diritto amministrativo europeo*, 3rd edition (Milan, Giuffrè, 2008), 105 ff.

7

The Implications of Globalisation for Public Law

THIS FINAL CHAPTER will strive to offer up a number of complementary comments on what is becoming public law under globalisation. What does this law—which is the law of the state, traditionally the organiser of public spheres and the principal regulator of relations between legal systems—become in the globalisation process, and in which ways do its various parts develop?[1] We will have to return to this question, as it is related to what may be the essential structures of law under globalisation.

The first section of this chapter will look at the implications of globalisation for public international law; the second, at the implications of globalisation for national public law; and the third, the influence of globalisation on relations between national public laws.

I. THE IMPLICATIONS OF GLOBALISATION FOR PUBLIC INTERNATIONAL LAW

We previously examined this issue[2] when we looked at the extent to which globalisation transforms the functional and conceptual relations between international law and domestic law, and in such a way that the distinction is both eroded and transformed in the global legal sphere.

The comments that we wish to add here are centred around two concepts. The first is that, even transformed—and, to a certain extent, *because* it is transformed—international law makes a significant contribution to globalisation. However, the price of that contribution is a change in its nature. This explains why jurisprudential works on theoretical renewal are now produced in this field.

---

[1] Jean-Bernard Auby, 'Globalisation et droit public' in *Mélanges offerts à Jean Waline, Gouverner. Administrer, Juger* (Paris, Dalloz, 2002) 135.

[2] See chapter 6, 'I. Globalisation and the Distinction between International Law and Domestic Law'.

A. Contributions to Legal Globalisation Processes

Ultimately, we cannot ignore the fact that public international law provides globalisation with a considerable proportion of its legal 'arsenal'—and this within certain confines, as we shall discuss.

i. International Organisations

The vast majority of international organisations derive from public international law; they are the instruments of the various openings that characterise globalisation.

This is true of economic globalisation. Public international law provides the latter with its global frameworks: the World Trade Organisation, the International Monetary Fund, the World Bank... It establishes globalisation's regional vectors, with regional economic integration in Europe, the Americas and South-East Asia.[3]

Equally, public international law provides non-economic globalisation— and particularly with regard to human rights protection—with tools in the form of various institutions which are simples forums, or centres of law-making, or seats for protective mechanisms (judicial or otherwise), as the case may be. Without going into too much detail here, mention must be made of a spectrum that ranges from the UN Human Rights Commission, to the Council of Europe and the Organisation of American States.[4]

ii. The Legal Technology of Public International Law

Public international law does not merely offer globalisation a number of institutional 'niches'. It also furnishes a significant proportion of its legal technology—which globalisation has, moreover, often pushed to be improved; the relationship is, in part, reciprocal.

The main economic treaties that public international law has produced, on both a global and a regional level, have placed legal techniques at the service of the opening-up of markets, techniques which have proved of decisive importance and which we have come across throughout this book: national treatment clauses, mutual recognition, etc.

In similar fashion, the main treaties have furnished the globalisation of human rights with its own unusual techniques which are specifically founded, as we know, on the possibility afforded to individuals of accessing

---

[3] See, eg, Dominique Carreau and Patrick Julliard, *Droit international économique*, 4th edn (Paris, LGDJ, 1998). See also above, chapter 1, 'iii Regional Integration and Globalisation'.

[4] See, eg, Frédéric Sudre, *Droit international et européen des droits de l'homme*, 9th edn (Paris, PUF, 2008).

international protection mechanisms, including those that are judicial in nature. We must also take into account the fact that, as in other contexts of economic integration, direct effect is sometimes aligned with international norms.[5]

iii. Competitors

Without over-emphasising the point, it must nevertheless be reiterated that public international law is not alone in fuelling the underlying architecture of legal globalisation.[6] It shares that function, on the international plane, with private international law and private—or partly private—schemes related to the leading role now played by a number of non-state entities. The same function is also shared with national legal systems, on which the practical implementation of global norms depends so heavily.

B. Transformation in the Very Nature of Public International Law?

The developments briefly mentioned above, together with those discussed in chapter 6, necessarily give rise to the question as to whether the very nature of public international law is undergoing radical change. The arguments hinting at this primarily concern the fact that its purpose and the scope of its subjects have been altered.[7]

i. A Shift in Purpose

Globalisation tends to alter the very purpose of public international law; the target of the rules that it produces.

This purpose and target consist less and less exclusively in the regulation of relations between states for the preservation of peace and development, and more and more in the position of citizens, businesses and other private organisations, for the sake of protecting their rights *vis à vis* states.

Other concerns, such as guaranteeing businesses the opportunity to trade together with the security of their investments, and protecting the human rights of private individuals and groups, play an increasingly significant part in public international law.

---

[5] On this, see, eg, the work of Frédéric Sudre *Droit international* (n 4).

[6] William Twining, 'The Province of Jurisprudence Re-examined' in Catherine Dauvergne (ed), *Jurisprudence for an Interconnected Globe* (Aldershot, Ashgate, 2003) 13.

[7] *cf*, eg, David J Bederman (2007–2008) 'Diversity and Permeability in Transnational Governance', 57 *Emory Law Journal* 201; *Globalization and International Law* (New York, Palgrave Macmillan, 2008).

Public international law now even goes so far as to place amongst its objectives the development of democracy, and in any event its protection in certain scenarios where it is under serious threat. As we have already indicated, the international community has twice responded vigorously to military coups: in Haiti in 1994 and Sierra Leone in 1998. The UN considers that the right to democracy is implicitly enshrined by the key legislation on human rights protection, and through the right to political participation.[8]

Correlatively, as has been identified above, it is to issues of domestic law—traditionally considered as such, at the very least—that public international law has extended the scope of its concerns, insofar as it takes an interest both in the fate of private individuals and groups, and in the democratic nature of political regimes. Its purpose then is one of taxation law, criminal law, labour law, even constitutional law.[9]

ii. A Shift in Subjects and Recipients

At the same time and as part of the same trend, public international law's sphere of subjects and intended recipients is also being transformed. It is almost trivial to say so nowadays, and the full scope has yet to be gauged, but public international law is no longer the preserve of states and international organisations. It is increasingly open to individuals, private organisations, businesses, sub-national authorities, etc.

The latter are increasingly the recipients of rights of which they are automatically holders and which they can implement themselves. The phenomenon is clear in the field of human rights; however, we have seen that it can also be observed in the economic sphere. Furthermore, it emerges that international economic litigation cases exclusively involve states less and less frequently. The same can be said, it would seem, for those cases where formally it is only they who remain concerned: in the functioning of the EU, for example, actions for failure to fulfil obligations—which, in theory, involve only Member States and EU bodies—are increasingly brought by businesses. International law could even be described as becoming increasingly public, in the sense of 'open to the public'.

iii. A Radical Change in Nature

Is the very nature of public international law currently undergoing radical change? If so, in which direction(s)?

---

[8] See Gregory H Fox and Brad R Roth (eds), *Democratic Governance and International Law* (Cambridge, Cambridge University Press, 2000), especially the introduction.

[9] See Slim Laghmani, 'Droit international et droits internes: vers un renouveau du *jus gentium*?' in Rafâa Ben Achour and Slim Laghmani (eds), *Droit international et droit interne. Développements récents* (Paris, Pedone, 1998) 23.

This is a complex question, in answer to which we can offer only two trends, whilst also suggesting that the current situation is a combination of classic law and what is grafted to it. It is not a complete switchover, but rather the co-existence of the old model and the new.

Less focused on the state (and international organisations as an extension of the state), which is criss-crossed with the various legal relations that concern it, public international law is increasingly becoming a transnational law[10] through the issues that it governs, the mechanisms by which it operates, and the legal relations with which it is concerned.

As has been very elegantly put, public international law:

> remains a law that is born between nations, but it is less and less a law that occurs between nations. Admittedly, it continues to govern international relations in such a way as to make both the coexistence and co-operation between States possible but, increasingly, it tends to unify domestic laws. International law tends to be transformed into a law that all nations use.[11,12]

As Joe Verhoeven explains,[13] while more classic Westphalian international law did not encompass any joint or 'social' project—striving as it was to navigate its way between various perils—'the assumption on which 'globalisation' is based is in this respect fundamentally different. It is not that of a fragmentation in relations that were initially between sovereign entities but rather their universalisation in spite of those entities'.

There is in fact a 'social' project under globalisation, simultaneously founded on the exponential opening-up of economic relations in the world, a worldwide blossoming of human rights protection, an international mixing of cultures, etc. Public international law is, like everything else, buffeted by those same winds, the dynamics of which are more difficult to withstand than the more complex and more often circumvented trends of the traditional law of peace and development.

In addition, as mentioned above, it would appear to be increasingly marked by general-interest concerns, the protection of common values, the production of global public goods, etc. The fact that behind the principles on display there sometimes lurk palpably different policies in no way undermines the legitimacy of the openings created by legal globalisation.

---

[10] *cf* in particular Carreau and Juillard, *Droit international* (n 3) 33 ff.

[11] Laghmani, *Droit international* (n 9).

[12] As we know, some authors (eg Jessup, Georges Scelle) had put forward a thesis on the transnational nature of international law. What Georges Scelle would not have thought, in any event, is that the same transnational nature could be achieved and reveal itself without national legal systems having to consent to monism: see Laghmani *Droit international* (n 9).

[13] Joe Verhoeven, 'Souveraineté et mondialisation: libres propos' in Eric Loquin and Catherine Kessedjian (eds), *La mondialisation du droit* (Paris, Litec, 2000) 43.

C. The Quest for Theoretical Renewal

Jurisprudence strives to identify, here and there, the intellectual avenues that will serve to account for the changes wrought by legal globalisation, and to renew the theoretical understanding of public international law.

Some writers consider that there is no reason to call fundamental theoretical balances into question, because it is simply a process of legal internationalisation that is at work here.[14] Giuliana Ziccardi Capaldo, for instance, argues that global law rests on four pillars:[15] verticality (the power of international organisations and especially the UN); legality (guaranteed in particular by the existence of the International Court of Justice); integration (integration and harmonisation of legal systems); and the development of collective guarantees.

According to this kind of theory, public international law does little more than accomplish its longstanding project of international legal integration.

Other writers have the sense that the traditional view cannot account for what is happening and that jurisprudential alternatives must necessarily be put forward.

Broadly speaking, they would appear to be sought along two main lines, the first focusing on a more syncretic approach, the second on an internal resourcing.

Writers subscribing to the former view include Paul Schiff Berman who argues that, faced with globalisation phenomena, international law has become an excessively restrictive framework; a broader perspective is required so as to allow an examination of the emergence of legal transnationalities through an amalgam of jurisprudential contributions drawn from comparative law, private international law, the law on new technologies and the cultural analysis of law, all combined with traditional public international law.[16] To this may also be added jurisprudential trends, which we have seen above, which strive to reflect on the 'constitutionalisation' of global bodies, and therefore attempt to add constitutional law to public international law's traditional 'baggage'.[17]

As to the latter view, this includes jurisprudence that is currently 'revisiting' public international law, highlighting the fact that global bodies are increasingly administrative in terms of nature and function—hence the revival of the 'international administrative law' theory, particularly in

---

[14] See above, chapter 1, 'D. The Scientific Scenario of Legal Globalisation and its Rivals'.

[15] Giuliana Ziccardi Capaldo *The Pillars of Global Law* (Aldershot, Ashgate, 2008) Introduction.

[16] Paul Schiff Berman (2005) 'From International Law to Law and Globalization', *Columbia Journal of Transnational Law* 43 485; see also Paul Schiff Berman (ed), *The Globalization of International Law* (Aldershot, Ashgate, 2005) Introduction.

[17] See above, chapter 4, 'B The Challenge of Constitutionalising Global Players' ff.

German jurisprudence,[18] and the emergence of 'global administrative law' (to which we shall return later in this chapter).[19]

II. THE IMPLICATIONS OF GLOBALISATION FOR NATIONAL PUBLIC LAW

Insinuating itself into national public law systems, confronting them with new issues, sometimes even putting them in competition with each other—globalisation can on occasion produce highly disruptive effects within the generally deeply entrenched construct that is national public law. Below we attempt to bring together several concepts that may shed light on these changes: following an overview of the mechanics of the globalisation of domestic legal frameworks and the specific vectors for globalisation's impact on public law, we will examine how globalisation generally meets constitutional law, administrative law and public finance law.

A. Globalisation of Domestic Legal Systems: Its Mechanics

In order to examine the way in which legal globalisation affects national legal systems in their various branches, a simple grid may be applied, representing four trends that emanate from globalisation:

— internationalisation: the penetration of external norms into the framework under consideration
— the need to adapt to the growing presence of various transnationalities
— the development of a genuinely global law that competes with national law
— the need to find new paradigms and conceptualisations in the face of the changes observed.

The aim of this chapter is to show the presence of these various changes within the major components of national public law, as these are delineated in the continental tradition. However, the same demonstration can no doubt be performed—and, indeed, this has occasionally been done—with regard to various segments of private law, with criminal law belonging either to public or private law depending on the legal tradition.

There are, for example, a number of works on the globalisation of labour law and social law more generally. They prove the considerable penetration of external norms within those branches of law: this is quite plain as regards

---

[18] See also Stefano Battini, *Amministrazione senza Stato. Profili di diritto amministrativo internazionale*, (Milan, Giuffrè, 2003).
[19] See below, chapter 7, 'The Theory of Global Administrative Law'.

labour law, particularly given the legislation produced by the ILO and the EU; this has, however, also been established with regard to social security law.[20] They show how frequently national social law is faced with transnational situations—migrant workers, combining different social security schemes with the principle of free movement within the EU sphere—along with the phenomenon of competition between systems that naturally results therefrom.[21] They also show how a genuinely global social law has been created, the heart of which is occupied by the basic principles enumerated by the ILO in its 1998 Declaration on Fundamental Principles and Rights at Work: freedom of association and the right to collective bargaining; the ban on forced labour; the abolition of child labour; non-discrimination, etc.[22] They highlight the search for new paradigms: for example, the current insistence on the social responsibility of businesses, or the significance of internal disciplinary procedures (codes of conduct, etc) that the latter impose on themselves in guaranteeing labour law norms.[23]

The same kind of demonstration can be performed with regard to of criminal law.[24] National criminal law now finds itself framed by a considerable number of European and international norms that either define behaviour that is prohibited internationally while leaving the task of punishing such behaviour to national law, or directly impact the punishment side of matters by setting the penalties themselves or conversely by prohibiting the punishment of certain acts.[25] It is also quite plain that criminal law is now faced with transnational situations that are sometimes very difficult to understand: money-laundering, corruption, terrorism, etc.[26] It is clear that there now exists a common 'heritage' or *acquis* of global criminal law: it is rooted in humanitarian law and human rights protection, the decline of immunities traditionally enjoyed by state officials and, of course, the creation of international criminal courts. The search for new paradigms can be

---

[20] Bettina Kahil-Wolff and Pierre-Yves Greber, *Sécurité sociale: aspects de droit national, international et européen* (Paris, LGDJ, 2006).

[21] eg Kevin Banks, 'The Impact of Globalization on Labour Standards' in John Craig and Michael Lynk (eds), *Globalization and the Future of Labour Law* (Cambridge, Cambridge University Press, 2006) 77.

[22] ibid, 1–14.

[23] Jill Murray, 'Relabelling the International Labour Problem: Globalization and Ideology' in Dauvergne, *Jurisprudence* (n 6) 29.

[24] Marc Henzelin and Robert Roth (ed), *Le droit pénal à l'épreuve de l'internationalisation* (Paris, LGDJ and Bruylant, 2002).

[25] André Huet and Marie Koering-Joulin, *Droit pénal international*, 3rd edn (Paris, PUF, 2005) 23 ff.

[26] Mark Findlay, 'Crime, Terror and Transitional Cultures in a Connecting Globe' in Dauvergne *Jurisprudence* (n 6) 231; Olaoluwa Olusanya, 'Double Jeopardy Without Parameters' (Schoten, Intersentia, 2004).

seen, for instance, amongst authors who argue in favour of an abandonment of the principle whereby one state's criminal courts may only apply national criminal law, never foreign criminal law—contrary to what private international law has long accepted in other branches of private law.[27]

Similar comments may be, and indeed have on occasion been, made with regard to other branches of private law, for instance concerning the effects of globalisation on the (civil) rights of persons.[28]

B. Specific Vectors for Globalisation's Impact on Public Law

The question considered here is that of whether and to what extent public law, owing to its own characteristics, is impacted by legal globalisation in a specific way. Two sets of comments may be made at this juncture.

i. Differences Between Public Law and Private Law

The reasons why public law is influenced by legal globalisation are not exactly the same as those applicable to private law. They are partly the same as, amongst the essential areas of legal globalisation, some have consequences for both public and private law: for example, that which, under legal globalisation, is related to the environment carries consequences not only for public regulations and public penalty systems, but also for private contract law, various kinds of self-regulation, etc.

There are, however, many factors that specifically call public law into question. As has been seen above,[29] national governance has in truth become a significant impact point for legal globalisation. The considerable development of human rights law mainly affects public institutions, owing to the frequently 'vertical' (as opposed to 'horizontal') nature of the corresponding norms. And we must not forget the increasingly common situations in which national public institutions contribute to European or international commitments:[30] the internationalisation of the functions of national public

---

[27] Huet and Koering-Joulin, *Droit pénal international* (n 25) 167.

[28] Françoise Dekeuwer-Defossez (ed), *Internationalisation des droits de l'homme et évolution du droit de la famille* (Paris, LGDJ, 1996); Kim Rubenstein, 'Globalization and Citizenship and Nationality' in Dauvergne *Jurisprudence* (n 6) 159.

[29] See above, chapter 2, 'D. (National) Governance' ff.

[30] Edoardo Chiti, *L'amministrazione militare tra ordinamento nazionale e ordinamento globale* (Milan, Giuffrè, 2006).

institutions automatically internationalises part of the law applicable to them.

ii. The Impact on National Public Law

Similarly, national public law is often affected in its various components (at least in part) through specific pathways or particular vectors. The following points may be made, for instance.

The permeation of constitutional law by globalisation comes about, in some instances, because the international community sticks its nose into the creation of national constitutions; we will return to this point later in the chapter. It is the result of the influence exerted by some international norms and standards, particularly in the field of human rights, on the conception of national constitutions. It comes from the reference made to such norms and standards in national constitutional litigation.

In the administrative law sphere, the most blatant aspect is the significant number of international agreements concluded on issues concerning administrative law and, correlatively, a growing number of cases, the settlement of which involves international agreements—and, where applicable, other international rules.[31]

There is another phenomenon, however, which is not necessarily linked to the previous one: this is the increasingly familiar discovery, in administrative litigation, of situations involving a foreign aspect, issues raised in relation to legal relationships that borrow in part from other legal systems. The imposing mass of litigation brought by foreign nationals—first by far in the French *Conseil d'Etat*'s statistics, for example[32]—testifies to this trend. However, this also reflects the regular appearance before administrative courts of issues of conflicts of laws or questions surrounding the enforcement of foreign judgments, which was not their common lot (although they did occasionally come across them).[33]

The economic opportunities created by globalisation have yielded an acceptance of international arbitration within a traditionally reluctant administrative law. If we look again at French law, Article 1492 of the

---

[31] This phenomenon can be seen in the law of all European states: see Gérard Marcou (ed), *Les mutations du droit de l'administration en Europe* (Paris, L'Harmattan, coll 'Logiques juridiques', 1995), particularly 20 ff.

[32] Conseil d'Etat, *Etudes et Documents du Conseil d'Etat*, 52 (Paris, La Documentation française, 2001) 55.

[33] Bernard Dolez, 'Le juge administratif et les conflits de lois' (*RDP [Revue du droit public]*, 1985) 4, 1029; Victor Haïm, 'Le choix du juge dans le contentieux des contrats administratifs' (*JCP*, 1992-I-8586); Olivier Dubos, 'Le droit administratif et les situations transnationales: des droits étrangers au droit comparé' in Fabrice Melleray (ed), *L'argument de droit comparé en droit administratif français* (Brussels, Bruylant, 2007) 69.

current *Code de procédure civile* (Civil Procedure Code) authorises public entities to resort to arbitration in order to settle disputes that challenge 'the interests of international trade'. The Law of 15 February 1982 on research grants the same authorisation in the context of research contracts with foreign organisations. As for the 'Disneyland' Law of 19 August 1986, this makes the same concession in the context of contracts concluded 'for carrying out operations in the national interest between multiple public entities acting together and foreign companies.'[34]

Globalisation's impact on public finance law essentially follows two main lines. In terms of taxation law, the need to deal with a considerable number of transnational situations, and systemic competition situations, has led to the development of a dense fabric of international agreements to which, in its own sphere, the EU has added its own harmonisation rules. As for public finance law, it is affected owing to powers conferred to certain international organisations: those allowing the World Bank or the IMF to array their aid packages with budgetary conditions; those allowing the EU's authorities to monitor Member State public deficits and occasionally call them to order.

C. Globalisation and Constitutional Law[35]

In which directions does globalisation influence the substance of constitutional law along the lines and for the reasons discussed previously?

With reference to the criteria proposed above, the following comments may be put forward.[36]

i. The Influence of Worldwide Law-making

The norms resulting from worldwide law-making, which come into contact with constitutional law, are not only plentiful but also concern essential points. The democratic principle has almost become a general principle—and in the European sphere, it is doubtless a binding norm—and the now considerable mass of global human rights law weighs heavily

---

[34] See Gérard Teboul (1997) 'Arbitrage international et personnes morales de droit public' *AJDA* January 25; and Daniel Labetoulle's commentary on the Opinion of 6 March 1986 in *Les grands avis du Conseil d'Etat* (Paris, Dalloz, 1997) 219.

[35] Antero Jyränki (ed), *National Constitutions in the Era of Integration* (The Hague, Kluwer Law International, 1999).

[36] To which we may add a reflection, which cannot be elaborated upon here, on the influence that globalisation sometimes has on the balances between powers within national systems: see, eg, on the benefit to be drawn by national courts from the European legal construct, Jean-Pierre Gridel, *Déclin des spécificités françaises et éventuel retour d'un droit commun européen* (Paris, Dalloz, 1999) 139.

on corresponding national norms which also lay at the heart of national constitutions.

In certain contexts, the pressure exerted by global law extends to all sorts of specific issues. The ECHR restricts the facility that states have to ban political parties, or deprive individuals of their right to vote. The European Charter on Local Self-Government and the European Charter for Regional and Minority Languages provide a framework for what the Member States of the Council of Europe that have ratified those Conventions can do as regards the organisation of the territorial pluralism of their public bodies and the status of their regional languages,[37] etc.

ii. Managing Transnationality and Extraterritoriality

Constitutional law must also learn how to manage situations of transnationality and extraterritoriality. Such situations were not completely unknown—eg governments in exile—but globalisation renders these more frequent and difficult to manage legally.

One basic factor that fuels their development is the growing frequency of scenarios in which national public bodies perform international functions or place themselves at the service of international institutions: as mentioned previously, this is the case for national armed forces taking part in humanitarian and peacekeeping operations. In such scenarios, the question arises as to whether domestic constitutional norms—for example those relative to human rights—apply to those sections of national public bodies that place themselves at the service of international tasks, be it norms protecting them (fundamental guarantees for civil servants) or norms with which they themselves must comply (rights of individuals in their dealings with the state). As matters stand, the answer to this question generally remains unclear.[38]

iii. The Development of Global Constitutional Law

The development of a global constitutional law, which supplements and competes with national constitutional law, even imposes binding norms on it, is quite apparent.[39]

---

[37] Luis-Maria Diez-Picaso (2006) 'Limites internationales du pouvoir constituant', *Revue européenne de droit public* 18, 109.

[38] Anne Peters, 'The Globalization of State Constitutions' in James Nijman and André Nollkaemper (eds) *New Perspectives in the Divide Between National and International Law* (Oxford, Oxford University Press, 2007) 251; Krysztof Wojticek, *Le champ territorial d'application d'une constitutional nationale*, Séminaire de la Chaire MADP de Sciences Po, 16 May 2008: www.sciencespo.fr/chaire-madp/sites/sciencespo.fr.chaire-madp/files/krzysztof_wojtyczek.pdf.

[39] David Feldman (2006) 'Modalities of Internationalization in Constitutional Law', *Revue européenne de droit public* 18, 131.

There is now a sort of broadly common constitutional *acquis*, the result of general international law mechanisms such as *jus cogens*, the emergence of the democratic principle within international law, and the large corpus of international human rights law.[40] It is around this common *acquis* that global law and constitutional law complete and compete, even come into conflict with one another.

iv. Globalisation and the Function of Constitutions

The unprecedented dialogue that globalisation maintains with national constitutional law gradually induces theoretical questions as to the function of constitutions—which, in particular, are no longer purely tools for the legal organisation of national sovereignty, but have also become instruments for regulating legal flows from internal to external—and as to the very notion of constitution.[41]

The growing awareness that, all in all, national constitutions are now little more than 'partial' constitutions leads to these reflections on global constitutionalism and multilevel constitutionalism.[42] The constitutional question can no longer be posed solely in the context of state institutions; whence the analysis of the constitutionalisation of international organisations, even globalisation's major private players.[43]

The theory of national constitutional law can no longer remain purely national, and this constitutes a major theoretical upheaval.

Globalisation and constitutional law

The consequences of legal globalisation that can be 'read' in terms of constitutional law fall into two categories. They consist of both a trend towards the internationalisation of national constitutions, and a quest to constitutionalise various global legal mechanisms.

---

[40] See above, chapter 2, 'C. Human Rights' ff; see also: Sedok Belaid, 'Droit international et droit constitutionnel: les développements récents' in Achour and Laghmani *Droit international* (n 9).

[41] Ann Peters, *The Globalization of State Constitutions* (n 38).

[42] See above, chapter 4, 'B. The Challenge of Constitutionalising Global Players' ff.; see also: Nicholas Bamforth and Peter Leyland, *Public Law in a Multi-Layered Constitution* (Oxford, Hart Publishing, 2003).

[43] See above, chapter 4, 'B. The Challenge of Constitutionalising Global Players'ff.

Internationalisation of national constitutions	— Dissemination of various international constitutional standards within national constitutional law (relative to democracy, the rule of law, etc). Such dissemination occasionally comes about through the courts, which draw inspiration from those standards (see boxed text 'Judicial dialogue and legal globalisation' in chapter 5). They are sometimes bound to incorporate those standards on the basis of consistent interpretation requirements: for example, some constitutions (eg Spain, Portugal, South Africa) provide that they must be interpreted in accordance with international human rights law.
	— Amendment of national constitutions to adapt the same to international requirements. Examples are:
	    — amendment of the Colombian constitution in that it provided for expropriation without compensation (David Schneidermann, (2000) 'Constitutional Approach to Liberalization. Inquiry into the Magnitude of Neo-Liberal Constitutionalism', *Law and Contemporary Problems* 63, 83)
	    — amendment of the Mexican and Canadian constitutions to allow the adoption of NAFTA (Gavin Anderson, *Constitutional Rights after Globalization* (Oxford, Hart Publishing, 2005) 114)
	    — amendment of various European constitutions to allow the adoption of various treaties of the EEC and the EU.

	— National constitutions elaborated internationally:
	    — Constitution of Cyprus in 1960
	    — Constitution of Bosnia in 1995.

Constitutionalisation of global legal mechanisms	In a certain number of scenarios, there has been and continues to be a desire to provide a constitutional basis for various (intergovernmental or otherwise) institutions that play a part in globalisation, in such a way as to clarify the nature and division of the powers that they hold, and secure their respect for public interest objectives and human rights. On this issue, see above, chapter 4, 'B The Challenge of Constitutionalising Global Players'ff.

See: Luis-Maria Diez-Picazo (2006) 'Limites internationales au pourvoir constituant' 18 *Revue Européenne de Droit Public* 1 109; David Felman (2006) 'Modalities of Internationalization in Constitutionalization Law' 18 *Revue Européenne de Droit Public* 1, 288; Jan Klabbers, Anne Peters and Geir Ulfstein, *The Constitutionalization of International Law* (Oxford, Oxford University Press, 2009); Anne Levade and Bertrand Mathieu (2006) 'L'internationalisation du droit constitutionnel. Acteurs. Domaines. Techniques' 18 *Revue Européenne de Droit Public* 1 161; Didier Maus, 'Où va le droit constitutionnel?', *Mélanges Franck Moderne* (Paris, Dalloz, 2004); Nicolas Maziau (2002) 'L'internationalisation du pouvoir constituant', *Revue générale de droit international public* 549; Anne Peters, 'The Globalization of State Constitutions' in Janne Nijman and André Nollkaemper (eds), *New Perspectives on the Divide Between National and International Law* (Oxford, Oxford University Press, 2007) 251.

D. Globalisation and Administrative Law[44]

The extent to which international norms have penetrated issues of administrative law is impressive.[45]

As has previously been pointed out,[46] this impacts questions relative to the relationship between public bodies and their environment—the impact of global human rights law is decisive here, but other factors come into play, for

---

[44] Eberhard Schmidt-Assman (2006) 'Internationalisation of Administrative Law: Actors, Fields and Techniques of Internationalisation' 18 *REDP* 1, 249; Juan-Cruz Alli Aranguren, *Derecho administrativo y globalizacion* (Madrid, Thomson-Civitas, 2004).

[45] Auby, 'Globalisation et droit public' (n 1); Giandomenico Falcon (2006) 'Internationalisation of Administrative Law, Impact of International Law on National Administrative Law' 18 *REDP* 1, 217.

[46] See above, chapter 2, 'D. (National) Governance' ff.

example as regards the internationalisation of public contracts—and questions relative to the organisation and internal operation of public bodies: decentralisation, the setting-up of government bodies as agencies, etc.

No area of administrative law remains unaffected by globalisation: whether it be acts and non-contentious procedure (eg the requirements under EU environmental law, or the administrative penalties drawn from EU law and from national competition law), contracts, administrative organisation, administrative liability, on which both EU law and ECHR law have an impact; or even administrative litigation, which is subject to the same influences.

European law has the most significant consequences, naturally, but it is not the sole vector for the internationalisation of domestic administrative law. Public contracts law is also influenced by WTO law, while non-European international legislation on the environment—such as the Aarhus Convention—have consequences for domestic legal procedures.

i. Extraterritorial and Transnational Administrative Situations

Domestic administrative law is increasingly driven to take into account situations of extraterritoriality or transnationality. The issue of international administrative contracts has become a matter of acute concern.[47] The treatment of administrative acts with transnational effects also presents growing problems.[48] The related question of the legal organisation of transnational administrative co-operation has become a major issue: not that this question is new in itself,[49] but it has acquired a particularly acute aspect in a globalising world—whence the questions surrounding the general mechanisms of such co-operation with, for example, the question of administrative arrangements which are concluded by ministers and are neither treaties nor international contracts,[50] or those surrounding certain specific spheres such as police co-operation in criminal matters.[51] These questions take on a particular significance in the sphere of the EU, where 'horizontal' co-operation between Member State administrations becomes a critical issue in the implementation of EU law. This highlights the fact that Community legislation is increasingly concerned with organising and providing a framework for such co-operation, as illustrated by the 2006 Services Directive.[52]

---

[47] See above, this chapter, and Olivier Dubos, 'Le droit administratif' (n 33).

[48] See boxed text 'Extraterritoriality in a context of legal globalisation', chapter 1.

[49] Rudolf Geiger, 'Legal Assistance Between States in Administrative Matters' in Rudolf Bernhardt (ed), *Encyclopedia of Public International Law*, vol III (Amsterdam, Oxford, North Holland Publishing Co., 1997) 186.

[50] Conseil d'Etat, *Les normes internationales en droit français* (Paris, La Documentation française, 2000) 9 ff.

[51] Huet and Koering-Joulin, *Droit pénal international* (n 25) 329 ff.

[52] Directive 2006/123/EC of the European Parliament and of the Council of 12 December 2006 on services in the internal market.

ii. A Common Acquis of Administrative Law

We are undoubtedly witnessing the emergence of a sort of common international *acquis* of administrative law: a certain number of principles and models which are becoming a common basis for administrative law under the rule of law and are thereby subject to international acceptance sometimes reflected in mandatory norms; the others remain amongst those standards conveyed by international organisations, sometimes providing inspiration to the courts, and expanded upon by jurisprudence.[53]

In particular, it is all those principles that are similar to those of good governance, be it transparency, matters relating to the integrity of public officials, the proper treatment of applications in the spirit of 'good administration', etc.

This sort of common global *acquis* of administrative law enhances and supplements national administrative law, sometimes compelling national law to redirect some of its constructs.

iii. Global Administrative Law

In the sphere of administrative law, all of this also sparks efforts to bring about theoretical renewal, new conceptualisations, which strive to account for globalisation permeating national administrative law.

At this juncture, we must mention the theory of global administrative law. This theory, the essential points of which can be found below, is driven by the fact that there are global administrative bodies, and the desire to reflect upon how these may be legally regulated more effectively. This does not lessen its impact on the very conception of national administrative law, particularly insofar as it takes account of the fact that some international mechanisms have in reality incorporated sections of national administration—in configuring networks, for example—and where it incorporates those sections in its descriptive and normative thinking. On that basis, it is therefore a tool for considering those aspects of multilevel governance that relate to national administrative law.

The theory of global administrative law

The theory of global administrative law is a research project which began at New York University and was then extended to Europe by Italian lawyers, under the stewardship of Sabino Cassese.

---

[53] Jacques Chevallier, 'La mondialisation de l'Etat de droit' in *Mélanges Ardant* (Paris, LGDJ, 1999) 325; Stefano Battini et al, *Il diritto amministrativo oltre i confini. Omaggio degli allievi a Sabino Cassese* (Milan, Giuffrè, 2008).

It is based on the observation of two phenomena. The first is the fact that, given the way in which the world is currently organised, there are numerous international entities—be they part of intergovernmental organisations or otherwise, public or private—which display all the characteristics of administrative bodies: they are responsible for typically administrative issues (fishing, medication, environmental issues, etc) and composed in whole or in part of experts rather than diplomats or politicians.

The theory identifies various categories of such global administrative entities: in addition to those that are found within formal international organisations, there are networks of national administrations, mechanisms involving public and private entities, and private entities performing regulatory functions.

The second phenomenon observed by the theory is the fact that these various global administrative bodies are not sufficiently accountable for their activities. This is the case for at least three reasons. The first is that they are not subject to the same legal disciplines applicable to national public bodies: they are either international or national entities but they then belong to networks, the operation of which cannot be entirely controlled by national law.

The second reason is that international law does not contain the same rules as those that make up the disciplines that are usually incumbent on domestic public bodies, in terms of transparency, adversarial procedure, stating reasons for decisions, etc.

The third reason is that some global administrative bodies are private, or semi-private, and are consequently exempt from national and international disciplines incumbent on public bodies.

Based on these observations, the theory of global administrative law has constructed an intellectual programme founded on the following concepts. In asking which legal corpus has the *savoir-faire* in the art of ensuring that public bodies abide by the law, transparency, proper procedures, etc, the answer is that administrative law has the best points of references in the field.

Taking that as its starting point, the theory has opened up a field of investigation consisting in reassessing global administrative bodies, identifying whether they are sufficiently subject to the rules and principles of accountability, and issuing proposals where that is not the case.

See: Sabino Cassese (2004) 'Gamberetti, tartaughe e procedure. "Standards" globali per i diritti amministrativi nazionali', *Rivista Trimestrale di Diritto Pubblico* 3, 657; Daniel Esty (2006) 'Good Governance at the Supranational Scale: Globalizing Administrative Law', *Yale Law Journal* 115, 1490; Eleanor Kinney (2002) 'The Emerging Field of International Law. Its Content and Potential' 54 *Administrative Law*

Review 1 415; Richard Kingsbury, Nico Krisch, Richard Stewart and Jonathan Wiener (2005) 'The Emergence of Global Administrative Law' 68 *Law and Contemporary Problems* 3–4.

Next, there is the theory of European administrative law—or, more precisely, the *theories*, as the concept is not limited identically by all the trends that may claim to it, as explained below. Specifically, one of the distinguishing variables is that while they all start on the basis of the observation that there is an administrative law within the EU, some include in their perspective the impact that the European construct (including, where applicable, the European Convention on Human Rights) has on national administrative law. In the latter scenario, the theory also becomes a tool for rethinking national administrative law in light of its Europeanisation.

The theories of European administrative law

There are at least two ways to approach the concept of European administrative law. The first is that upheld by Jürgen Schwarze in his reference work, and uses a definition of 'European administrative law' as meaning the proportion of EU law that can be taken as administrative law. The second, broader approach also includes in the field of study defined as European administrative law everything related to the links between EU law and national administrative law.

European administrative law certainly includes, first of all, the proportion of EU law that may be deemed to be administrative law, ie that which, under EU law, relates not to law-making but to the execution and implementation of EU legislation.

It is true that within EU mechanisms, the line between legislation and execution is not always easy to identify. The same can be said for reasons that are both organisational and formal. Organisational, because the leading EU bodies are not readily sorted into legislative bodies and enforcement bodies. The European Council is neither a legislative nor an executive body. The Council of Ministers is both legislative and executive. The Commission is an executive body, but also part of the legislative process. Formal, owing to the incomplete nature of the typology of acts which, occasionally, are also difficult to categorise into legislative and executive acts.

European administrative law may also be understood as including everything relating to the links between EU law and national administrative law. This may mean two types of relationship: firstly, those relative to the legal constraints that EU law brings to bear on national administrative law—correlatively, to the way in which national administrative law places itself, efficiently or otherwise, at the service of EU law and ensures, efficiently or otherwise, the sanction of any breach of EU law; and, secondly, those relative to the relations of pure influence, relations of inspiration that may exist between the respective intellectual constructs of EU law and national administrative law.

The EU's legal system serves as a crucible, where EU law acts on national law, which in turn may influence the former. However, the national laws of the various Member States also influence each other, in such a way that they compete to influence EU law—this is true especially of administrative law, as the areas covered by EU law very much fall within the remit of public policy.

Just as the implications of EU law are not confined to the legal obligations that it brings to bear, the Community crucible is not home only to vertical legal relations. It is the receptacle for a multilateral exchange of laws, an exchange which also occurs in other contexts and particularly that of the Council of Europe, through various review mechanisms implemented by the European Court of Human Rights. This applies to administrative law.

See: Jean-Bernard Auby and Jacqueline Dutheil de la Rochère (eds), *Traité de droit administratif européen* (Brussels, Bruylant, 2014); Jack Beatson and Takis Tridimas (eds), *New Directions in European Public Law* (Oxford, Hart Publishing, 1998); Paul Beaumont, Carole Lyons and Neil Walker, *Convergence and Divergence in European Public Law* (Oxford, Hart Publishing, 2002); Patrick Birkinshaw, *European Public Law* (London, Butterworths, 2003); Mario Chiti, *Diritto amministrativo europeo*, 3rd edn (Milan, Giuffrè, 2008); Paul Craig, *EU Administrative Law* (Oxford, Oxford University Press, 2006); Giandomenico Falcon (ed), *Il diritto amministrativo dei paesi europei tra ommogenizzazzione e diversita culturali* (Padova, Dedam, 2005); Antonio Gil Ibanez, *The Administrative Supervision of EC Law. Powers, Procedures and Limits* (Oxford, Hart Publishing, 1999); Jan Jans, Roel de Lange and Sacha Prechal, *Europeanization of Public Law* (Europa Law Publishing, 2007); Luis Ortega (ed), *Studies on European Public Law. The Europeanization of Public Law and the European Constitution* (Valladolid, Editorial Lex Nova, 2005); Luciano Parejo Alfonso et al, *Manual de derecho administrativo comunitario* (Madrid, Editorial Centro de Estudios Ramón Aceres, 2000); Jürgen Schwarze, *Droit administratif européen*, 2nd edn (Brussels, Bruylant, 2009); Jürgen Schwarze (ed), *Le droit administratif sous l'influence de l'Europe* (Baden-Baden, Nomos Verlagsgesellschaft and Bruxelles, Bruylant, 1996); Luciano Vandelli, Carlo Bottari and Daniele Donati (eds), *Diritto amministrativo comunitario* (Rimini, Miggiolo Editore, 1994).

On a different note, the development of transnationalities in the sphere of administrative law has generated new discussions around the concept of transnational administrative law, to which we will return below.

E. Globalisation and Public Finance Law[54]

i. The Impact of Globalisation

The intrusion of external norms can clearly be seen in the area of taxation law, but also in budgetary law.

National taxation law is now heavily influenced by international norms, particularly owing to the existence of a considerable number of international agreements in that field.[55] In the European sphere, naturally, that influence is conveyed by EU law's own legal instruments and is especially strong; some fields of taxation are now even steered outright by EU law.[56]

Budgetary law is influenced firstly by international standards developed in the areas of good governance and the transparency of public finances in particular. In the EU sphere, it is especially influenced by the requirements instigated from the Maastricht Treaty onwards, to provide a framework for public deficits.[57]

ii. Taxation Law

Taxation law obviously has to deal with a growing number of transnational situations, connected in particular to the expansion of international trade[58]—hence the dense fabric of agreements, as noted above, and the growing legal improvement of co-operation mechanisms between national tax authorities.[59]

iii. Public Financial Law

While this is undoubtedly less obvious than in the constitutional or administrative spheres, a European and international corpus of common public

---

[54] Marie-Christine Esclassan, 'Le modèle français de finances publiques à l'épreuve de l'internationalisation du droit et de la politique' in Michel Bouvier (ed), *Réforme des finances publiques, démocratie et bonne gouvernance* (Paris, LGDJ, 2004) 361.

[55] Loïc Levoyer (2003) 'Juge administratif, hiérarchie des normes et droit fiscal', *AJDA*, June 1350.

[56] Guy Gest, 'Les contraintes d'origine communautaire en matière de fiscalité directe' (*RFPP*, 1997) 60.

[57] 'L'Union européenne et les finances publiques nationales' (*RFPP*, 1999) 68; Loïc Levoyer, *L'influence du droit communautaire sur le pouvoir financier du Parlement français* (Paris, LGDJ, 2002).

[58] Bernard Castagnède, *Précis de fiscalité internationale* (PUF, 2002): Introduction.

[59] See *Juris-Classeur Fiscal*, fasc. 17; Blaise Knapp, 'L'entraide administrative vue de la Suisse' in *Mélanges Moderne* (Paris, Dalloz, 2004) 849.

financial law is being developed. This is clear in the field of budgetary law where, as mentioned previously, common norms on good financial governance are being created.[60] This is also true of the taxation sphere, where some techniques constitute a common international body of law, such as those on how to handle issues surrounding double taxation.[61]

iv. Influence on Concepts

Public financial law is not spared by the need for theoretical questions linked to globalisation. The concepts are sometimes mishandled owing to the latter: for example, European law requires a re-evaluation to varying degrees of concepts such as budget balance or taxation.[62] Competition between tax systems, mentioned previously,[63] demands legal and economic reflections on its consequences and how to adapt thereto.[64]

III. GLOBALISATION'S INFLUENCE ON RELATIONS BETWEEN NATIONAL PUBLIC LAWS

Lastly, we offer up several observations on that which globalisation brings about in the horizontal relations between national public laws.

A. The Impact of General Globalising Factors

Firstly, it is perfectly clear that those relations are impacted in their entirety by the general developments which affect relations between legal systems under globalisation. The phenomena of 'permeabilisation', competition and harmonisation[65] identified above affect public law as much as they do private law. All kinds of examples given in the developments discussed above testify to that.

---

[60] Esclassan, 'Le modèle français' (n 54).

[61] See Castagnède, *Précis de fiscalité internationale* (n 58).

[62] Jean-Bernard Auby (ed), *L'influence du droit européen sur les catégories du droit public français* (Paris, LGDJ, 2010).

[63] See above, chapter 3, 'B. Competition between Legal Systems'.

[64] eg Tsilly Dagan, 'The Costs of International Tax Cooperation' in Eyal Benvenisti and Georg Nolte (eds), *The Welfare State, Globalization and International Law* (Berlin, Heidelberg, Springer, 2003) 49.

[65] See above, chapter 3, 'II. Systemic Relations' ff.

B. Regulating Relations Between National Public Laws

We must tarry a little on the issue of the regulation of relations between national public laws under globalisation.

As noted at several points over the course of this book, globalisation multiplies and intensifies situations with a foreign aspect, situations involving transnationality and extraterritoriality falling within the remit of public law. This presents problems concerning the legal organisation of co-operation between public bodies. However, it also raises issues as to how to establish which law is applicable and which court has jurisdiction in the event of a dispute. These issues are the subject of increasingly complex reflections, to which both public law and private international law experts have contributed, and which have given in particular to the idea of constructing a theory of transnational administrative law.[66] The task is by no means an easy one, for various reasons (many of which are of general principle), such as whether it is possible to break as little as possible with the traditional rule on the exclusivity of public law—according to which only national public law can apply within the national territory—or whether to borrow from conflict of laws concepts and techniques as put forward by private international law, or even whether there is a need to create specific concepts and techniques for managing the coexistence of national public laws.

[66] See the monitoring of transnational administrative law, regularly conducted by Mathias Audit in *Droit administratif*.

Conclusion

WERE WE TO attempt to summarise the effects that globalisation has on the world's legal organisation, we could say that they are primarily linked to the following five phenomena:

— A development in the sense of a growing interdependence between systems (other terms may be used: interoperability, inter-relevance, inter-functionality, or even interconnection);
— The growing presence of transnationality situations (and of extraterritoriality situations, which are another form thereof);
— The significant weight of non-state (and non-intergovernmental) players, including regulators;
— The development of networks as the modern and characteristic form of international governance;
— The fact that all the above phenomena are both 'vertical' and 'horizontal', legal globalisation being both multilevel and made up of horizontal interrelations.

These phenomena do not constitute the whole of the modern world's legal structure. They are powerful trends that shape it. They have their limitations, which have been discussed. The examination conducted here has sought never to ignore that the realities that it looked to highlight were more or less marked depending on the sphere or on the regions of the world, and could witness ups and downs depending on the period. They are, however, the dominant direction, and major crises in recent decades—after 9/11, or the economic and financial crash of 2008—have borne this out. They barely affected the opening of international trade and the development of its global law, barely altered the legal operation of EU mechanisms or those of the European Convention on Human Rights, and have in no way set back worldwide networks and the legal problems that their operation can raise. This was illustrated, for example, by the issue raised by the handing over of customer databases belonging to various airlines to the US customs authorities.

There may be an argument that what we impute to globalisation here relates more generally to facts of modernity or post-modernity: the dispersal of power, the decline of existing hierarchies are not specially due to globalisation, driven as they are by the prevailing winds of modernity or post-modernity. As Ulrich Beck points out, modern society has no control centre.[1]

The reply is undoubtedly that globalisation is a specific tributary to modernity or post-modernity, and that legal globalisation is a specific tributary to legal modernity or post-modernity. In the political order, its primary dimension is the challenge that it brings to the Westphalian organisation of international society into states; the division of political territories; the national segmentation of the world.

In the legal sphere, it is a challenge to the state's legal centrality, the territoriality of law, the differentiation between national legal systems, as well as the traditional connections between national and international legal orders.

This creates difficulties, with more to come in future. Weighty issues will demand considerable investigative efforts in the three basic areas underpinning the organisation of legal systems: norms; powers; and bodies. In the first of these spheres, it is the issue of the multilateral management of the interconnections between systems that is raised, in a context where hierarchical models are clearly inadequate. In the second sphere, it is the definition of legitimate public action that is in question, in a context of a plurality of cultures and ideologies that have become increasingly intertwined. In the third sphere, what is at issue is the proper organisation of public action, from the perspective of both effectiveness and democracy, in a context of the vertical and horizontal interconnectedness of systems.

---

[1] Ulrich Beck, *La société du risque. Sur la voie d'une autre modernité* (Paris, Aubier, 2001) 485.

Bibliography

PUBLICATIONS IN ENGLISH

Allison, J, *A Continental Distinction in the Common Law. A Historical and Comparative Perspective on English Public Law* (Oxford, Clarendon Press, 1996).

Aman, A, *The Democracy Deficit. Taming Globalization through Law Reform* (New York University Press, 2004).

Anderson, G, *Constitutional Rights after Globalization* (Oxford, Hart Publishing, 2005).

Anthony, G, Auby, J-B, Morison, J and Zwart, T (eds), *Values in Global Administrative Law* (Oxford, Hart Publishing, 2010).

Appadurai, A, *Modernity at Large: Cultural Dimension of Globalisation* (Minneapolis, University of Minnesota Press, 1997).

Arrowsmith, S and Davies, A (eds), *Public Procurement: Global Revolution* (The Hague, Kluwer Law International, 1998).

d'Aspremont, J (2006) 'Contemporary International Rulemaking and the Public Character of International Law', IILJ Working Paper, New York University, 12.

Auby, J-B, 'Three Questions Concerning the Public-Private Divide in Legal Globalization', report to the Law of the Future Conference, The Hague, 8–9 October 2009.

Axtmann, R, *Globalization and Europe. Theoretical and Empirical Investigation* (London and Washington, Pinter, 1998).

Barrett, S, *Why Cooperate? The Incentive to Supply Global Public Goods* (Oxford, Oxford University Press, 2010).

Basedow, J, and Kono, T (eds), *Legal Aspects of Globalization* (The Hague, Kluwer Law International, 2000).

Bayly, CA, *The Birth of the Modern World 1780–1914. Global Connections and Comparisons* (Oxford, Blackwell, 2004).

Beaumont, P, Lyons C, and Walker N (eds), *Convergence and Divergence in European Public Law* (Oxford, Hart Publishing, 2002).

Beatson, J and Tridimas T (eds), *New Directions in European Public Law* (Oxford, Hart Publishing, 1998).

Beck, U, *What is globalization?* (Cambridge, Polity Press, 2000).

Bederman, DJ, *Globalisation and International Law* (New York, Palgrave Macmillan, 2008).

Benvenisti, E and Nolte, G (eds), *The Welfare State. Globalization and International Law* (Berlin, Heidelberg, Springer, 2003).

Berhardt, R (ed), *Encyclopedia of Public International Law*, Vol III (1997).

Bernie, P, Boyle, A and Redgwell, C, *International Law and the Environment* (Oxford, Oxford University Press, 2009).

Birkinshaw, P, *European Public Law* (London, Butterworths, 2003).

Birkinshaw, P and Varney, M (eds), *The European Legal Order after Lisbon* (The Hague, Kluwer Law International, 2010).

Bolewski, W, *Diplomacy and International Law in Globalized Relations* (Berlin, Heidelberg, Springer, 2007).

Bratspies, R and Miller, R (eds), *Transboundary Harm in International Law* (Cambridge, Cambridge University Press, 2006).

Brysk, A (ed), *Globalization and Human Rights* (Berkeley, University of California Press, 2002).

Burchill, R, *Democracy and International Law* (Aldershot, Ashgate, 2006).

Busch, A, *Banking Regulation and Globalization* (Oxford, Oxford University Press, 2009).

Byers, M (ed), *The Role of Law in International Politics. Essays in International Relations and International Law* (Oxford, Oxford University Press, 2000).

Craig, J and Lynk, M, (eds), *Globalization and the Future of Labour Law* (Cambridge University Press, 2006).

Craig, P, *Administrative Law*, 5th edn (London, Sweet & Maxwell, 2003).

Curtin, D, *Postnational Democracy* (The Hague, Kluwer Law International, 1997).

Cutler, C, *Private Power and Global Authority* (Oxford, Oxford University Press, 2003).

Dahlgaard Dingel, D, *Public Procurement. A Harmonization of the National Judicial Review of the Application of European Community Law* (The Hague, Kluwer Law International, 1999).

Dauvergne, C (ed), *Jurisprudence for an Interconnected Globe* (Aldershot, Ashgate, 2003).

Dowdle M (ed), *Public Accountability* (Cambridge, Cambridge University Press, 2006).

Drolshammer, J and Pfeifer, M, *The Internationalization of the Practice of Law* (The Hague, Kluwer Law International, 2001).

Edge, I (ed), *Comparative Law in Global Perspective* (New York, Transnational Publishers, 2000).

Falk, R, *Law in an Emerging Global Village. A Post-Westphalian Perspective* (Ardsley, NY, Transnational Publishers Inc, 1998).

Faundez, J, Footer, ME and Norton, JJ (eds), *Governance, Development and Globalization* (Oxford, Blackstone Press Limited, 2000).

Ferran, E and Goodhart, C, *Regulating Financial Services and Markets in the 21st Century* (Oxford, Hart Publishing, 2001).

Fitzpatrick, P and Tuitt, P, *Critical Beings, Law, Nation and the Global Subject* (Cambridge, Cambridge University Press, 2004).

Fox, GH and Roth, BR (eds), *Democratic governance and international law* (Cambridge, Cambridge University Press, 2000).

Freedland, M and Sciarra S (eds), *Public Services and Citizenship in European Law* (Oxford, Oxford University Press, 1998).

Friedman, T, *The World is Flat: A Brief History of the Twenty-First Century* (New York, Farrar, Strauss and Giroux, 2005).

Gessner, V, and Budak, AC (eds), *Emerging Legal Certainty: Empirical Studies on the Globalization of Law (Onati International Series in Law and Society)* (Aldershot, Ashgate, 1998).

Gil Ibanez, A, *The Administrative Supervision of EC Law. Powers, Procedures and Limits* (Oxford, Hart Publishing, 1999).

Gilpin, R, *Global Political Economy. Understanding the International Economic Order* (Princeton, NJ, Princeton University Press, 2001).

Gray, J, *False Dawn. The Delusions of Global Capitalism* (London, Granta, 1998).

van Harten, G, *Investment Treaty Arbitration and Public Law* (Oxford, Oxford University Press, 2007).

Hirst, P and Thompson, G, *Globalization in Question*, 2nd edn (Cambridge, Polity Press, 1999).

Hoeckman, B and Mavroidis, P, *Law and Policy in Public Purchasing—The WTO Agreement on Government Procurement* (Ann Arbor, University of Michigan Press, 1997).

Jacobsen, T, Sampford, C and Thakur, R (eds), *Re-envisioning Sovereignty* (Aldershot, Ashgate, 2008).

Jans, J, de Lange, R, Prechal, S and Widershoven, R (eds), *Europeanisation of Public Law* (Groningen, Europa Law Publishing, 2007).

Joerges, C and Petersmann, E-U (eds), *Constitutionalism, Multilevel Trade Governance and Social Regulation* (Oxford, Hart Publishing, 2006).

Joerges, C, Sand, I-J and Teubner G (eds), *Transnational Governance and Constitutionalism* (Oxford, Hart Publishing, 2004).

Jyränki, A (ed), *National Constitutions in the Era of Integration* (The Hague, Kluwer Law International, 1999).

Kaul, I and Conceição, P (eds), *Providing Global Public Goods: Managing Globalization* (Oxford, Oxford University Press, 2003).

Kaul, I, Gurndberg, I and Stern, M (eds), *Global Public Goods: International Cooperation in the 21st Century* (Oxford,Oxford University Press, 1999).

Keck, M and Sikking, K, *Activists Beyond Borders: Advocacy Networks in International Politics* (Ithaca, Cornell University Press, 1998).

Klabbers, J, Peters, A and Ulfstein, G, *The Constitutionalization of International Law* (Oxford, Oxford University Press, 2009).

Kolm, H-H and Sorensen, G (eds), *Whose World Orders?* (Boulder, Colorado, Westview Press, 1995).

Ladeur, K-H (ed), *Public Governance in the Age of Globalization* (Aldershot, Ashgate, 2004).

Leylands, P and Woods, T, *Administrative Law Facing the Future: Old Constraints and New Horizons* (Oxford, Blackstone, 1999).

MacLeod, S and Parkinson, J (eds), *Global Governance and the Quest for Justice*, Vol II: Corporate Governance (Oxford, Hart Publishing, 2004).

Maminho, C (ed), *The Dublin Convention on Asylum: Its Essence, Implementation and Prospects, European Institute of Public Administration* (Maastricht, European Institute of Public Administration, 2000).

Mattei, U, *Comparative Law and Economics* (Ann Arbor, The University of Michigan Press, 2000).

Nijman, J and Nollkaemper, A (eds), *New Perspectives on the Divide between National and International Law* (Oxford, Oxford University Press, 2007).

Oliver, D, *Common Values and the Public–Private Divide* (London, Butterworths, 1999).

Olusanya, O, *Double Jeopardy Without Parameters* (Antwerp, Intersentia, 2004).

Ortega, L (ed), *Studies on European Public Law. The Europeanization of Public Law and the European Constitution* (Valladolid, Editorial Lex Nova, 2005).

Perez, FX, *Cooperative Sovereignty. From Independence to Interdependence in the Structure of International Law* (The Hague, Kluwer Law International, 2000).

Peters, A, Koechlin, L Förster, T and Zinkernagel, GF (eds), *Non-State Actors as Standard Setters* (Cambridge, Cambridge University Press, 2009).

Reich, A, *International Public Procurement Law—The Evolution of International Regimes on Public Purchasing* (The Hague, Kluwer Law International, 1999).

Rose-Ackerman, S and Lindseth, P (eds), *Comparative Administrative Law* (Aldershot, Ashgate, 2010).

Ross-Harper, J (ed), *Global Law in Practice* (The Hague, Kluwer Law International, 1997).

Sassen, S, *A Sociology of Globalization* (New York, WW Norton & Company, Inc, 2007).

Schiff Berman, P (ed), *The Globalization of International Law* (Aldershot, Ashgate, 2005).

Scholte, JA, *Globalization. A critical introduction* (London, Macmillan and New York, St Martin Press Inc, 2000).

Schneiderman, D, *Constitutionalizing Economic Globalization* (Cambridge, Cambridge University Press, 2008).

de Senarclens, P and Kazancigil, A (eds), *Regulating Globalization: Critical Approach to Global Governance* (United Nations, United Nations University Press, 2007).

Shams, H, *Legal Globalisation, Money Laundering Law and Other Cases*, Sir Joseph Gold Memorial Series (London, British Institute of International and Comparative Law, 2004).

Shan, W, Simons, P and Singh, D (eds), *Redefining Sovereignty in International Economic Law* (Oxford, Hart Publishing, 2008).

Slaughter, A-M, *A New World Order* (Princeton, NJ, Princeton University Press, 2004).

Snyder, F (ed), *Regional and Global Regulation of International Trade* (Oxford, Hart Publishing, 2002).

da Sousa Santos, B, *Law and Globalization from Below* (Cambridge, Cambridge University Press, 2005).

Taylor, P, *International Organization in the Age of Globalization* (London, Continuum, 2003).

Teubner, G, *Global Law without a State* (Aldershot, Dartmouth, 1997).

Twining, W, *Globalization & Legal Theory* (London, Butterworths, 2000).

Verhoosel, G, *National Treatment and WTO Settlement. Adjudicating the Boundaries of Regulatory Autonomy* (Oxford, Hart Publishing, 2002).

Vandamme, TAJA and Reestman, J-H (eds), *Ambiguity in the Rule of Law. The Interface Between National and International Systems* (Groningen, Europa Law Publishing, 2001).

Vogler, J, The Global Commons. Environmental and Technological Governance (Chichester, John Wiley, 2000).

Walker, N (ed), *Sovereignty in Transition* (Oxford, Hart Publishing, 2002).

Wiener, J, *Globalization and the Harmonization of Law* (London and New York, Pinter, 1999).

World Bank. *World Development Report 1997: The State in a Changing World* (New York, Oxford University Press, 1997).

World Trade Organization, 'European Communities—Protection of Trademarks and Geographic Indication for Agricultural Products and Foodstuffs', Panel Report, 15 March 2005, WTO Doc WT/DS174/R.

Yerglin, D, and Stanislaw, J, *The Commanding Heights* (New York, Touchstone, 1999).

Ziccardi Capallo, G, The Pillars of Global Law (Aldershot, Ashgate, 2008).

PUBLICATIONS IN FRENCH

Agostini, E, *Droit comparé* (Paris, PUF, 1988).

Alland, D (ed), *Droit international public*, coll 'Droit fondamental' (Paris, PUF, 2000).

Allard, J and Garapon, A, *Les juges dans la mondialisation. La nouvelle révolution du droit* (Paris, Le Seuil, 2005).

Amouts, M-C, *Forêt tropicale, jungle internationale* (Paris, Presses de Sciences Po, 2001).

Arnaud, A-J (ed), *Dictionnaire encyclopédique de théorie et de sociologie du droit* (Paris, LGDJ, 1993).

Arnaud, A-J, *Critique de la raison juridique. Gouvernants sans frontières. Entre mondialisation et post-mondialisation* (LGDJ, 2003).

Aspects économiques du droit internationalprivé, Académie de Droit International de La Haye, Recueil des Cours, tome 307 (2004).

Auby, J-B, *La décentralisation et le droit* (LGDJ, 2006).

Auby, J-B and Dutheil de la Rochère, J (eds), *Traité de droit administratif européen*, 2nd edn, (Brussels, Bruylant, 2014).

Audit, M, *Les conventions transnationales entre personnes publiques* (Paris, LGDJ, 2002), Bibl de Droit Privé.

Badie, B, *La fin des territoires* (Paris, Fayard, 1995).

—— *Un monde sans souveraineté* (Paris, Fayard, 1999).

Batselé, D, Dony, M., Durviaux, A-L., *Les marchés publics à l'aube du XXIe siècle* (Bruxelles, Bruylant, 2001).

Bayart, J-F, *Le gouvernement du monde. Une critique politique de la globalisation* (Paris, Grasset, 2004).

Beck, U, *La société du risque. Sur la voie d'une autre modernité* (Paris, Aubier, 2001).

Ben Achour, R and Laghmani, S (eds), *Droit international et droit interne. Développments récents* (Paris, Pedone, 1998).

Bénoit, F-P (ed), *Collectivités locales* (formerly updated regularly, last published 2004, Paris, Dalloz.).

Berkovicz, G, *La place de la Cour pénale internationale dans la société des Etats* (Paris, L'Harmattan, 2005).

Bettinger, C, *La gestion déléguée des services publics dans le monde* (Paris, Berger-Levrault, 1997).

Blum, R, *Mondialisation: chances et risques* (Rapport de la Commission des Affaires étrangères de l'Assemblée Nationale, No 1963, 1999).

Bourdin, A, *La question locale* (Paris, PUF, 2000).

Bouretz, P (ed), *La force du droit. Panorama des débats contemporains* (Paris, Editions Esprit, 1991).

Bouvier, M, *Introduction au droit fiscal général et à la théorie de l'impôt*, 5th edn (Paris, LGDJ, 2003).

—— (ed), *Réforme des finances publiques, démocratie et bonne gouvernance* (Paris, LGDJ, 2004).

Carpano, E, *Etat de droit et droits européens* (Paris, L'Harmattan, 2008).

Carreau, D, *Droit international*, 5th edn, (Paris, Pedone, 1997).

Carreau, D and Julliard, P, *Droit international économique*, 4th edn (Paris, LGDJ, 1998).

Castagnède, B, *Précis de fiscalité internationale* (Paris, PUF, 2002).

Chaltiel, F, *La souveraineté de l'Etat et l'Union européenne. L'exemple français. Recherches sur la souveraineté de l'Etat membre* (LGDJ, 2000).

Chatillon, G (ed), *Le droit international de l'internet* (Brussels, Bruylant, 2009).

Chauvier, S, *Justice et droits à l'échelle globale* (Paris, Vrin—Ehess, 2006).

Chevallier, J, *L'Etat postmoderne*, coll 'Droit et société' (Paris, LGDJ, 2003).

Cohen, E, *L'ordre économique mondial* (Paris, Fayard, 2001).

Combacau, J and Sur, S, *Droit international public* (Paris, Montchrestien, 1999).

Comment améliorer la performance économique des territoires? (Paris, Caisse des Dépôts et des Consignations, 2000).

Commerce mondial et protection des droits de l'homme, Publications de l'Institut international des Droits de l'Homme (Brussels, Bruylant, 2001).

Conseil d'Etat, *Internet et réseaux numériques* (Paris, La Documentation française, 1998).

Conseil d'Etat, *Les normes internationales en droit français* (Paris, La Documentation française, 2000).

Council of Europe/Conseil de l'Europe, *Les mutations de l'Etat-nation en Europe à l'aube du XXIᵉ siècle* (Strasbourg, Conseil de l'Europe Eds., 1998).

Crépeau, F (ed), *Mondialisation des échanges et fonctions de l'Etat* (Bruxelles, Bruylant, 1997).

Daillier, P and Pellet, A, *Droit international public*, 6th edn (Paris, LGDJ, 1999).

Daudet, Y (ed), *Les Nations unies et la restauration de l'Etat* (Paris, Pedone, 1995).

Dekeuwer-Defossez, F (ed), *Internationalisation des droits de l'homme et évolution du droit de la famille* (Paris, LGDJ, 1996).

Delas, O and Deblock, C (ed), *Le bien commun comme réponse politique à la mondialisation* (Brussels, Bruylant, 2003).

Delmas Marty, M, *Trois défis pour un droit mondial* (Paris, Le Seuil, 1997).

—— 'La mondialisation du droit: chances et risques' (Paris, Dalloz, 1999).

—— (ed), *Critique de l'intégration normative* (Paris, PUF, 2004).

La démocratie locale. Représentation, participation et espace public (Paris, PUF, 1999).

Dieux, X Fagnart, J-L, Fesler, D, Simonart, V, Steenbergen J, *L'autorégulation* (Brussels, Bruylant, 1995).

Fauroux, R and Spitz, B (eds), *Notre Etat. Le livre-vérité sur la fonction publique* (Paris, Robert Laffont, 2000).

Flory, T, *L'Organisation mondiale du commerce. Droit institutionnel et substantiel* (Brussels, Bruylant, 1999).

le Galès, P and Thatcher, M, *Les réseaux de politique publique. Débat autour des policy networks* (Paris, L'Harmattan, 1995).

Grewe, C and Ruiz-Fabri, H, *Droits constitutionnels européens* (Paris, PUF, 1995).

Gridel, J-P, *Déclin des spécificités françaises et éventuel retour d'un droit commun européen* (Paris, Dalloz, 1999).

Les grands avis du Conseil d'Etat (Paris, Dalloz, 1997).

Gurvitch, G, *L'idée du droit social* (Paris, Sirey, 1932).

Hamoniaux, T, *L'intérêt général et le juge communautaire* (Paris, LGDJ, 2001).

Henzelin, M and Roth, R (ed), *Le droit penal à l'épreuve de l'internationalisation* (Paris, LGDJ and Bruxelles, Bruylant, 2002).

Huet, A and Koenig-Joulin, M, *Droit pénal international*, 3rd edn (Paris, PUF, 2005).

Isaac, G, *Droit communautaire général*, 7th edn (Paris, Armand Colin, 1999).

Jacqué, J-P, *Droit institutionnel de l'Union européenne*, 3rd edn (Paris, Dalloz, 2004).

Jacquet, J-M and Delebecque, P, *Droit du commerce international* (Paris, Dalloz, 2001).

Jouanet, E, Ruiz-Fabri, H and Sorel, J-M, *Regards d'une génération de juristes sur le droit international* (Paris, Pedone, 2008).

Kahil-Wolff, B and Greber, P-Y, *Sécurité sociale: aspects de droit national, international et européen* (Paris, LGDJ, 2006).

Kebadjian, G, *Les théories de l'économie politique internationale* (Paris, Le Seuil, 1999).

Kieffer, B, *L'OMC et l'évolution du droit international* (Paris, Larcier, 2008).

Kiss, A and Beurier, J-P, *Droit international de l'environnement*, 2nd edn (Paris, Pedone, 2000).

La mer et son droit, Mélanges offerts à Laurent Lucchini et Jean-Pierre Queneudec (Paris, Pedone, 2003).

Laazouzi, M, *Les contrats administratifs à caractère international* (Paris, Economica, 2008).

Laidi, Z, *La norme sans la force. L'énigme de la puissance européenne* (Paris, Presses de Sciences Po, 2008).

Leben, C, *La théorie des contrats d'Etat et l'évolution du droit des investissements*, Recueil des Cours de l'Académie de Droit International, tome 302 (2003).

Leclerc, G, *La mondialisation culturelle. La civilisation à l'épreuve* (Paris, PUF, 2000).

Lemaire, S, *Les contrats internationaux de l'administration* (Paris, LGDJ, 2005).

Leresche, J-P (ed), *Gouvernance territoriale et citoyenneté urbaine* (Paris, Pedone, 2001).

Lévêque, F, *Economie de la réglementation* (Paris, La Découverte, 2004).

Levoyer, L, *L'influence du droit communautaire sur le pouvoir financier du Parlement français* (Paris, LGDJ, 2002).

Levrat, N, *L'Europe et les collectivités territoriales. Réflexions sur l'organisation et l'exercice du pouvoir territorialisé dans un monde globalisé* (Brussels, Bern, Berlin, PIE Peter Lang, 2005).

Levy, J (ed), *L'invention du Monde. Une géographie de la mondialisation* (Paris, Presses de Sciences Po, 2008).

Lignières, P, *Partenariat public-privé*, 2nd edn (Paris, Litec, 2005).

Loquin, E and Kessedjian, C, *La mondialisation du droit* (Paris, Litec, 2000).

Mackaay, E and Rousseau, S, *Analyse économique du droit* (Paris, Dalloz, 2008).

Manciaux, S, *Investissements étrangers et arbitrage entre Etats et ressortissants d'autres Etats* (Paris, Litec, 2004).

du Marais, B (ed), *Des indicateurs pour mesurer le droit? Les limites des rapports* Doing Business *de la Banque Mondiale* (Paris, Editions Société de Législation Comparée, 2006).

Marcou, G (ed), *Les mutations du droit de l'administration en Europe*, coll 'Logiques juridiques' (Paris, L'Harmattan, 1995).

Mayer, P, *La neutralisation du pouvoir normatif de l'Etat en matière de contrats d'Etat* (Paris, Clunet, 1986).

—— *Droit international privé*, 6th edn (Paris, Montchrestien, 1998).

Mayer, P and Heuzé, V, *Droit international privé*, 7th edn (Paris, Montchrestien, 2001).

Mélanges Borella (Nancy, Presses Universitaires de Nancy, 1999).

Mélanges Cohen-Jonathan (Brussels, Bruylant, 2004).

Mélanges Fenet, Un droit pour les hommes libres (Paris, Dalloz, 2008).

Mélanges offerts à Franck Moderne (Paris, Dalloz, 2004).

Mélanges offerts à Jean Waline, Gouverner. Administrer. Juger (Paris, Dalloz, 2002).

Mélanges offerts au président Benoît Jeanneau (Paris, Dalloz, 2002).

Mélanges Philippe Ardant, Droit et politique à la croisée des cultures (Paris, LGDJ, 1999).

Mélanges Philippe Kahn (Souveraineté étatique et marchés internationaux à la fin du 20ᵉ siècle (Paris, Litec, 2000).

Mélanges Puissochet (Paris, Pedone, 2008).

Melleray, F (ed), *L'argument de droit comparé en droit administrative français*, coll 'Droit Administratif/Administrative Law' (Brussels, Bruylant, 2007).

Michalet, C-A, *Le capitalisme mondial*, coll Quadrige (Paris, PUF, 1998).

Mockle, D (ed) *Mondialisation et Etat de droit* (Brussels, Bruylant, 2002).

Morand, C-A (ed), *Le droit saisi par la mondialisation* (Brussels, Bruylant, 2001).

Moreau Defarges, P, *L'ordre mondial* (Paris, Armand Colin, 2000) 155.

Nallet, H, *Les réseaux pluridisciplinaires et les professions du droit* (Paris, La Documentation française, 2000).

Ost, F and van der Kerchove, M, *Le système juridique entre ordre et désordre* (Paris, PUF, 1988).

—— *De la pyramide au réseau. Pour une théorie dialectique du droit* (Brussels, Publications des facultés universitaires Saint-Louis, 2002).

Paquin, S, *Paradiplomatie et relations internationales. Théorie des stratégies internationales des régions* (Brussels, Bern, Berlin, PIE Peter Lang, 2004).

Peyro Llopis, A, *La compétence universelle en matière de crimes contre l'humanité* (Brussels, Bruylant, 2003).

Redor, M-J (ed), *L'ordre public: ordres publics ou ordre public. Ordre public et droits fondamentaux* (Brussels, Bruylant, 2001).

Rideau, J, *Droit institutionnel de l'Union et des Communautés européennes* (Brussels, Publications des facultés universitaires Saint-Louis LGDJ, 2006).

Rigozzi, A, *L'arbitrage international en matière de sport* (Basel, Helbing et Lichtenhahn, 2005).

Robin-Olivier, S and Fasquelle, D (ed), *Les échanges entre les droits, l'expérience communautaire. Une lecture des phénomènes de régionalisation et de mondialisation du droit* (Brussels, Bruylant, 2008).

Romano, S, *L'ordre juridique* (Paris, Dalloz, 2002).

Roy, O, *L'islam mondialisé* (Paris, Le Seuil, 2002).

Salah, M, *Les contradictions du droit mondialisé* (Paris, PUF, 2002).

Schwarze, J (ed), *Le droit administratif sous l'influence de l'Europe* (Baden-Baden, Nomos Verlagsgesellschaft and Bruxelles, Bruylant, 1996).

—— *Droit administratif européen*, 2nd edn (Brussels, Bruylant, 2009).

de Senarclens, P, *La mondialisation*, 2nd edn (Paris, Armand Colin, 2001).

—— *La mondialisation. Théories, enjeux et débats*, 4th edn (Paris, Armand Colin, 2005).

Simonnot, P, *L'invention de l'Etat. Economie du droit* (Paris, Les Belles Lettres, 2003).

Sociéte française de Droit international, *Droit international et droit communautaire: perspectives actuelles* (Paris, Pedone, 2000).

Société française de Droit international, *Les collectivités territoriales non-étatiques dans le système juridique international* (Paris, Pedone, 2002).

Sudre, F (ed), *L'interprétation de la Convention européenne des droits de l'homme* (Brussels, Bruylant, 1998).

—— *Droit international et européen des droits de l'homme*, 9th edn (Paris, PUF 2008).

Territoires et libertés, Mélanges offerts à Yves Madiot (Brussels, Bruylant, 2000).

Weil, P, *Ecrits de droit international* (Paris, PUF, 2000).

PUBLICATIONS IN ITALIAN

d'Alberti, M, *Poteri pubblici, mercati e globalizzazione* (Bologna, Il Mulino, 2008).

Allegretti, U, *Diritti e Stato nella mondializzazione* (Troina, Città Aperta, 2002).

Battini, S, *Amministrazioni nazionali e controversie globale* (Milan, Giuffrè, 2007).

—— *Amministrazione senza Stato. Profili di diritto amministrative internazionale* (Milan, Giuffrè, 2003).

Battini, S, D'Auria, G, Della Cananea, G, Franchini, AM, Mattarella, BG, Napolitano, G, Sandulli, AJ, Torchia, L, Vesperini, G, *Il diritto amministrativo oltre i confini. Omaggio degli allievi a Sabino Cassese* (Milan, Giuffrè, 2008).

Cassese, S, *La crisi dello Stato* (Bari, Editori Laterza, 2002).

—— *Lo spazio giuridico globale* (Bari, Editori Laterza, 2003).

—— *Il diritto globale. Giustizia e democrazia oltre lo stato* (Einaudi, 2009).

Chiti, M, *Diritto amministrativo europeo*, 3rd edn (Milan, Giuffrè, 2008).

Falcon, G (ed), *Il diritto amministrativo dei paesi europei tra ommogenizzazzione e diversita culturali* (Padova, Dedam, 2005).

Ferrarese, MR, *Diritto sconfinato, enventiva giuridica e spazi nel mondo globale* (Bari, Editori Laterza, 2006).

Napolitano, G and Brescia, M, *Analisi economica del diritto pubblico* (Bologna, Il Mulino, 2009).

Vandelli, L, Bottari, C and Donati, D (eds), *Diritto amministrativo comunitario* (Rimini, Miggiolo Editore, 1994).

PUBLICATIONS IN SPANISH

Alli Aranguren, J-C, *Derecho administrativo y globalización* (Madrid, Thomson-Civitas, 2004).

Ballbé, M and Padros, C, *Estado competitivo y armonización europea* (Madrid, Ariel Sociedad Económica, 1997).

Innerarity, D, *El nuevo espacio público* (Madrid, Espasa, 2006).

Moreno Molina, AM, Parejo Alfonso, L, de la Quadra Salcedo, T, *Manual de derecho administrativo comunitario* (Madrid, Editorial Centro de Estudios Ramón Aceres, 2000).

Index

Ingram Content Group UK Ltd.
Milton Keynes UK
UKHW020611080323
418160UK00004B/71